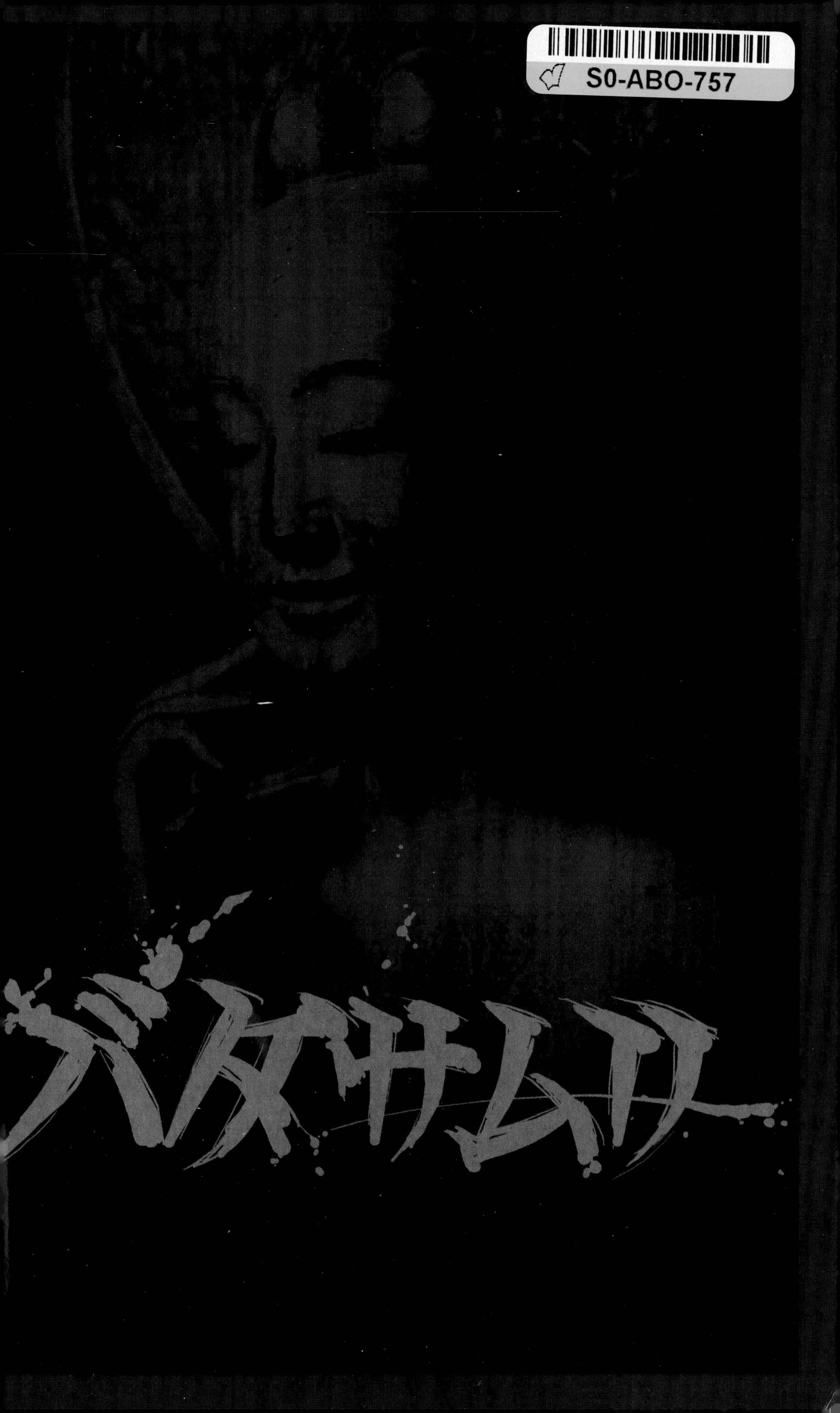

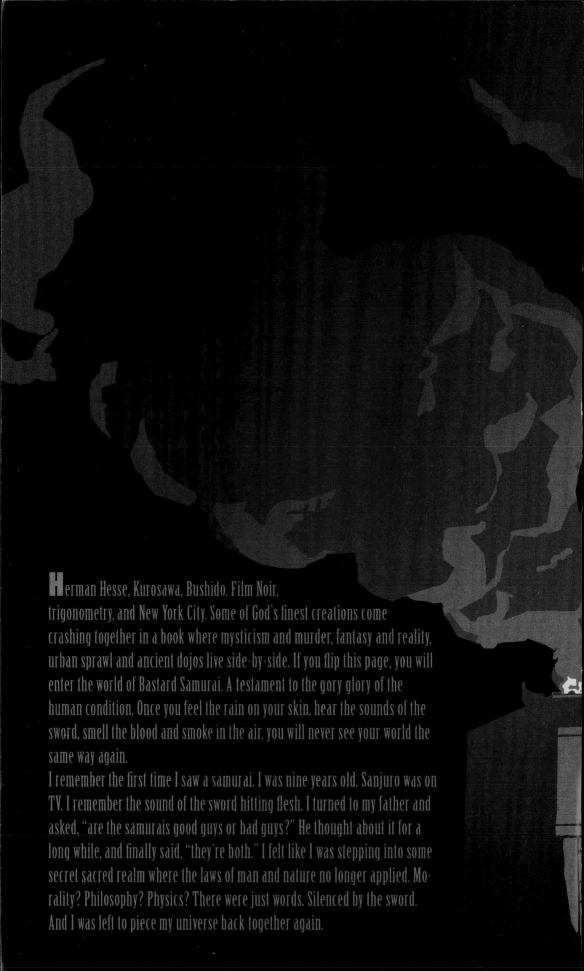

Herman Hesse, Kurosawa, Bushido, Film Noir, trigonometry, and New York City. Some of God's finest creations come crashing together in a book where mysticism and murder, fantasy and reality, urban sprawl and ancient dojos live side-by-side. If you flip this page, you will enter the world of Bastard Samurai. A testament to the gory glory of the human condition. Once you feel the rain on your skin, hear the sounds of the sword, smell the blood and smoke in the air, you will never see your world the same way again.

I remember the first time I saw a samurai. I was nine years old. Sanjuro was on TV. I remember the sound of the sword hitting flesh. I turned to my father and asked, "are the samurais good guys or bad guys?" He thought about it for a long while, and finally said, "they're both." I felt like I was stepping into some secret sacred realm where the laws of man and nature no longer applied. Morality? Philosophy? Physics? There were just words. Silenced by the sword. And I was left to piece my universe back together again.

Nowadays, I spend my time making movies. Telling stories on screen. But I first learned to tell stories from comic books. And I'm still learning. Bastard Samurai was a new lesson, a book as graphic and cinematic and visually arresting as any flick out there. It moves, it speaks, it spits and breathes like a movie. It jumps off the page and grabs you by the throat and rips you into the dark, wet, blood-soaked rooftops of its own secret world. You will go to sleep dreaming of this twisted universe, and wake up with its images tattooed on your brain — just like Jiro wakes with his skin covered in tatts.

So be forewarned. This is not a book for the feint of heart, because once you flip this page, there's no going back to a world where the old laws apply. Once you flip the page, you will be hooked. And as they say in Sanjuro, "killing people is just a bad habit."

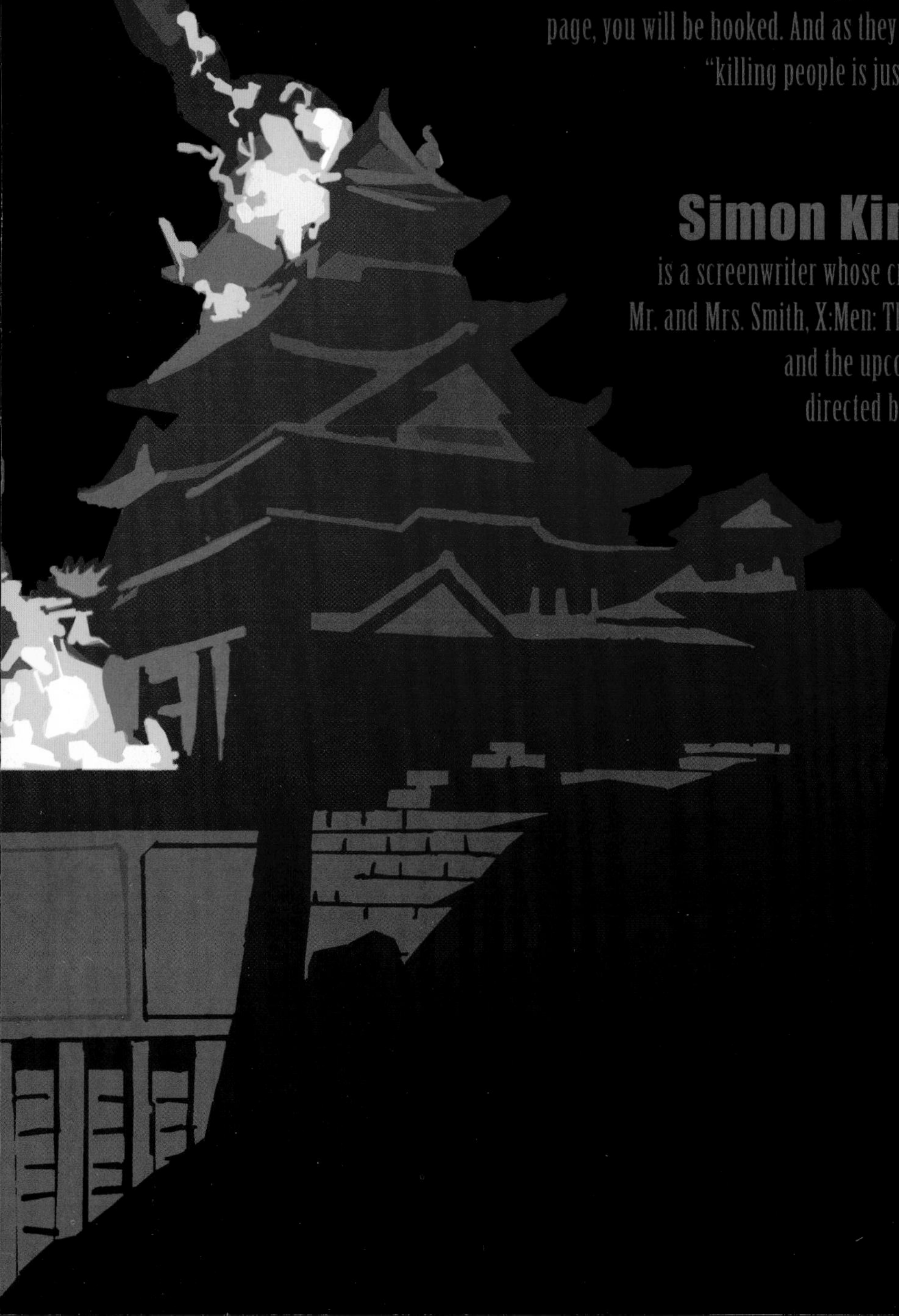

Simon Kinberg

is a screenwriter whose credits include Mr. and Mrs. Smith, X:Men: The Last Stand, and the upcoming Jumper, directed by Doug Liman.

BUSHIDO SUCKS
By Ric Meyers

They're all bastards. At least that's what their movies say. And that's the definition of bastard which reads: "a vicious or despicable person," not "an illegitimate child." Just about the only title character who fits the latter description is Norman Chu in the Shaw Brothers Studio Productions, Bastard Swordsman and Return of the Bastard Swordsman. Neither should be confused with Bastard Samurai, which is an entirely different animal altogether.

But now, with further ado, let's get one thing straight before we continue. Samurai is Japanese. Swordsman is Chinese. Karate is Japanese. Kung-fu is Chinese. White uniforms with colored belts is Japanese. Coolie costumes are Chinese. Topknots are Japanese. Ponytail "queues" are Chinese. Sonny Chiba did "karate flicks." Jackie Chan and Jet Li do kung-fu films. People who say different might as well be calling the New York Yankees a great football team ("Hey, it's a sport using a ball, right?!").

That settled, let's get to the meat of the matter. Scratch the surface of virtually any good film or book incorporating a samurai or ninja sword and you'll discover an attack on Bushido ­ that cultural dictum which nominally preached rectitude, but actually was an intellectual straightjacket which took no human frailty into consideration. It essentially set up a police state (with 3% of the population dominating 97%), demanded people not have any shades of gray, and created a strict code with a load of dangerous, destructive loopholes.

Through one of those cracks the ninja crawled: angry, desperate slaves hired to do the dishonorable things Bushido didn't "permit" samurai to do. Yet Bushido still allowed samurai willing to hire these assassin/spies into heaven while barring their dark agents. This resulted in thousands, even millions, of marred lives, but also a handful of brilliant Japanese "Shinobi No Mono" ninja films which beautifully recreated the world of these tortured infiltrators as people with no place on earth (they were hated even by those who hired them) and none in heaven.

Now the good news. Bushido reality made for tragedy, but the fantasy made for stirring, enduring entertainment that can impress whoever it's seen by wherever it's seen. Lone Wolf and Cub (a.k.a. Ogami Itto, a.k.a. the Baby Cart series) still thrives in comics, videos, and pastiches (Road to Perdition anyone?). Zatoichi (the Blind Swordsman) has more than two dozen films to his credit, and counting. The brilliant, bloody Son of Black Mass movie series has been released here under the misleading and seriously unevocative new blanket title Sleepy Eyes of Death. Get onto the web or into Chinatown to find these as well as the aforementioned ninja classics (and find out how badly those lousy Sho Kosugi hunks of celluloid junk loused things up for the rest of us).

The final proof? What you hold in your hands. Not this intro, but the still, yet cinematic, story of a contemplative, wet-dreaming, reiki-lacking, walking yin-yang who thinks he'll find balance through beheading. It's Kurosawa, Kenji-Misumi-style (the director of the best Zatoichis and Itto Ogamis, not to mention Razor Hanzo, flicks). It's Kyoshiro Nemuri (the Son of Black Mass himself) with A Touch of Zen thrown in for good measure. It's Wong Kar-wai framing with Johnny To lighting. It's Hideo Gosha (director of Sword of the Beast) battling Kihachi Okamoto (director of Kill!) to get the first slice in. It's everything. It's its own thing. It's what happens when the Shinto hits the fan.

Beyond all that, this comic, those films, and much more mighty morphing power media exist to point the finger of doom at Bushido. Unlike democracy, socialism, and even communism, it wasn't a good idea ruined once people got involved. It was unrealistic, eminently pervertable wishful thinking -- a pipe dream, a fantasy, a reverie, a bar set way too high for virtually anyone with chromosomes to clear it. But it sure makes for great viewing (and reading), doesn't it?

Bastards.

RIC MEYERS is the bastard (in the despicable person sense, although the jury is still out on the illegitimate child context) who writes the movie columns in Inside Kung-fu and Asian Cult Cinema magazines, wrote the first book on the genre (Martial Arts Movies: From Bruce Lee to the Ninja) as well as the latest (Great Martial Arts Movies: From Bruce Lee to Jackie Chan & More), supplied audio commentaries for more than twenty DVDs (including Once Upon a Time in China and Drunken Master), inspired and/or appeared on documentaries on A&E, Bravo, the Discovery Channel, and Starz Encore, was inducted into both the World and Worldwide Martial Arts Hall of Fames, and has contributed to Atlas, DC, Topps, and Image comics.

conceived, co-written and inked by

Mike Avon Oeming

written and co-created by

Miles Gunter

penciled, colored and co-created by

Kelsey Shannon

lettered by

Ken Bruzenak

book design and cover by *Kelsey Shannon*

Special Thanks

David Mack, Brian Stelfreeze, Dave Johnson, Andy Lee,
Jacen Burrows, Ric Myers, Ivan Brandon, Brett, Brent, Sean,
and the rest at Image comics. Without all of you guys, this would
have been much more of a pain in the ass. , The number 13,
Duncan Fegredo (you rock!) Akira Kurosawa, Mike Patton,
David Fincher, Tool, All the Gods, Hiroaki Samura,
Jason Pearson, Macintosh, Gainax, and Mary Jane!

and Thank You.

IMAGE COMICS, INC.
Erik Larsen - *Publisher*
Todd McFarlane - *President*
Marc Silvestri - *CEO*
Jim Valentino - *Vice-President*

Eric Stephenson - *Executive Director*
Mark Haven Britt - *Director of Marketing*
Thao Le - *Accounts Manager*
Rosemary Cao - *Accounting Assistant*
Traci Hui - *Administrative Assistant*
Joe Keatinge - *Traffic Manager*
Allen Hui - *Production Manager*
Jonathan Chan - *Production Artist*
Drew Gill - *Production Artist*
Chris Giarrusso - *Production Artist*

www.imagecomics.com

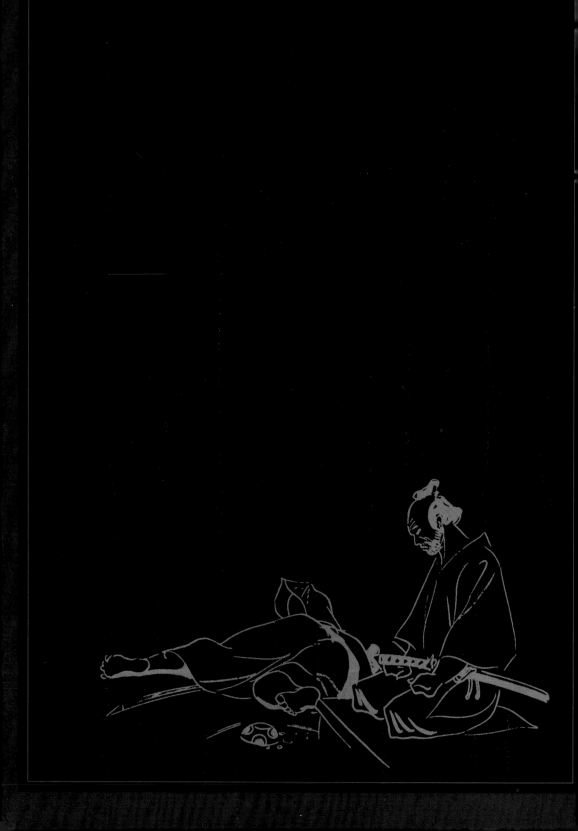

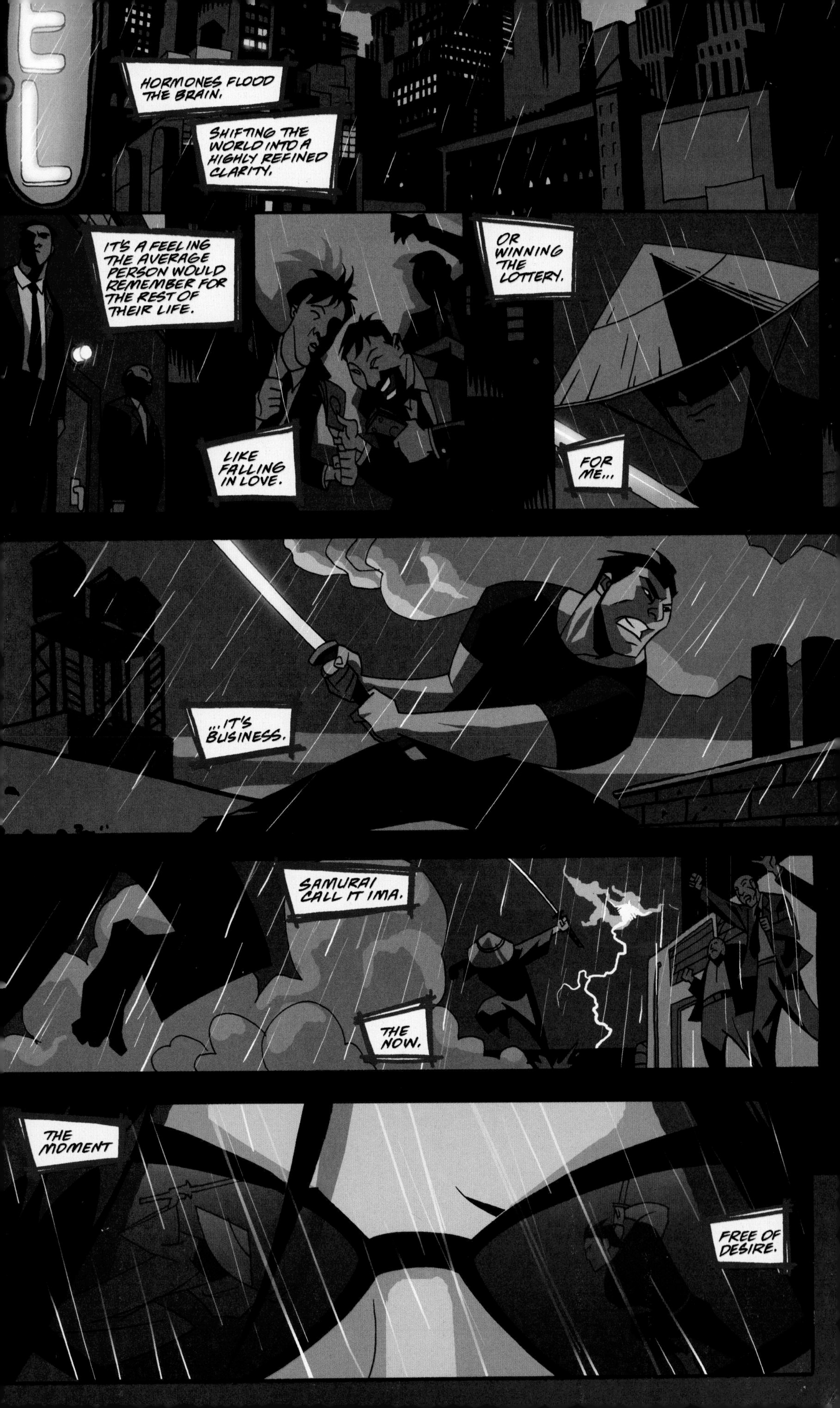
HORMONES FLOOD THE BRAIN.
SHIFTING THE WORLD INTO A HIGHLY REFINED CLARITY.
IT'S A FEELING THE AVERAGE PERSON WOULD REMEMBER FOR THE REST OF THEIR LIFE.
LIKE FALLING IN LOVE.
OR WINNING THE LOTTERY.
FOR ME...
...IT'S BUSINESS.
SAMURAI CALL IT IMA.
THE NOW.
THE MOMENT
FREE OF DESIRE.

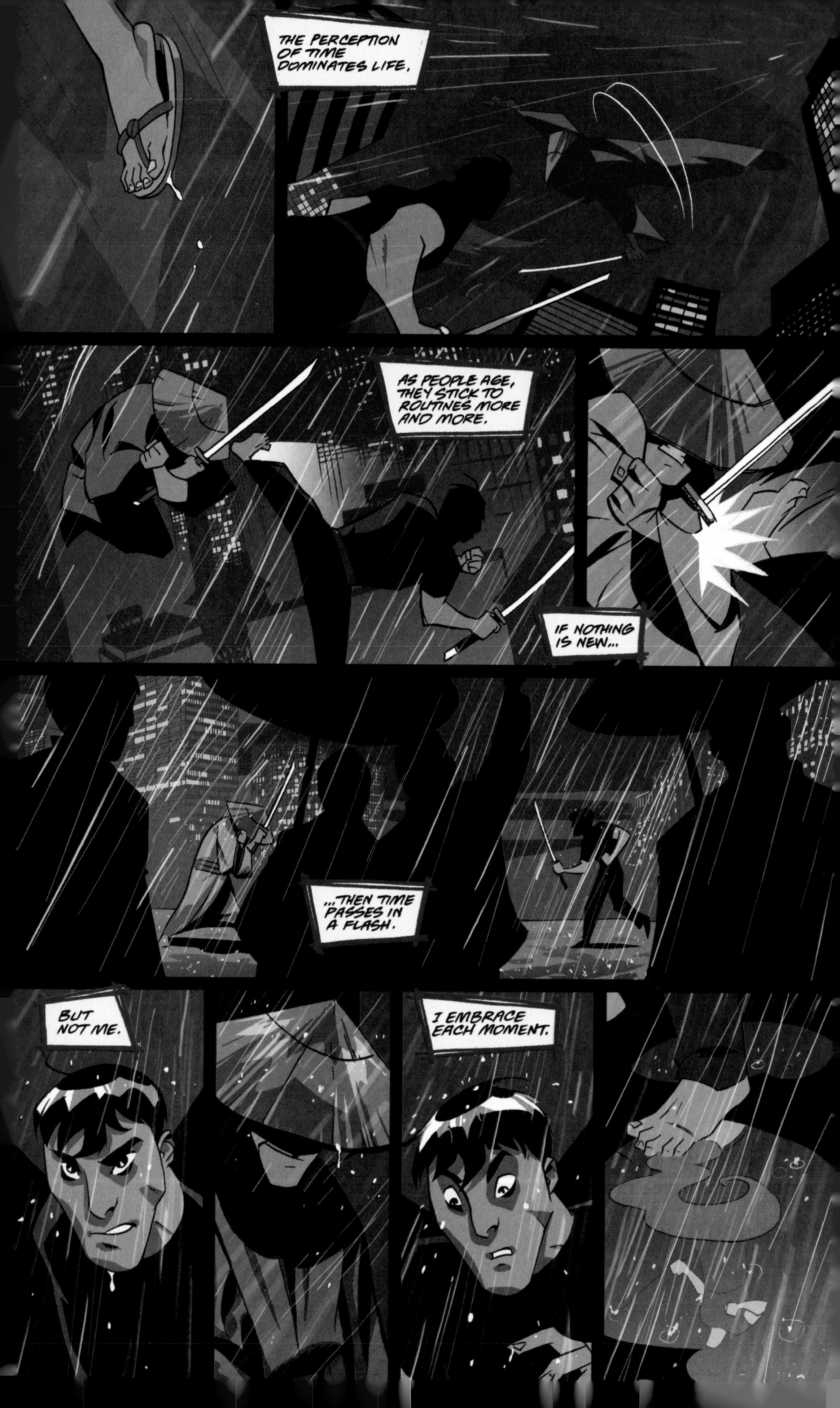
THE PERCEPTION OF TIME DOMINATES LIFE.
AS PEOPLE AGE, THEY STICK TO ROUTINES MORE AND MORE.
IF NOTHING IS NEW...
...THEN TIME PASSES IN A FLASH.
BUT NOT ME.
I EMBRACE EACH MOMENT.

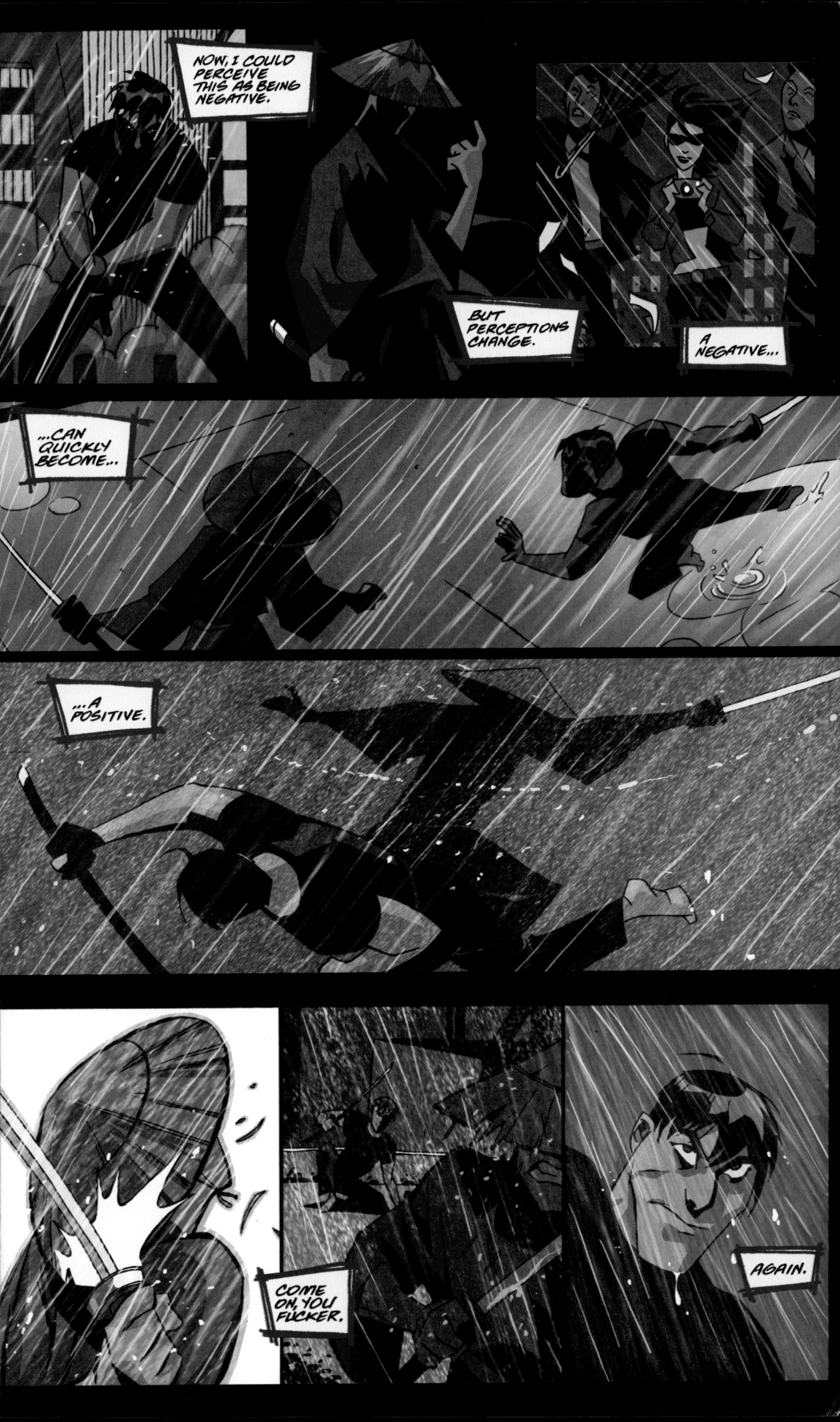
NOW, I COULD PERCEIVE THIS AS BEING NEGATIVE.
BUT PERCEPTIONS CHANGE.
A NEGATIVE...
...CAN QUICKLY BECOME...
...A POSITIVE.
COME ON, YOU FUCKER.
AGAIN.

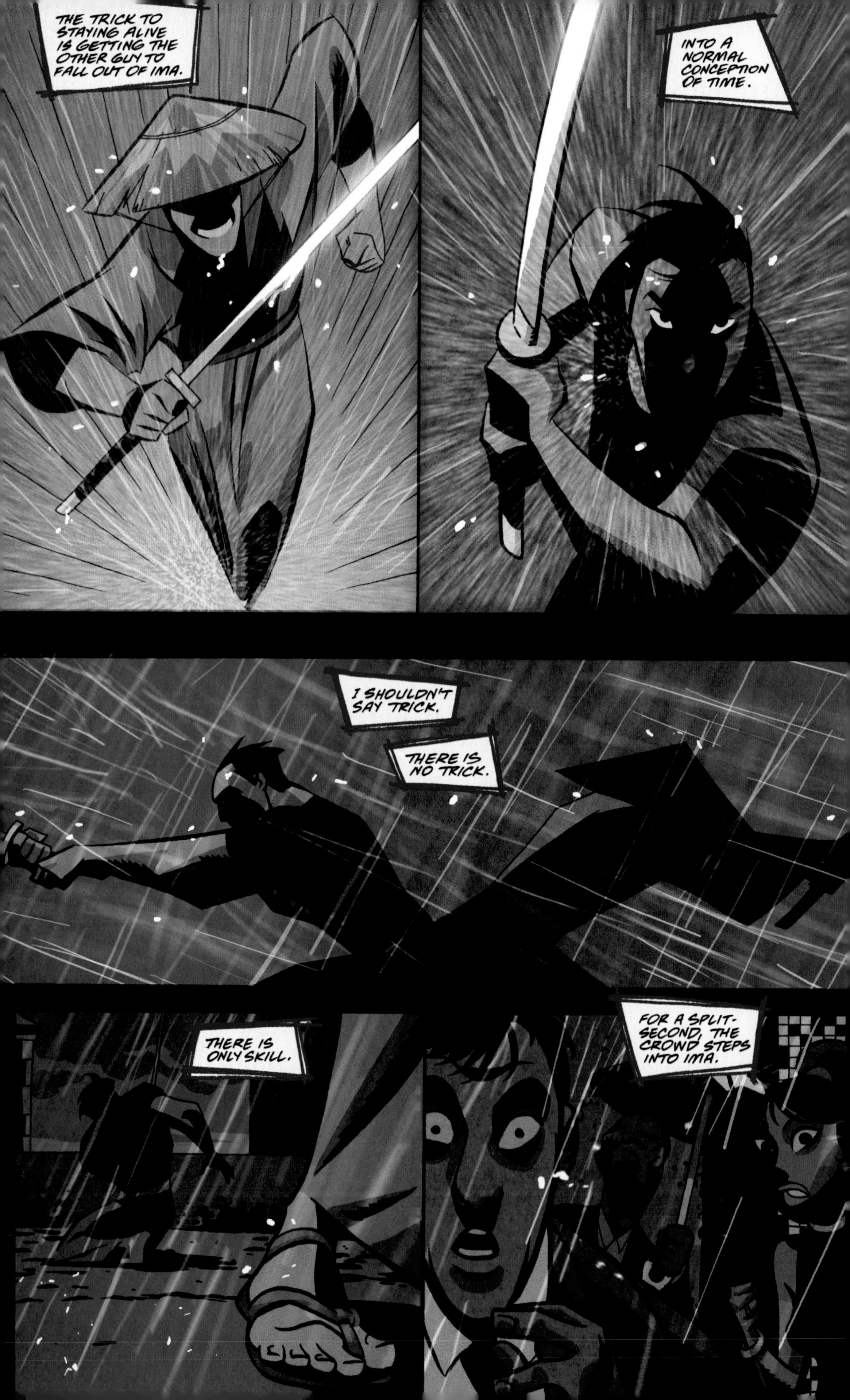
THE TRICK TO STAYING ALIVE IS GETTING THE OTHER GUY TO FALL OUT OF IMA.
INTO A NORMAL CONCEPTION OF TIME.
I SHOULDN'T SAY TRICK.
THERE IS NO TRICK.
THERE IS ONLY SKILL.
FOR A SPLIT-SECOND, THE CROWD STEPS INTO IMA.

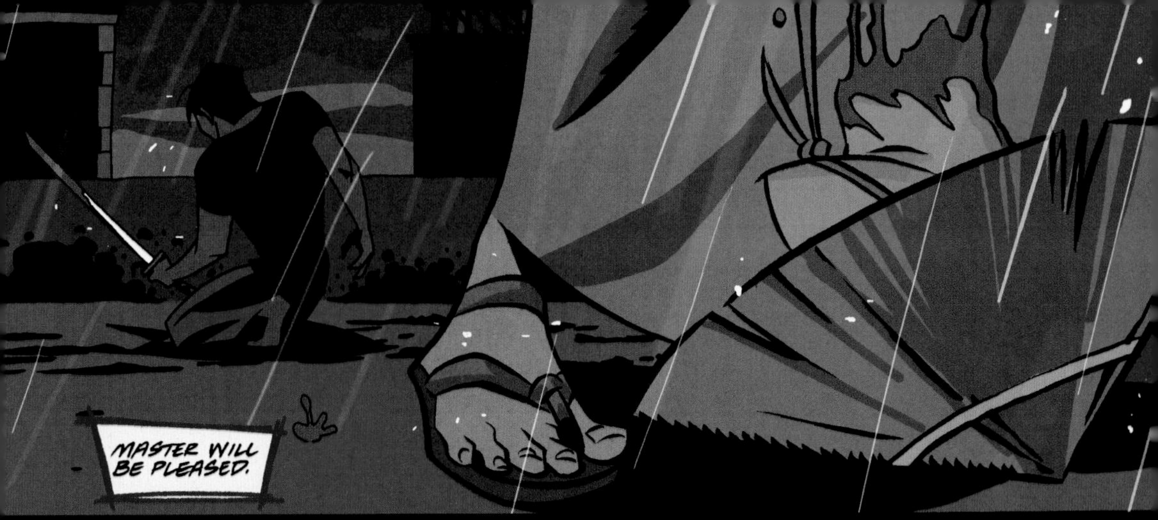
MASTER WILL BE PLEASED.

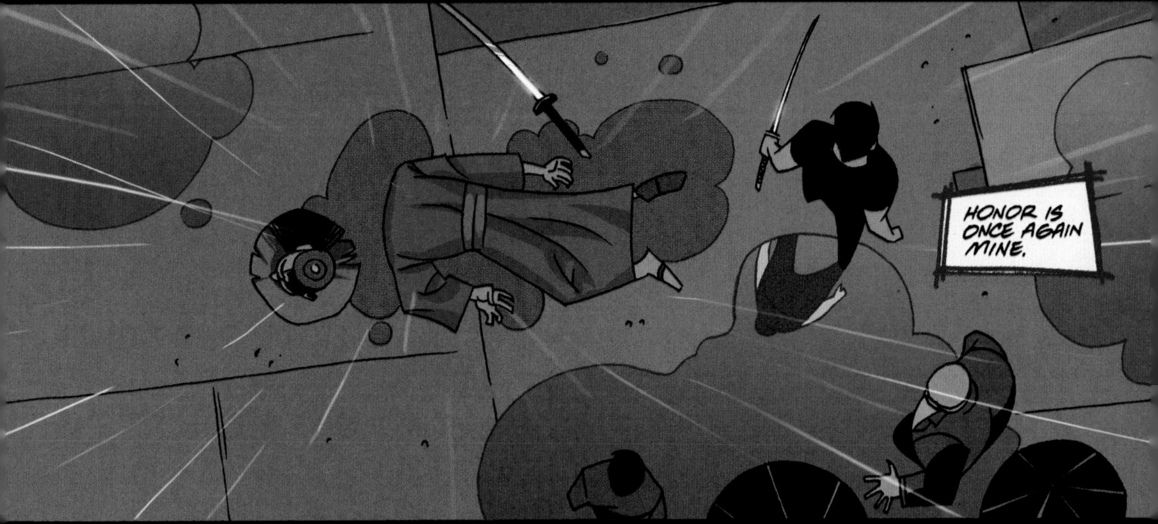
HONOR IS ONCE AGAIN MINE.

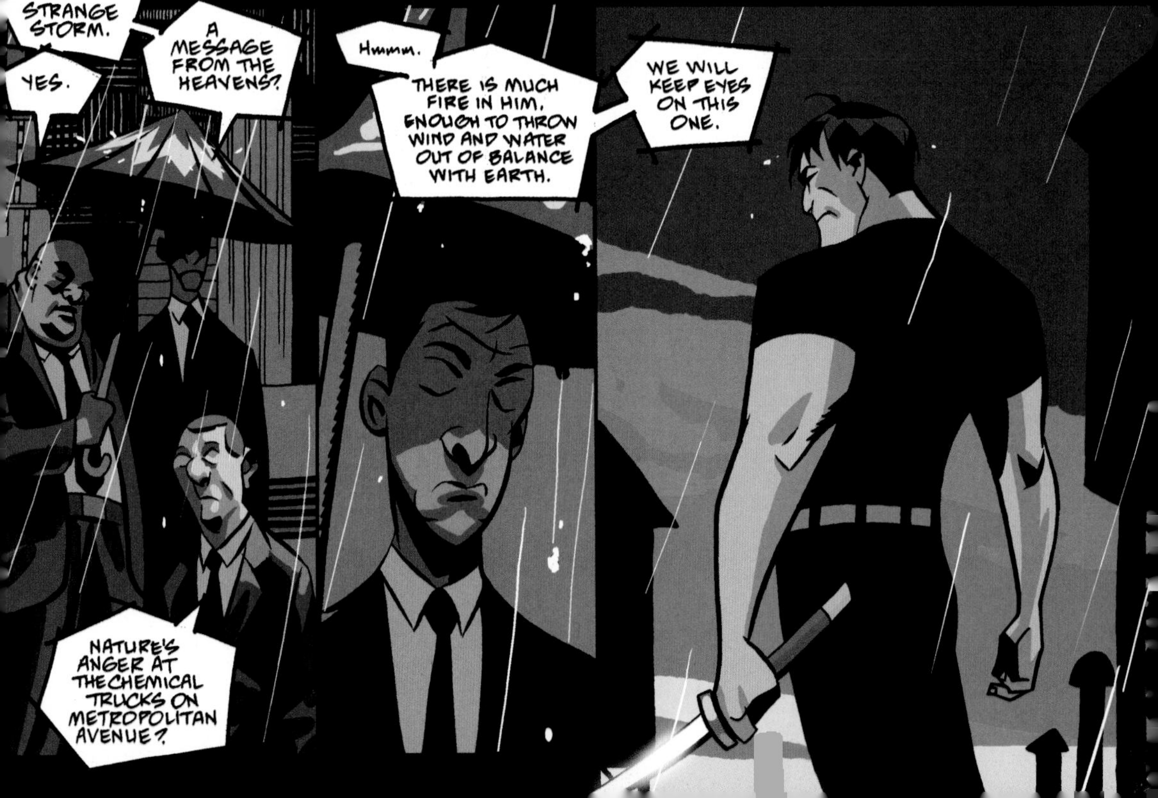
STRANGE STORM.
YES.
A MESSAGE FROM THE HEAVENS?
NATURE'S ANGER AT THE CHEMICAL TRUCKS ON METROPOLITAN AVENUE?
Hmmm.
THERE IS MUCH FIRE IN HIM, ENOUGH TO THROW WIND AND WATER OUT OF BALANCE WITH EARTH.
WE WILL KEEP EYES ON THIS ONE.

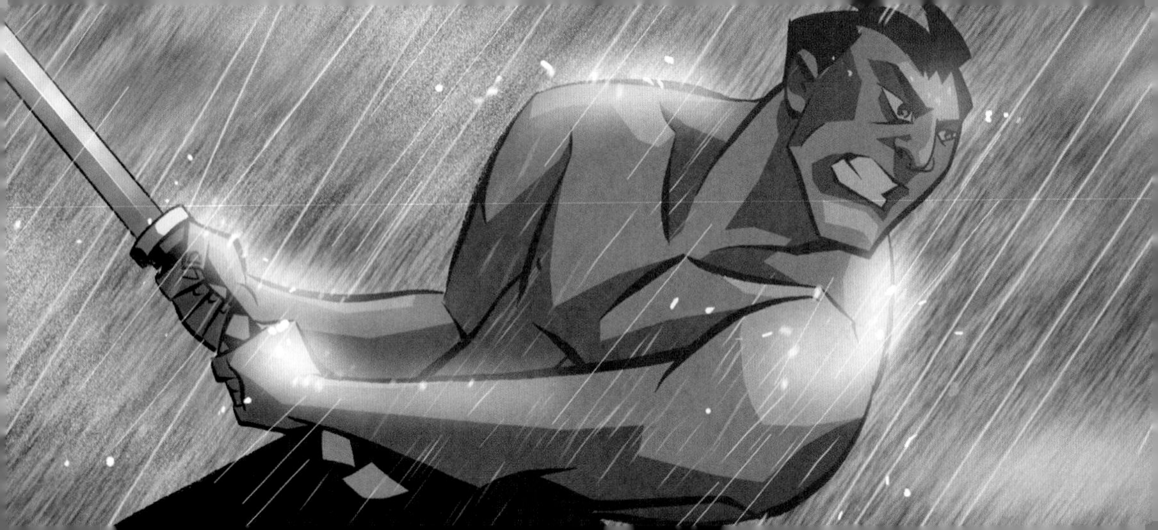

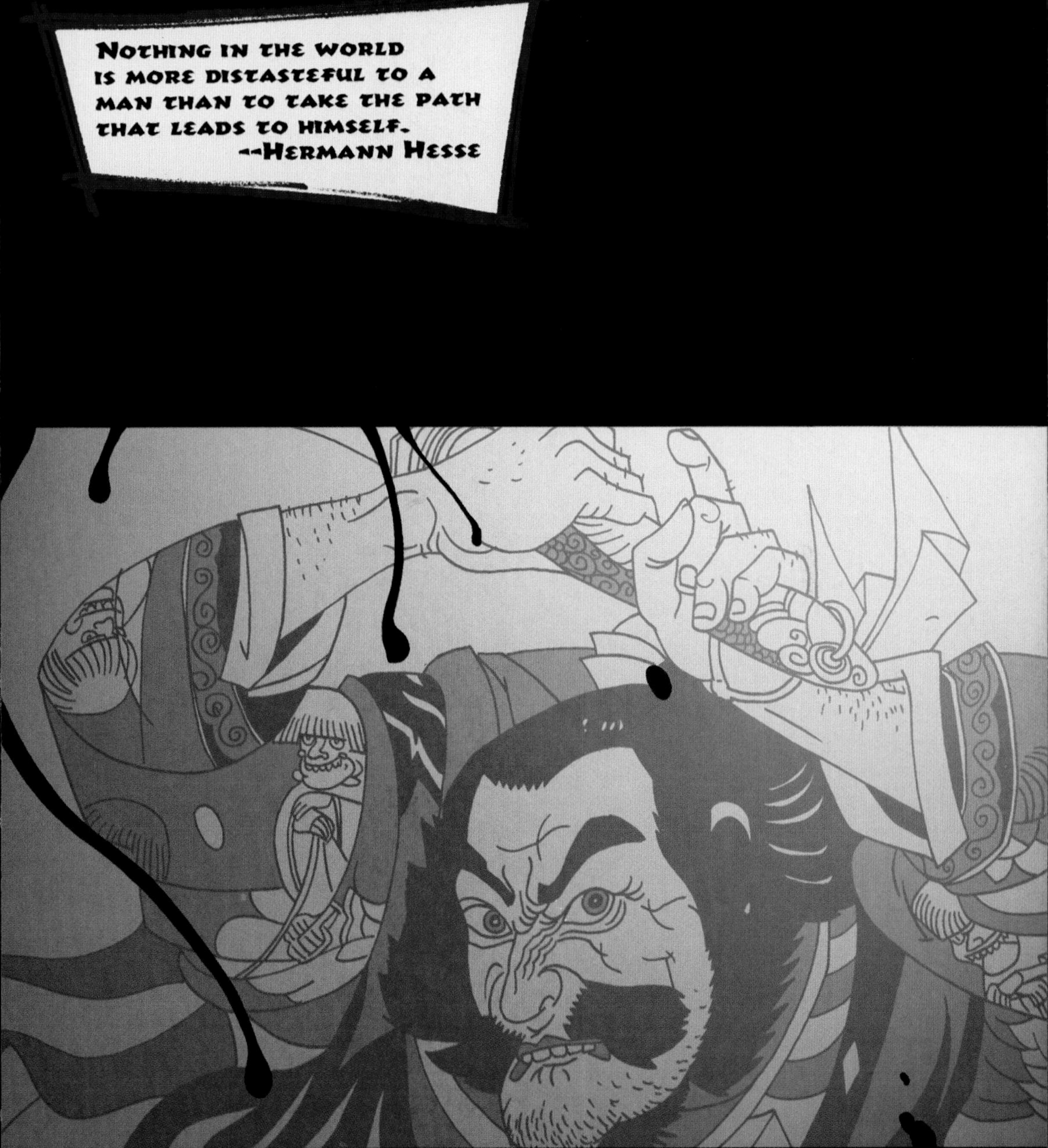
Nothing in the world is more distasteful to a man than to take the path that leads to himself.
--Hermann Hesse

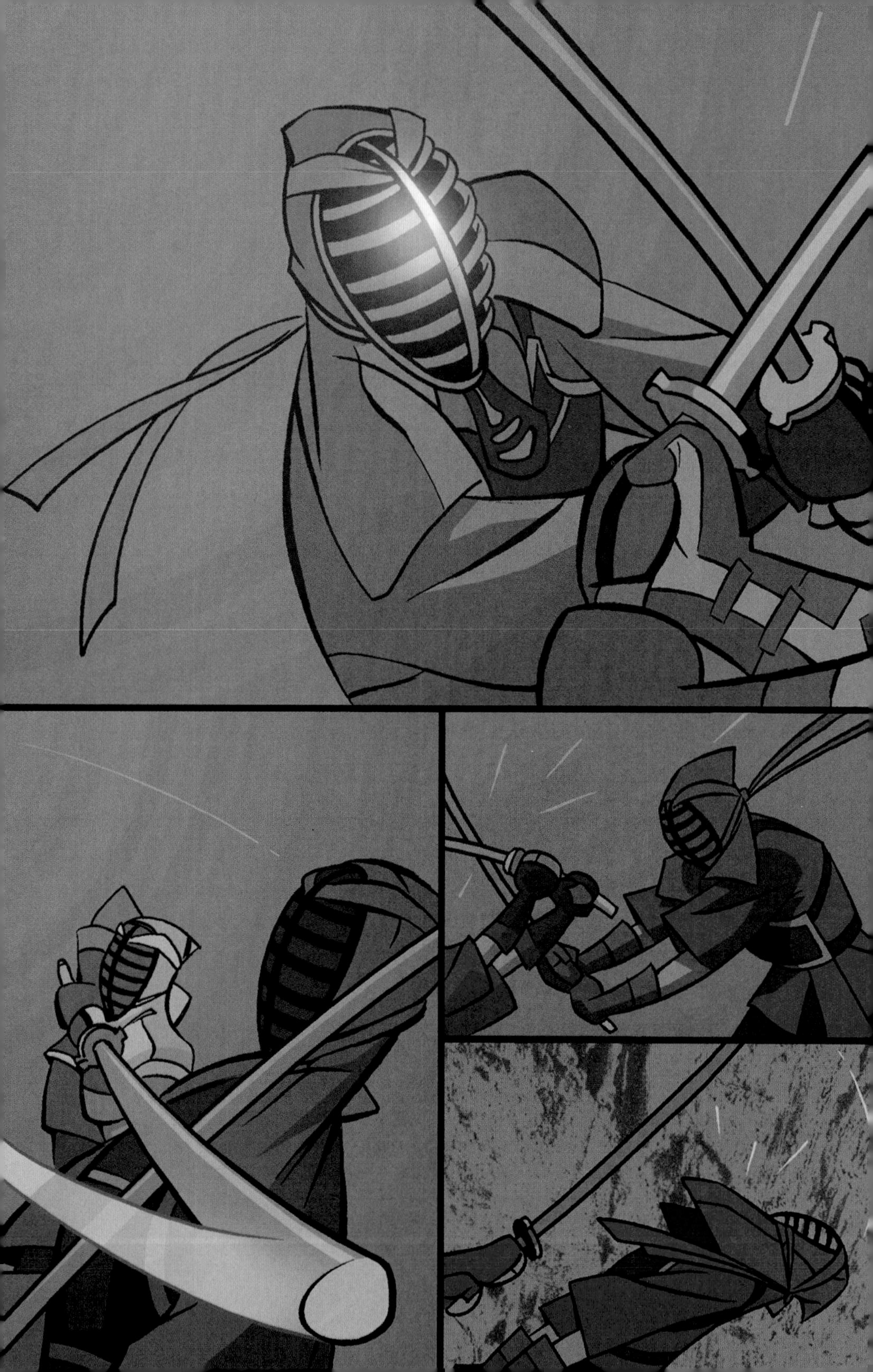

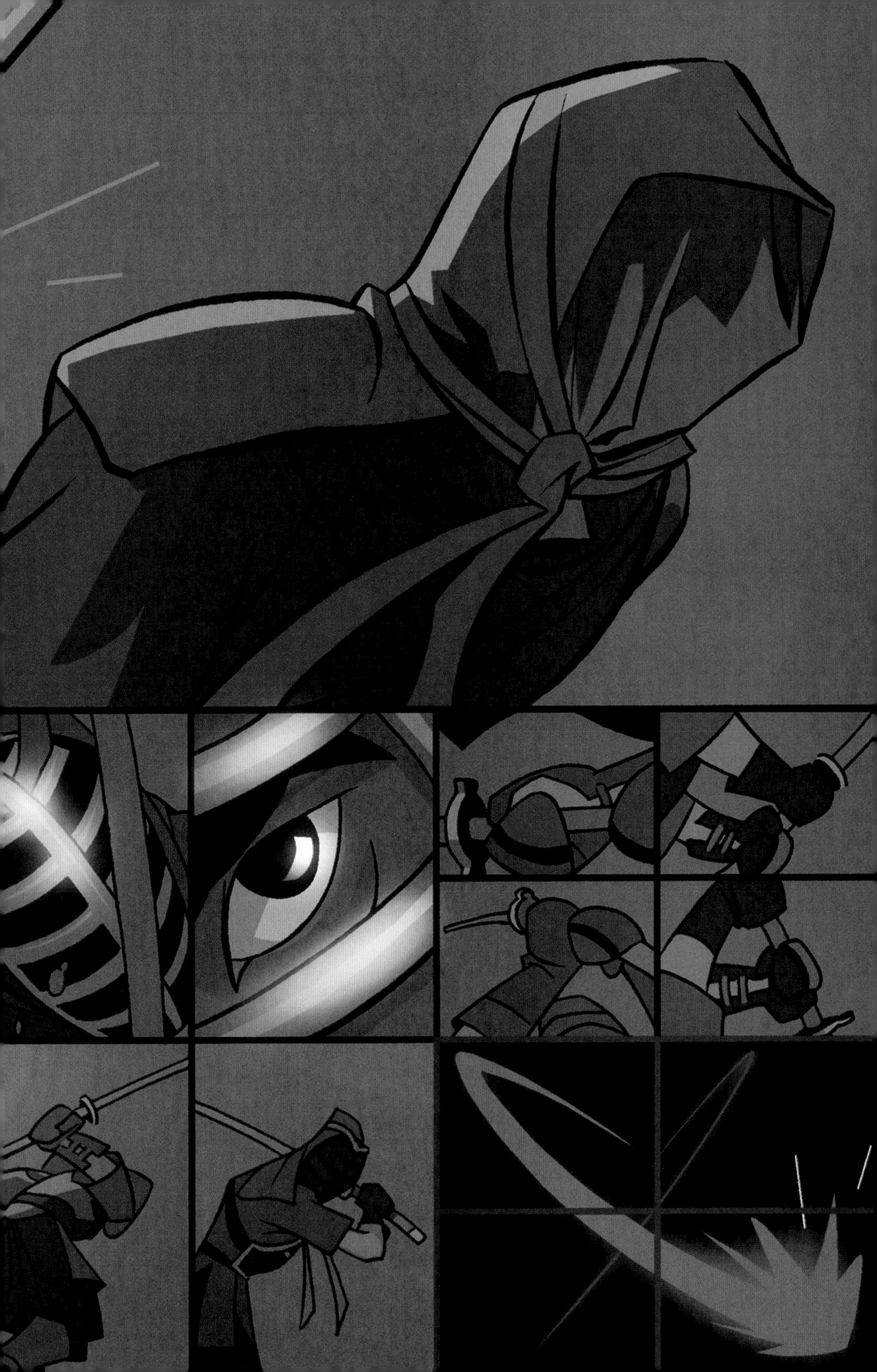

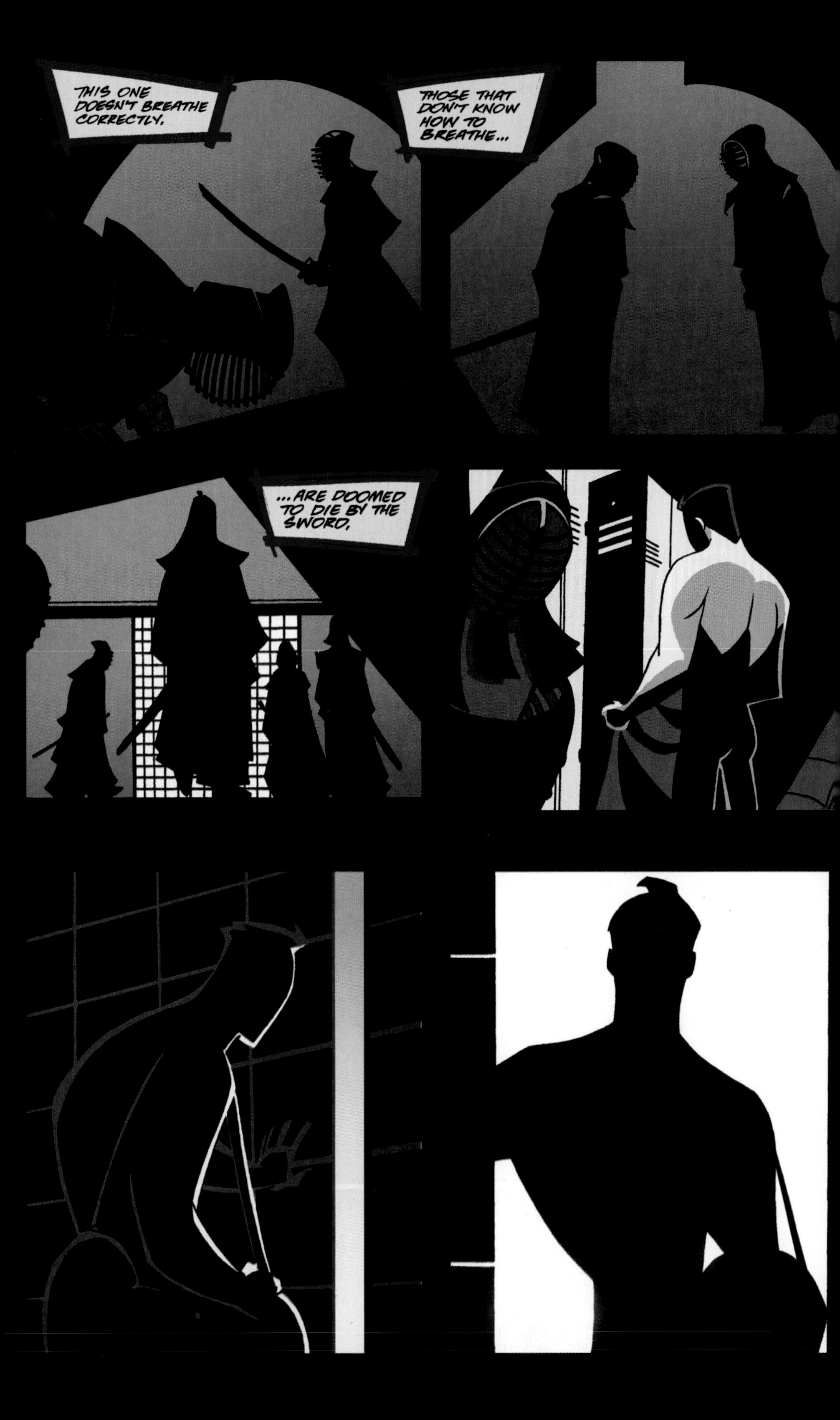
THIS ONE DOESN'T BREATHE CORRECTLY.
THOSE THAT DON'T KNOW HOW TO BREATHE...
...ARE DOOMED TO DIE BY THE SWORD.

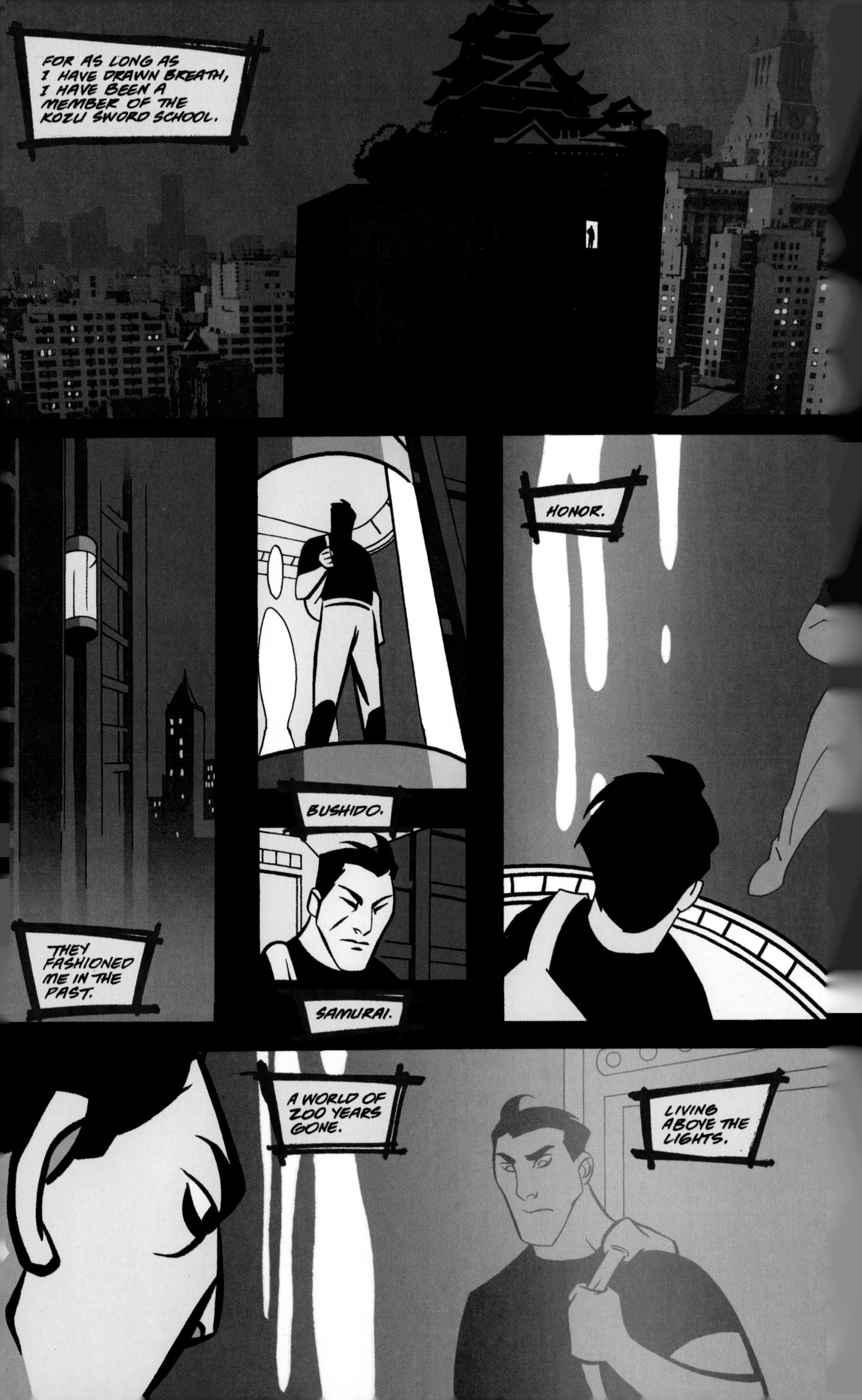
FOR AS LONG AS I HAVE DRAWN BREATH, I HAVE BEEN A MEMBER OF THE KOZU SWORD SCHOOL.
HONOR.
BUSHIDO.
THEY FASHIONED ME IN THE PAST.
SAMURAI.
A WORLD OF 200 YEARS GONE.
LIVING ABOVE THE LIGHTS.

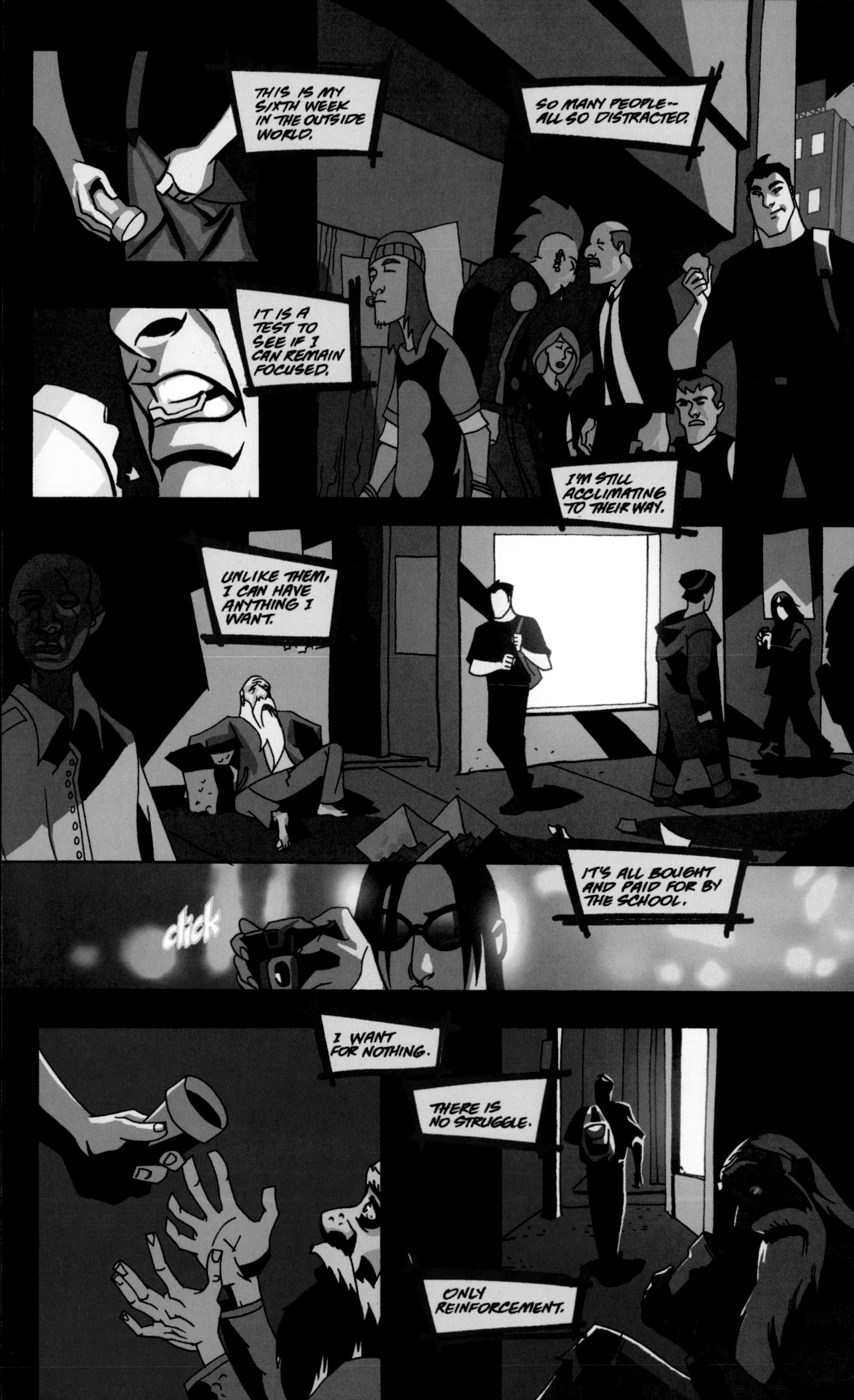
THIS IS MY SIXTH WEEK IN THE OUTSIDE WORLD.
SO MANY PEOPLE-- ALL SO DISTRACTED.
IT IS A TEST TO SEE IF I CAN REMAIN FOCUSED.
I'M STILL ACCLIMATING TO THEIR WAY.
UNLIKE THEM, I CAN HAVE ANYTHING I WANT.
click
IT'S ALL BOUGHT AND PAID FOR BY THE SCHOOL.
I WANT FOR NOTHING.
THERE IS NO STRUGGLE.
ONLY REINFORCEMENT.

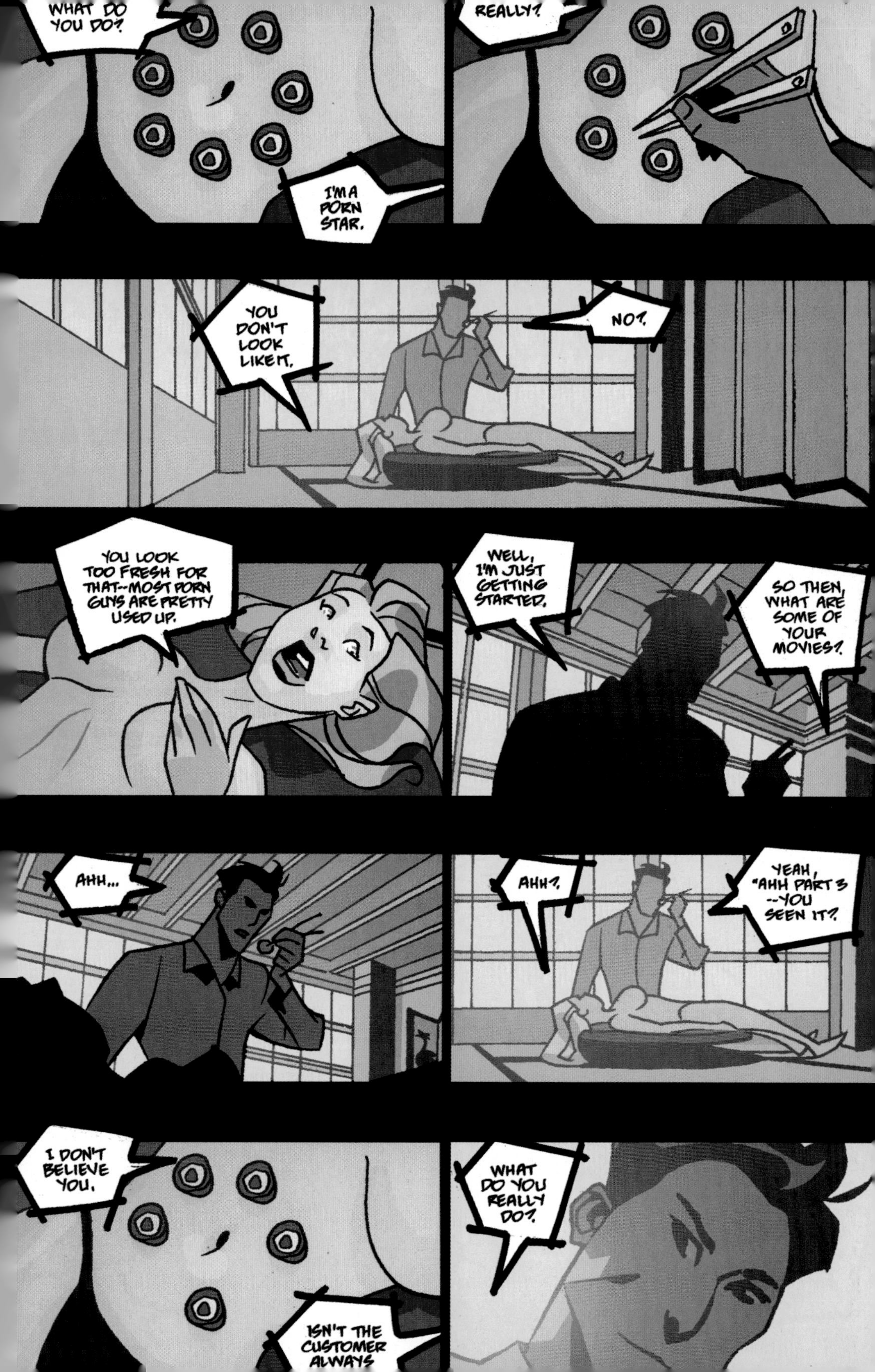
WHAT DO YOU DO?
I'M A PORN STAR.
REALLY?
YOU DON'T LOOK LIKE IT.
NO?
YOU LOOK TOO FRESH FOR THAT--MOST PORN GUYS ARE PRETTY USED UP.
WELL, I'M JUST GETTING STARTED.
SO THEN, WHAT ARE SOME OF YOUR MOVIES?
AHH...
AHH?
YEAH, "AHH PART 3 --YOU SEEN IT?
I DON'T BELIEVE YOU.
ISN'T THE CUSTOMER ALWAYS
WHAT DO YOU REALLY DO?

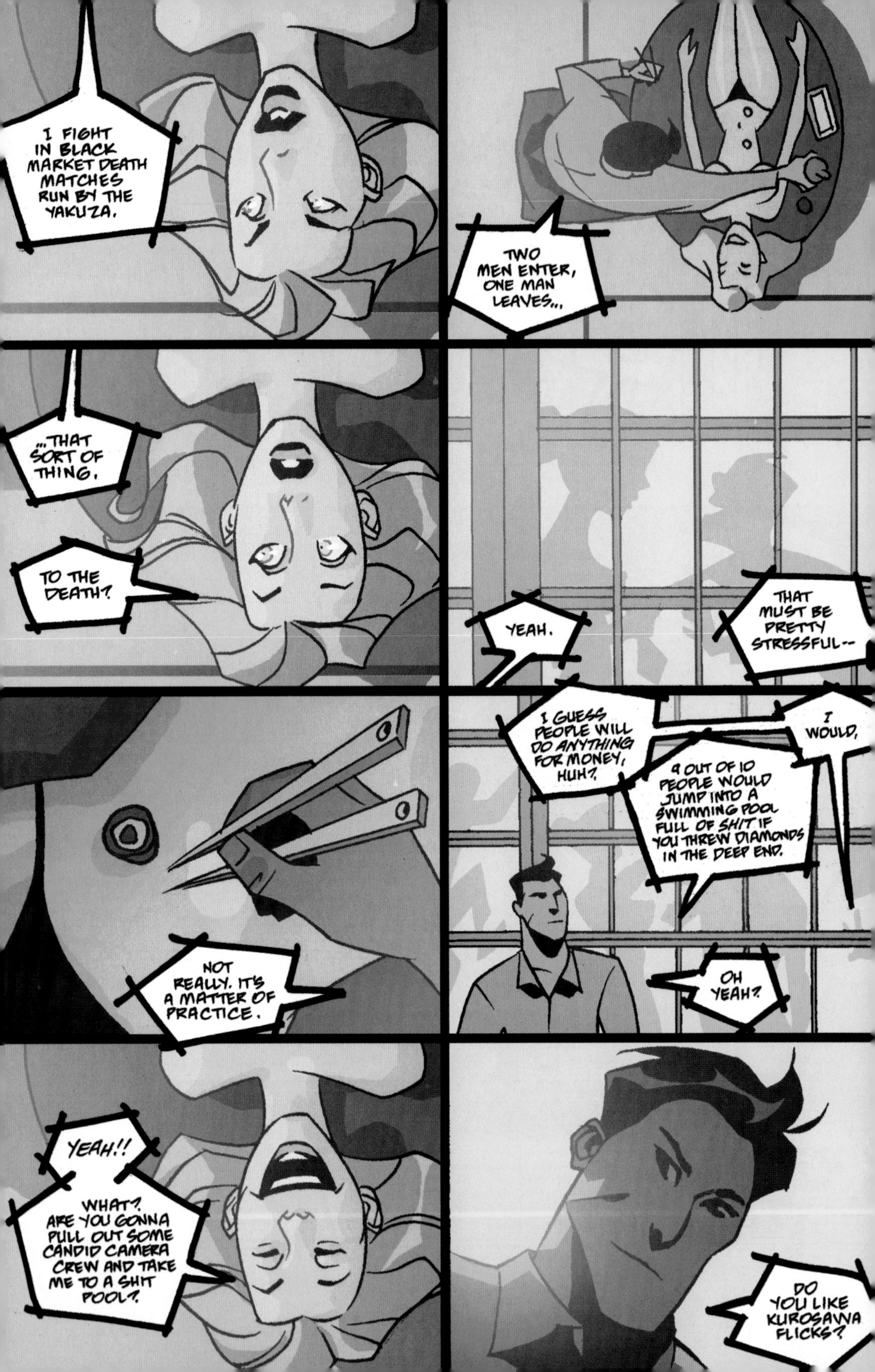

I FIGHT IN BLACK MARKET DEATH MATCHES RUN BY THE YAKUZA.
TWO MEN ENTER, ONE MAN LEAVES...
...THAT SORT OF THING.
TO THE DEATH?
YEAH.
THAT MUST BE PRETTY STRESSFUL--
NOT REALLY. IT'S A MATTER OF PRACTICE.
I GUESS PEOPLE WILL DO ANYTHING FOR MONEY, HUH?
I WOULD.
9 OUT OF 10 PEOPLE WOULD JUMP INTO A SWIMMING POOL FULL OF SHIT IF YOU THREW DIAMONDS IN THE DEEP END.
OH YEAH?
YEAH!!
WHAT? ARE YOU GONNA PULL OUT SOME CANDID CAMERA CREW AND TAKE ME TO A SHIT POOL?
DO YOU LIKE KUROSAWA FLICKS?

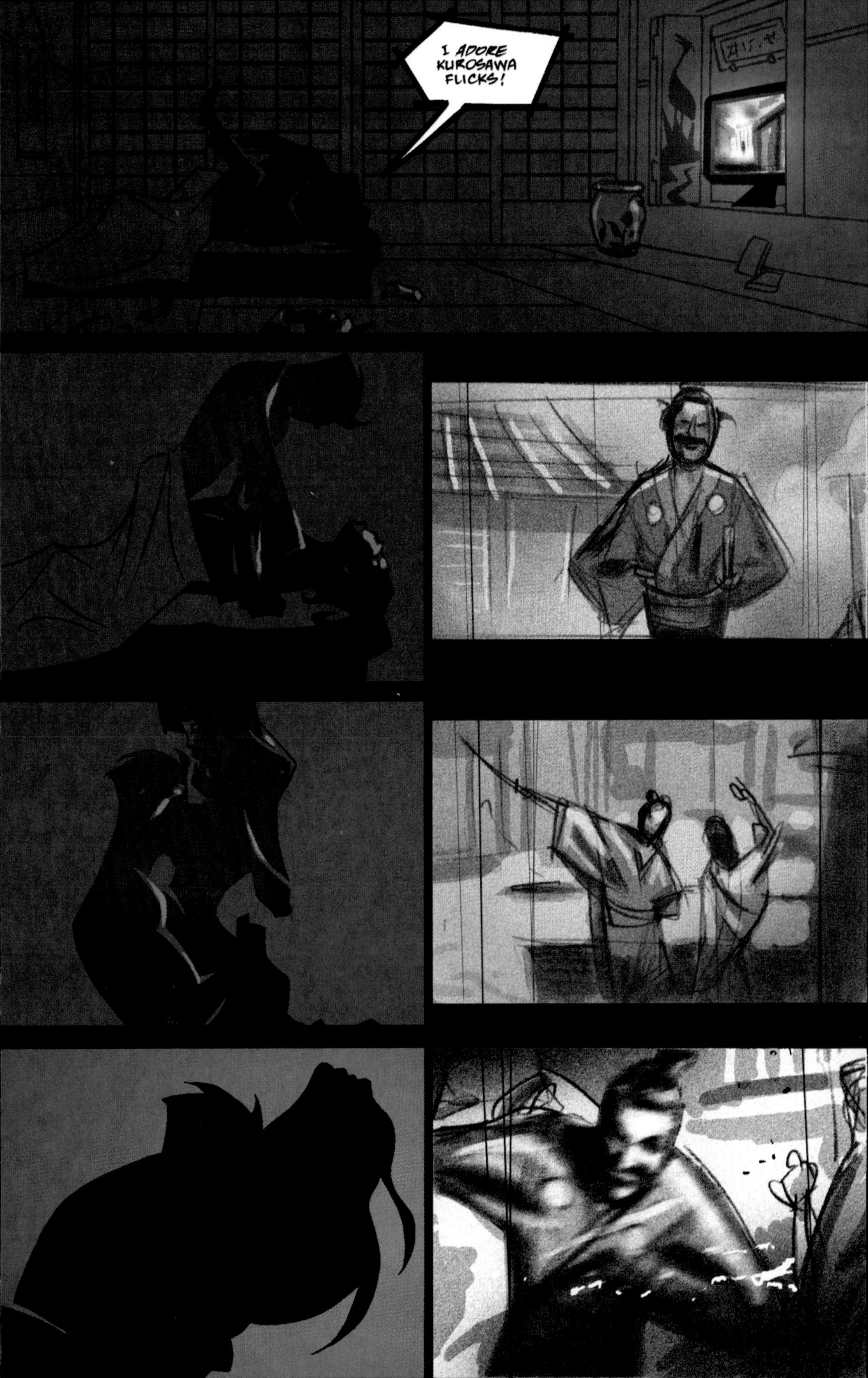
I ADORE KUROSAWA FLICKS!

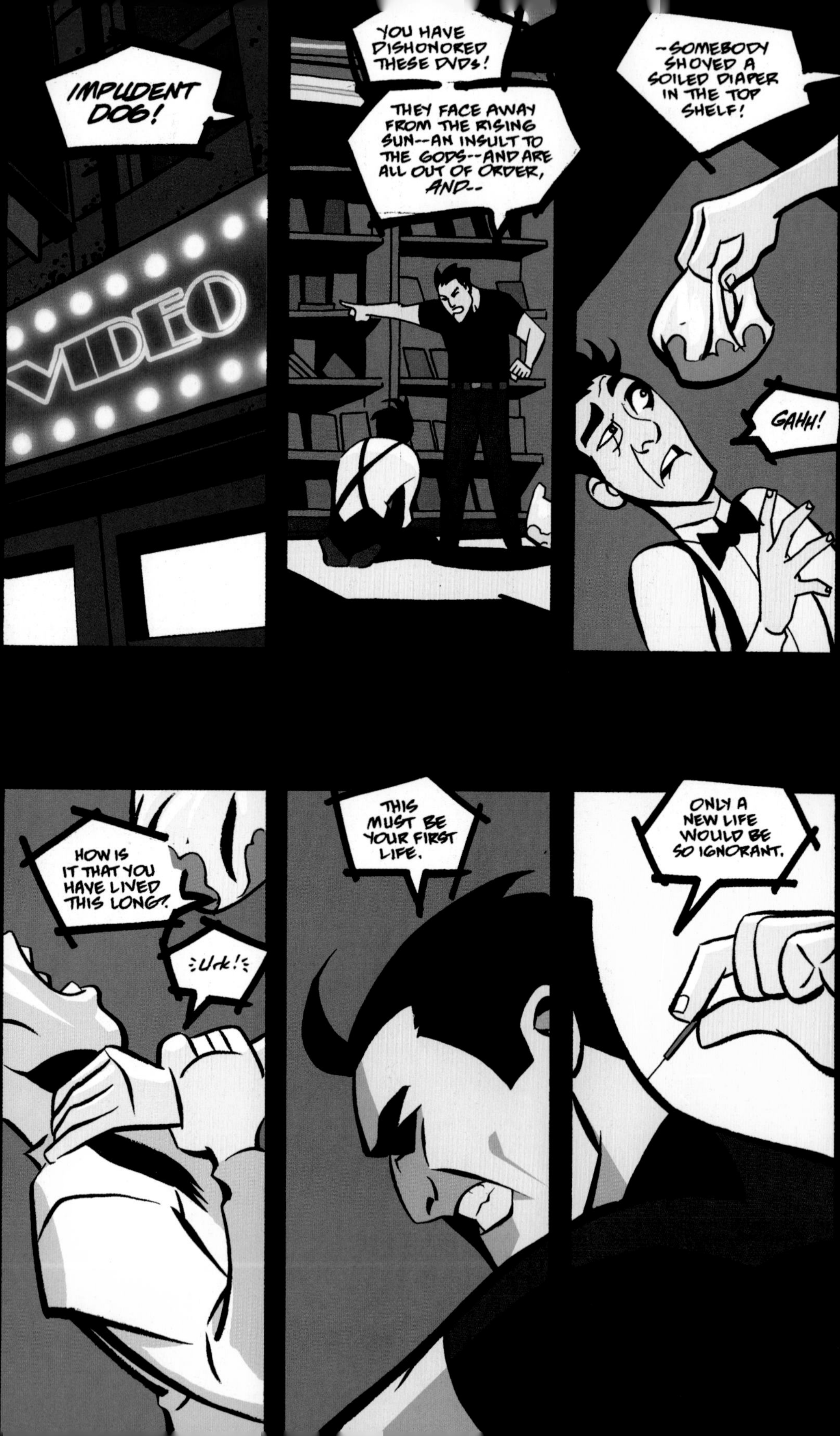
IMPUDENT DOG!
VIDEO
YOU HAVE DISHONORED THESE DVDs!
THEY FACE AWAY FROM THE RISING SUN--AN INSULT TO THE GODS--AND ARE ALL OUT OF ORDER, AND--
--SOMEBODY SHOVED A SOILED DIAPER IN THE TOP SHELF!
GAHH!
HOW IS IT THAT YOU HAVE LIVED THIS LONG?
Urk!
THIS MUST BE YOUR FIRST LIFE.
ONLY A NEW LIFE WOULD BE SO IGNORANT.

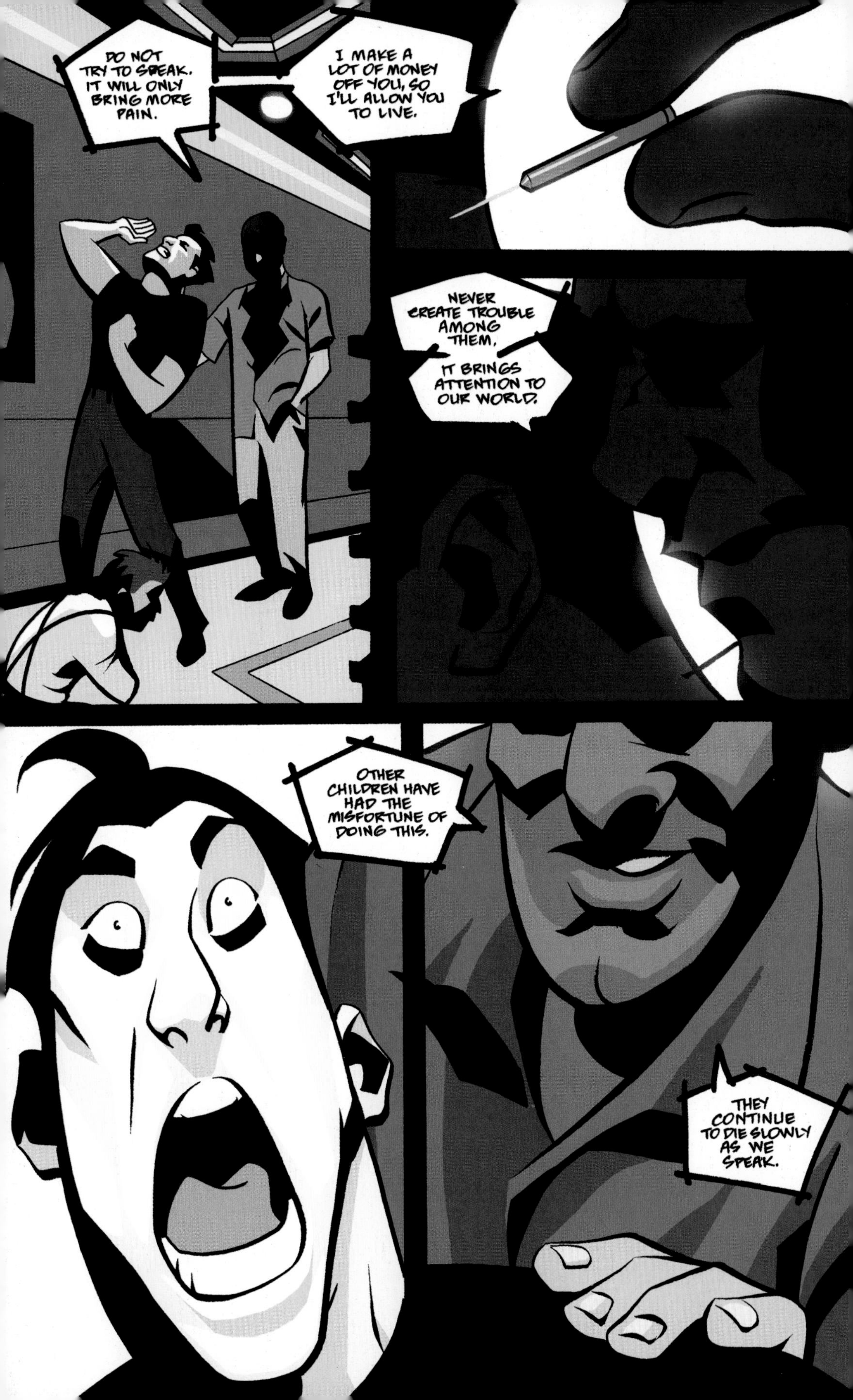
DO NOT TRY TO SPEAK. IT WILL ONLY BRING MORE PAIN.
I MAKE A LOT OF MONEY OFF YOU, SO I'LL ALLOW YOU TO LIVE.
NEVER CREATE TROUBLE AMONG THEM,
IT BRINGS ATTENTION TO OUR WORLD.
OTHER CHILDREN HAVE HAD THE MISFORTUNE OF DOING THIS.
THEY CONTINUE TO DIE SLOWLY AS WE SPEAK.

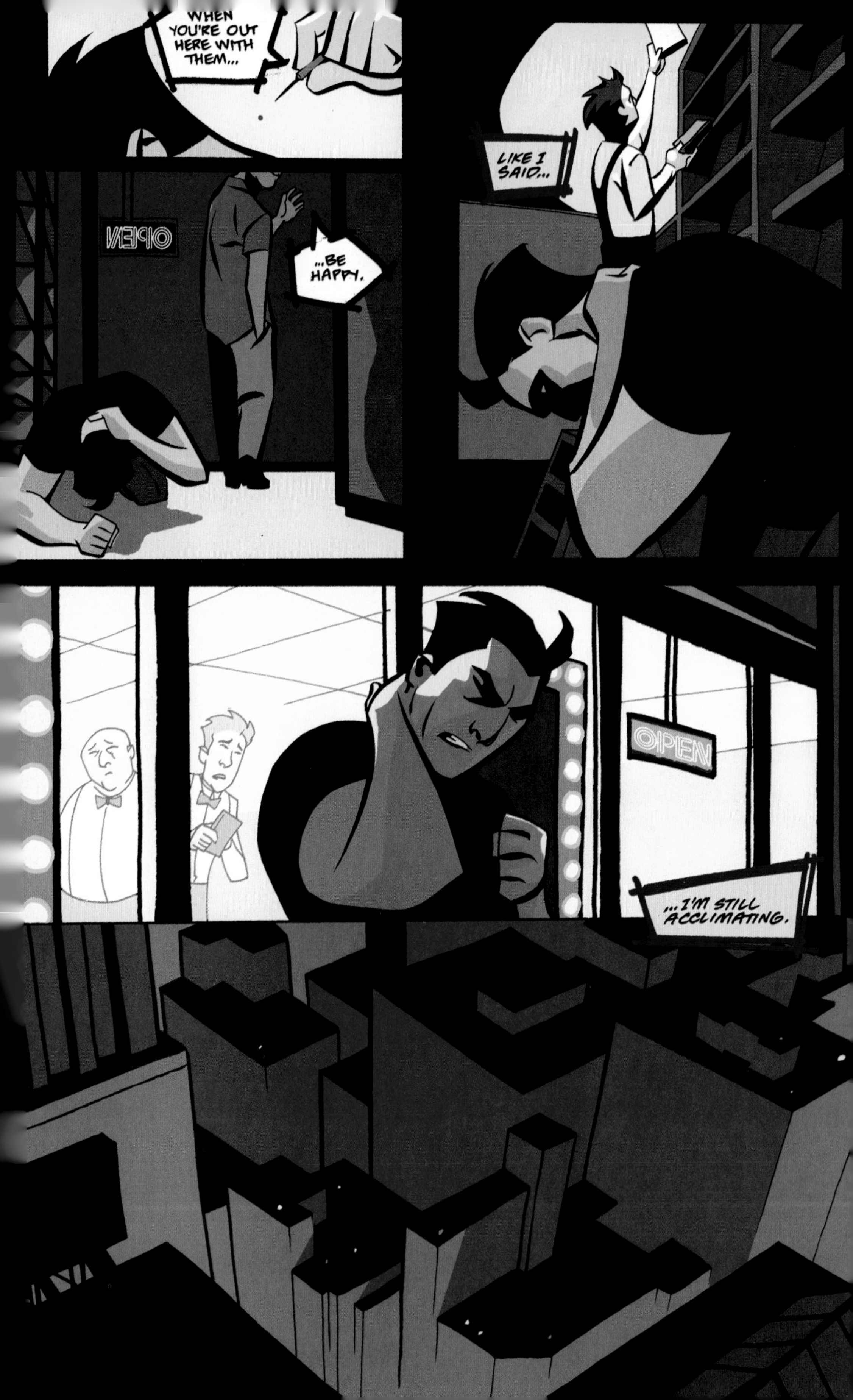
WHEN YOU'RE OUT HERE WITH THEM...
LIKE I SAID...
OPEN
...BE HAPPY.
OPEN
...I'M STILL ACCLIMATING.

KUJI
NO HO

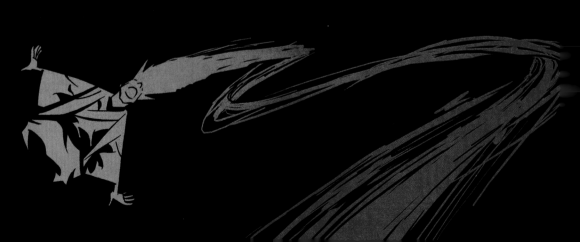

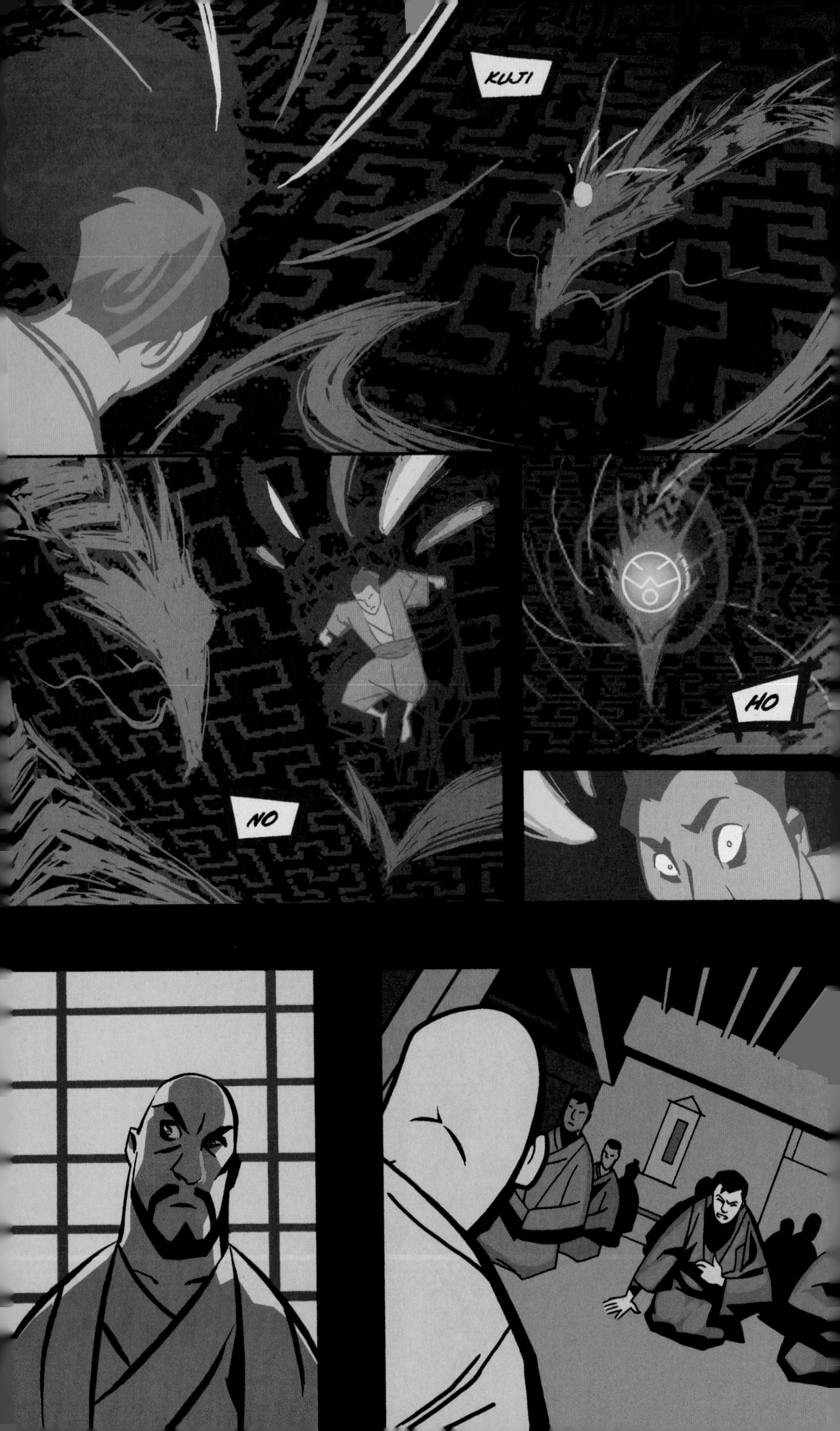
KUJI
NO
HO

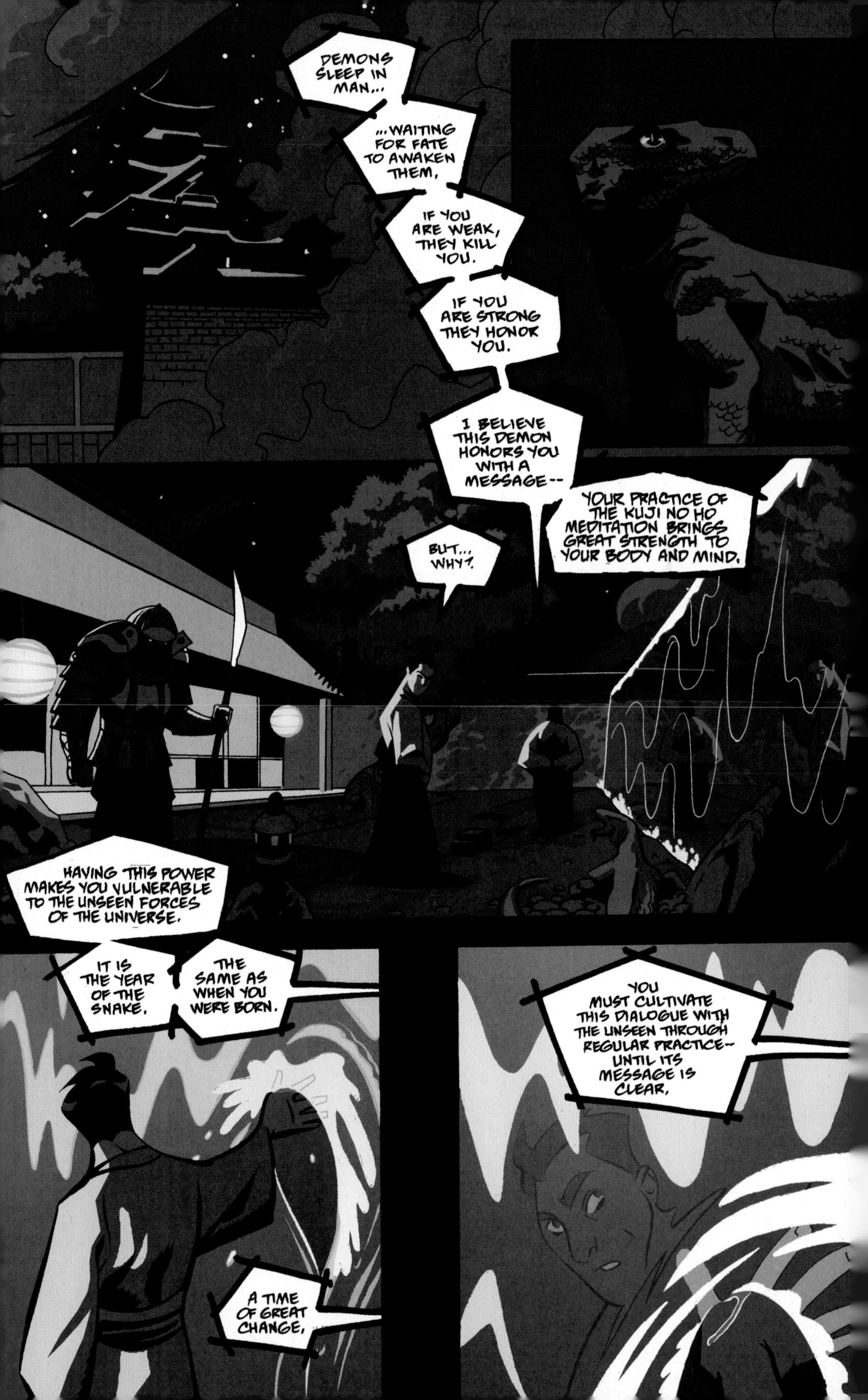
DEMONS SLEEP IN MAN...
...WAITING FOR FATE TO AWAKEN THEM.
IF YOU ARE WEAK, THEY KILL YOU.
IF YOU ARE STRONG THEY HONOR YOU.
I BELIEVE THIS DEMON HONORS YOU WITH A MESSAGE--
BUT... WHY?
YOUR PRACTICE OF THE KUJI NO HO MEDITATION BRINGS GREAT STRENGTH TO YOUR BODY AND MIND.
HAVING THIS POWER MAKES YOU VULNERABLE TO THE UNSEEN FORCES OF THE UNIVERSE.
IT IS THE YEAR OF THE SNAKE.
THE SAME AS WHEN YOU WERE BORN.
A TIME OF GREAT CHANGE.
YOU MUST CULTIVATE THIS DIALOGUE WITH THE UNSEEN THROUGH REGULAR PRACTICE-- UNTIL ITS MESSAGE IS CLEAR.

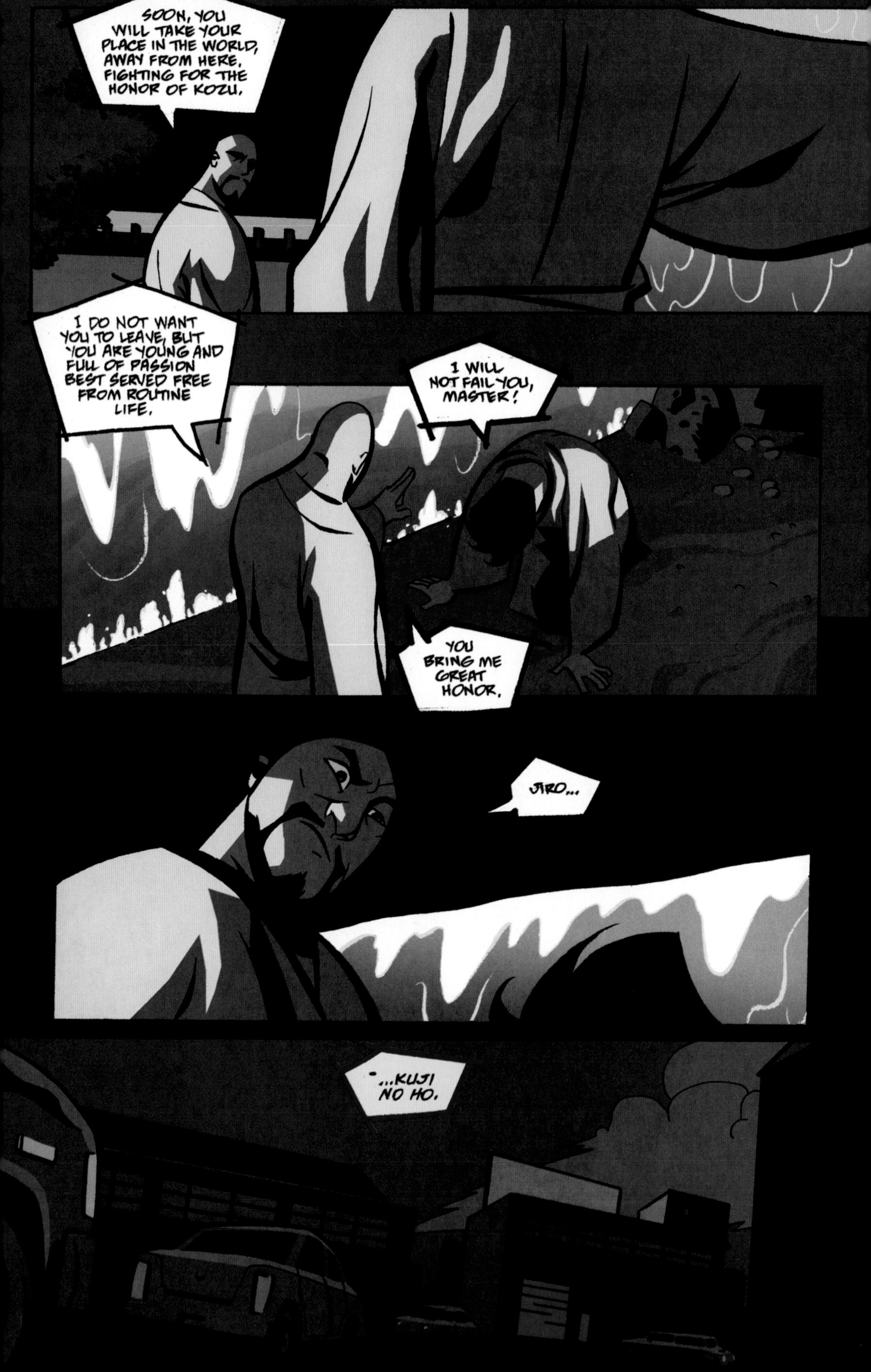
SOON, YOU WILL TAKE YOUR PLACE IN THE WORLD, AWAY FROM HERE, FIGHTING FOR THE HONOR OF KOZU.
I DO NOT WANT YOU TO LEAVE, BUT YOU ARE YOUNG AND FULL OF PASSION BEST SERVED FREE FROM ROUTINE LIFE.
I WILL NOT FAIL YOU, MASTER!
YOU BRING ME GREAT HONOR.
JIRO...
...KUJI NO HO.

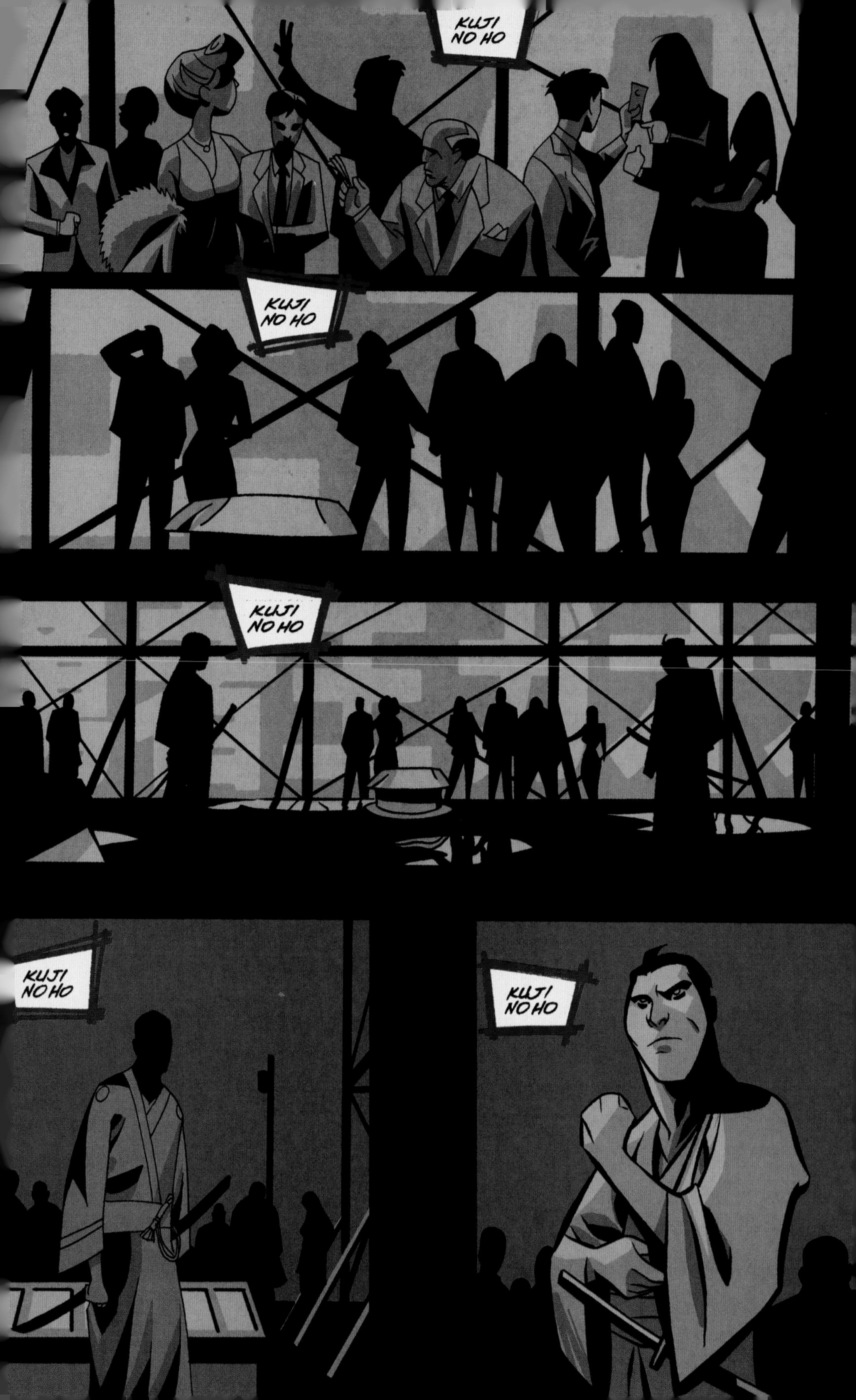
KUJI NO HO
KUJI NO HO
KUJI NO HO
KUJI NO HO
KUJI NO HO

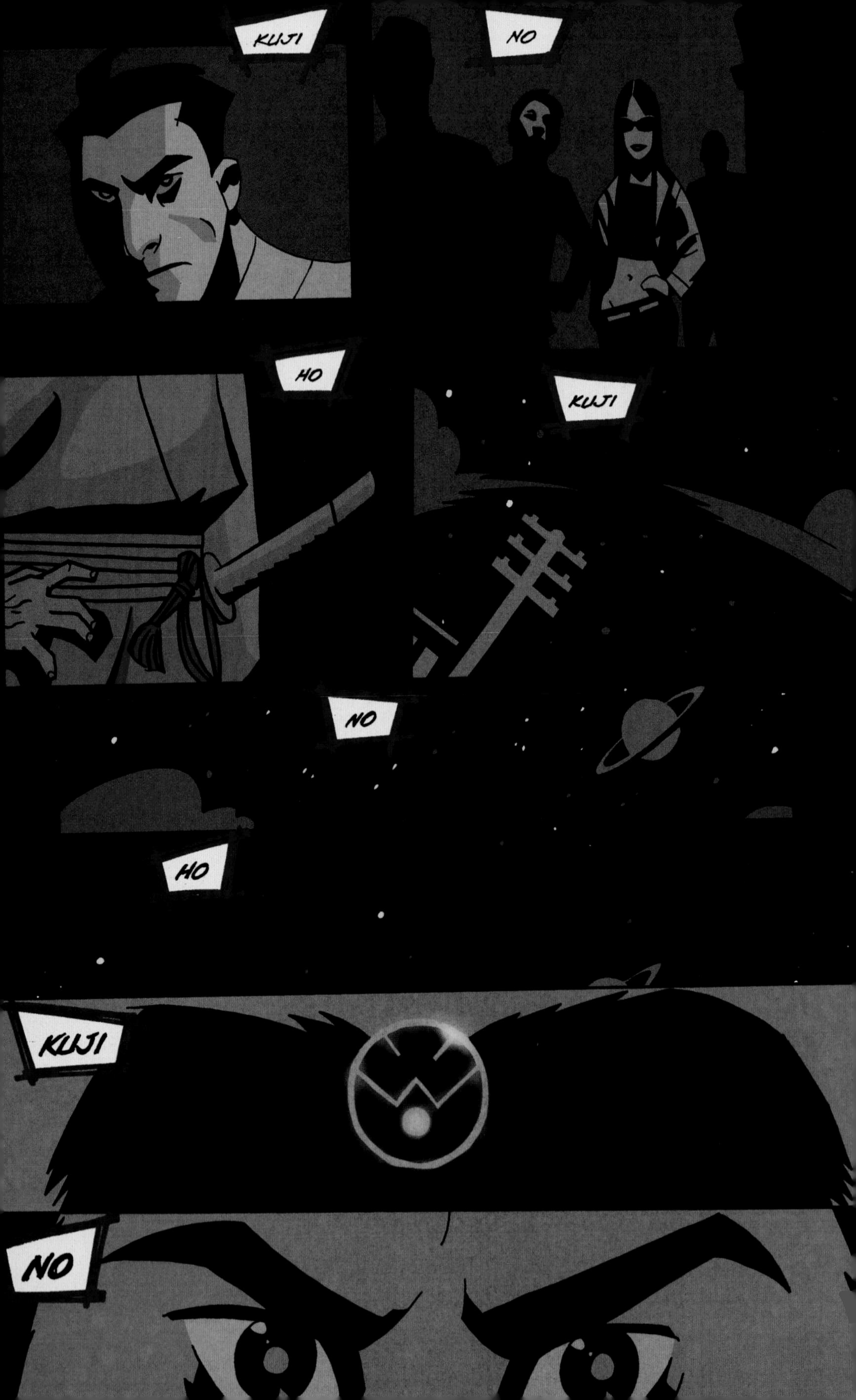
KUJI
NO
HO
KUJI
NO
HO
KUJI
NO

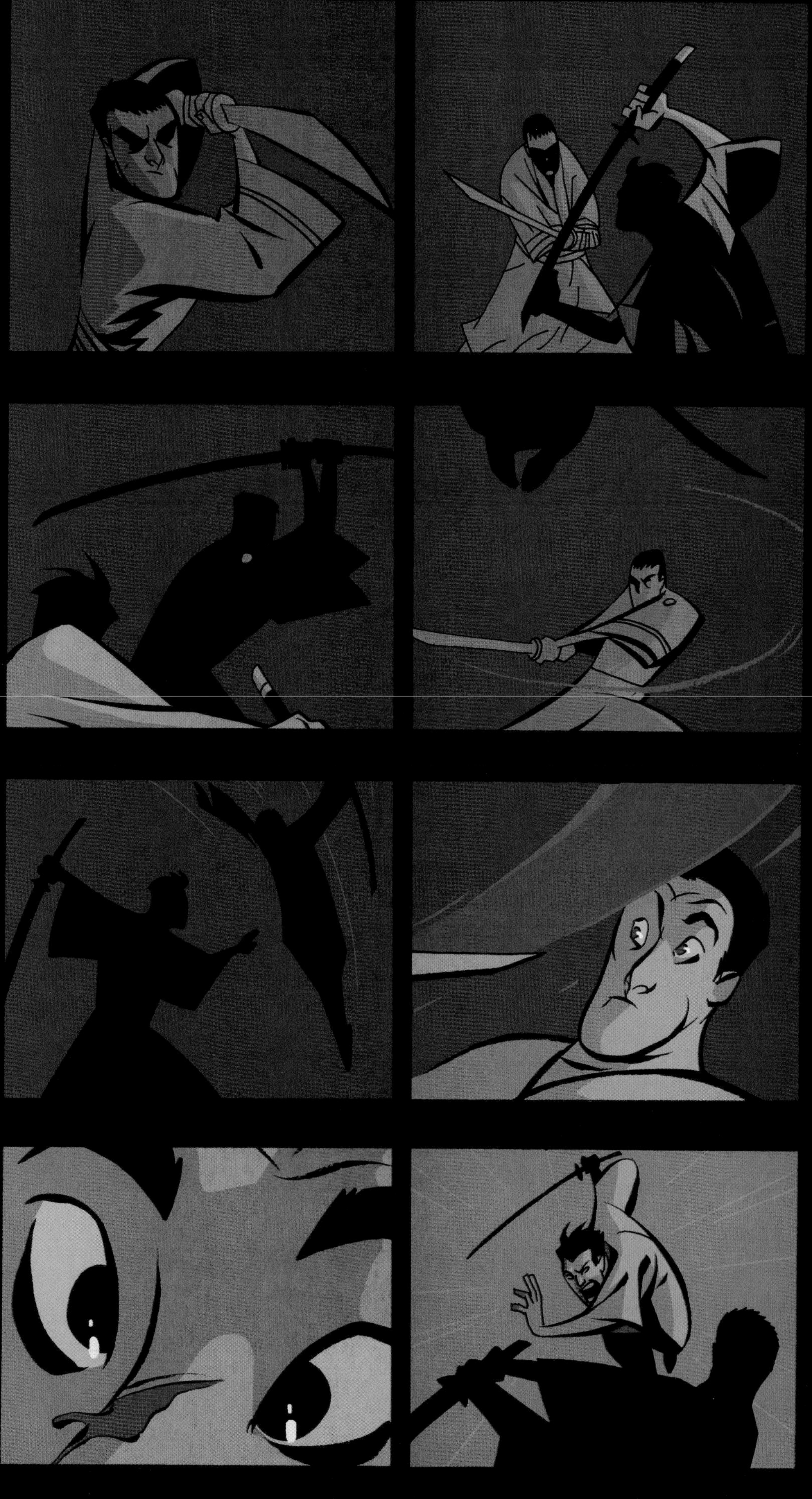

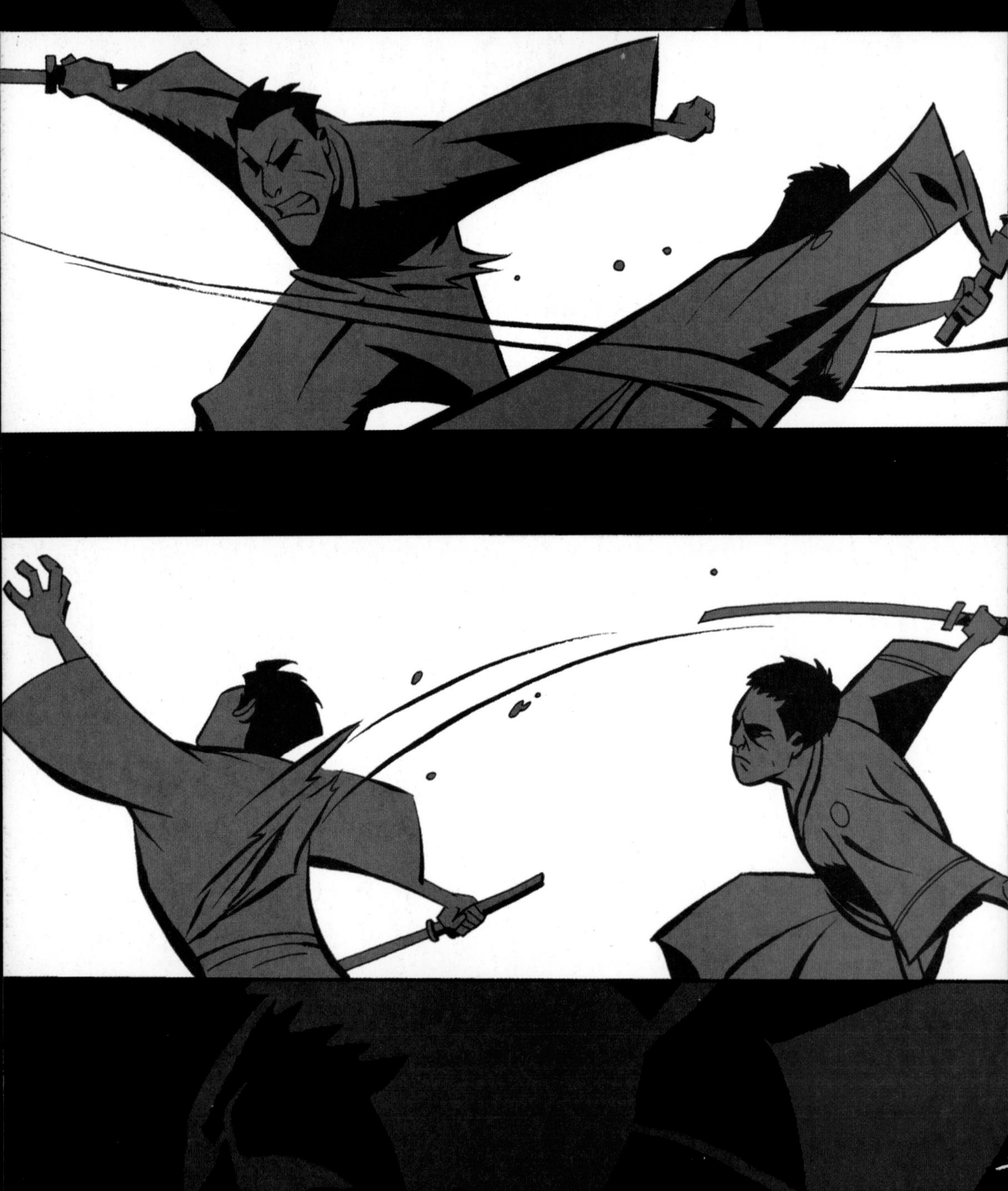

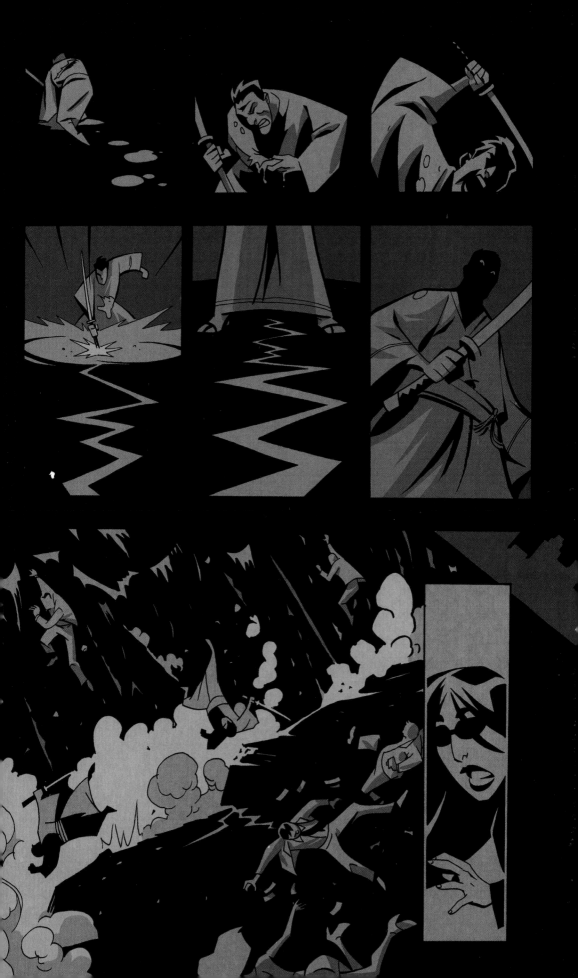

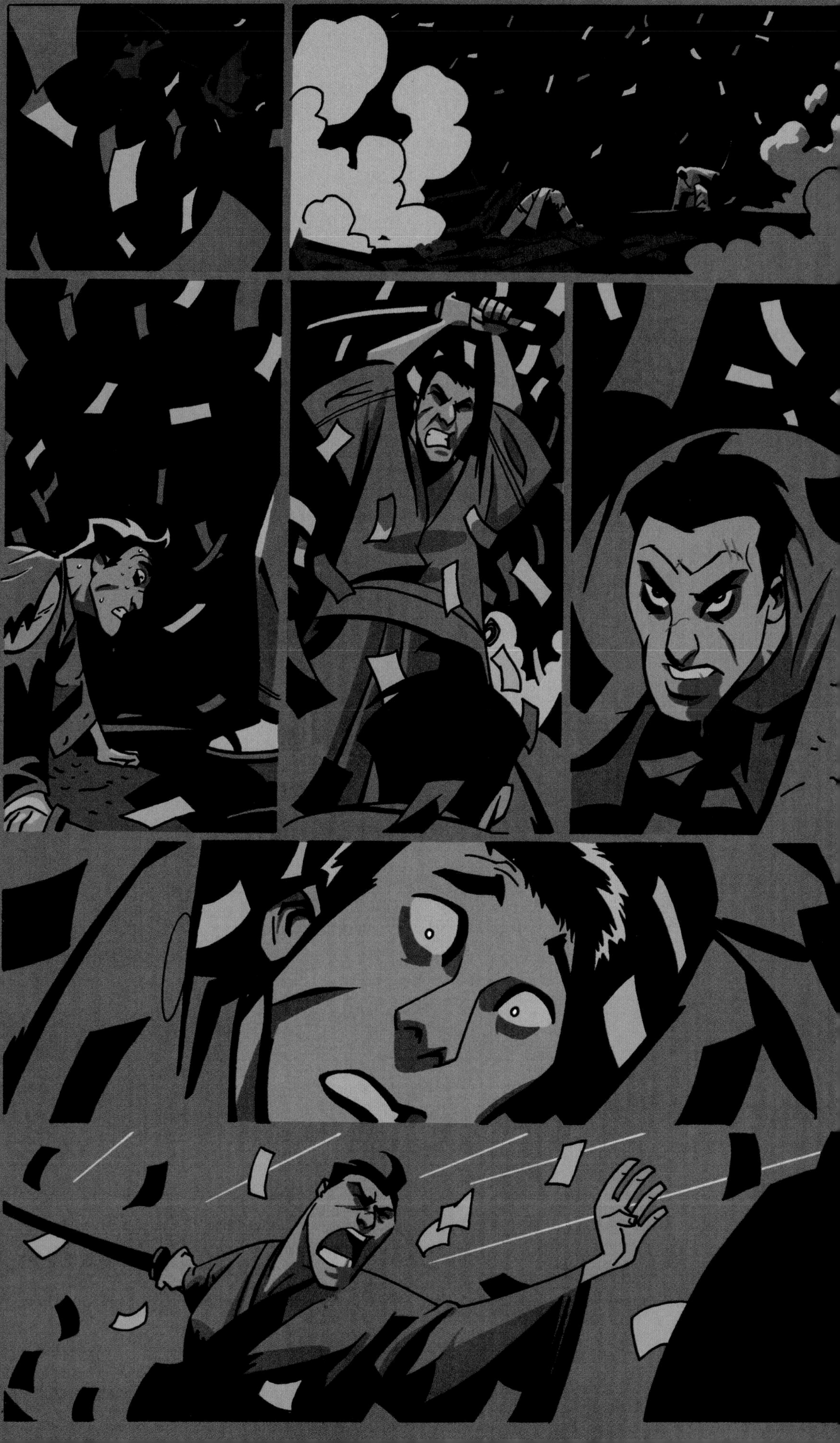

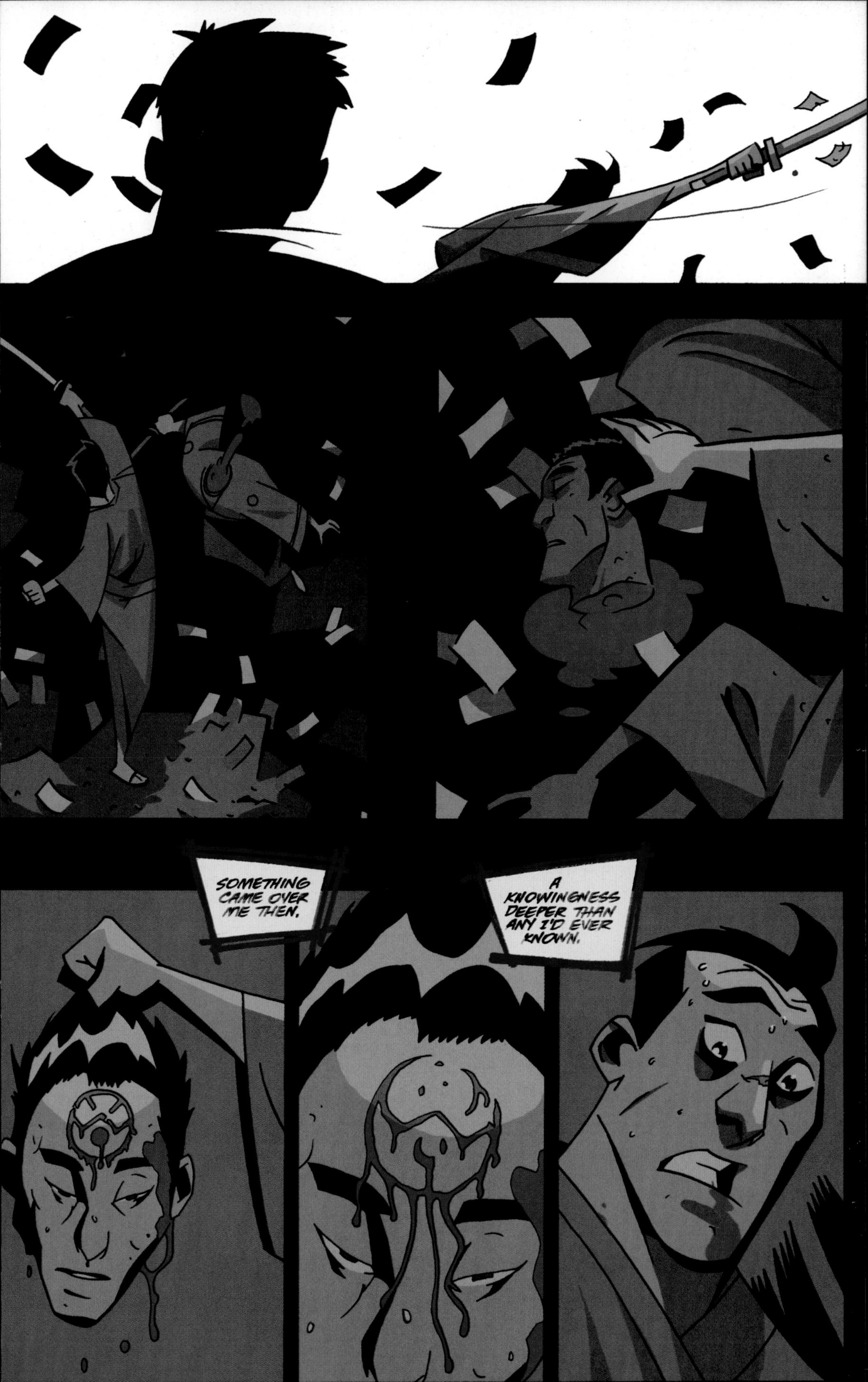
SOMETHING CAME OVER ME THEN.
A KNOWINGNESS DEEPER THAN ANY I'D EVER KNOWN.

THIS RONIN...

...IS MY BROTHER...

...MY OLDER BROTHER.

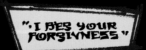
シーホルト！

"MY BROTHER.

"...I BEG YOUR FORGIVNESS"

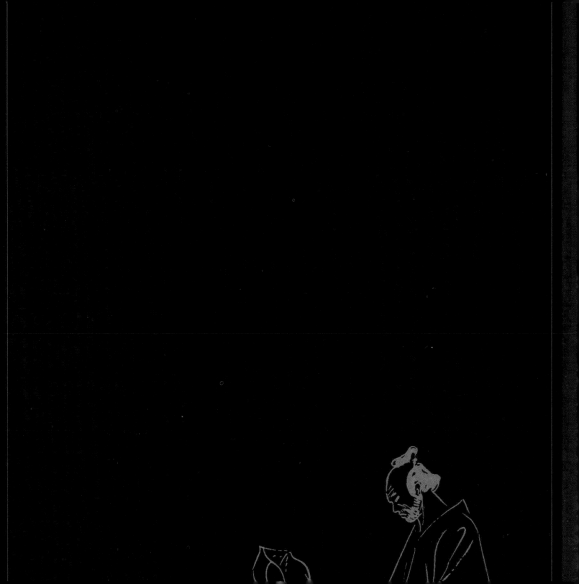

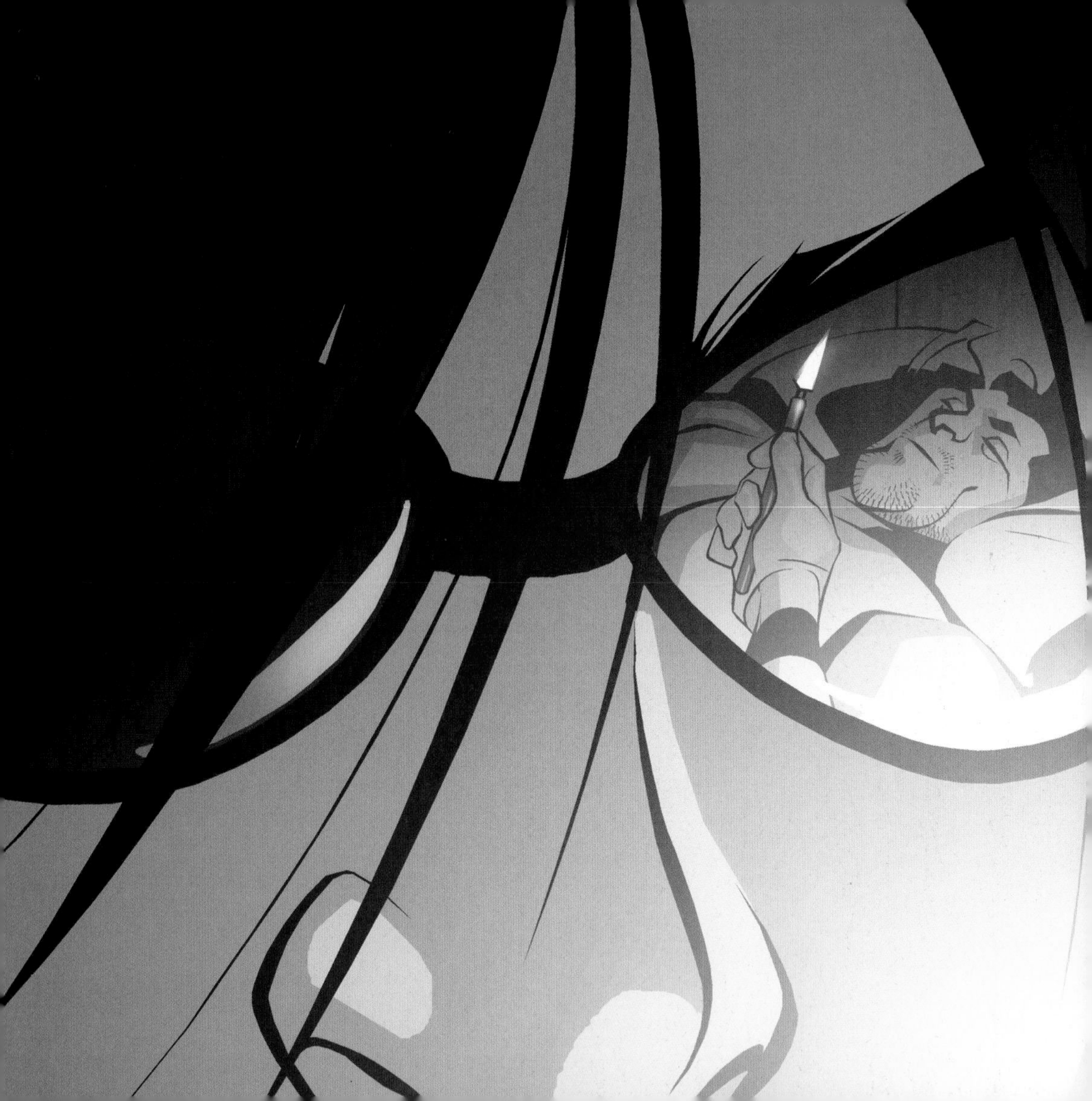

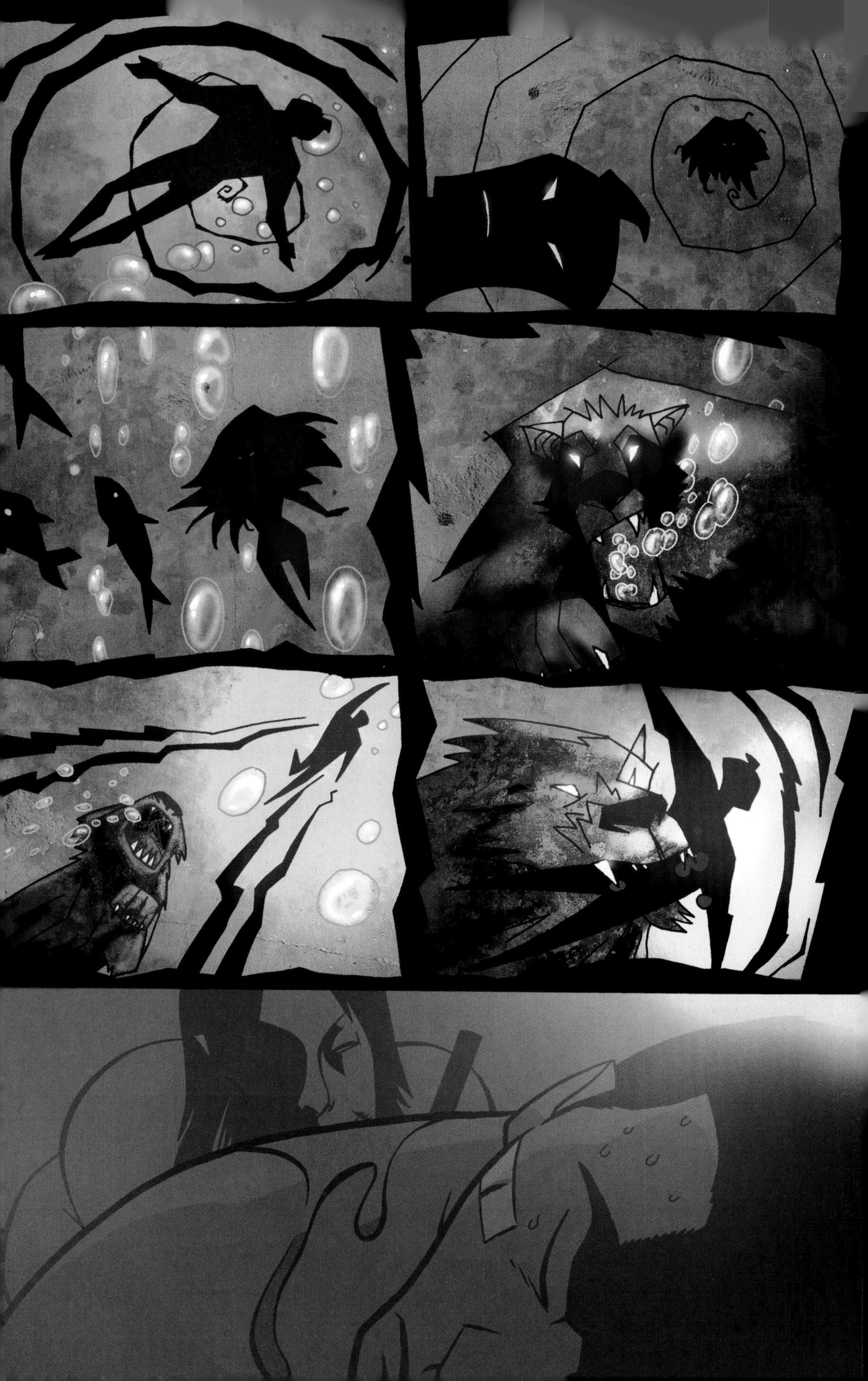

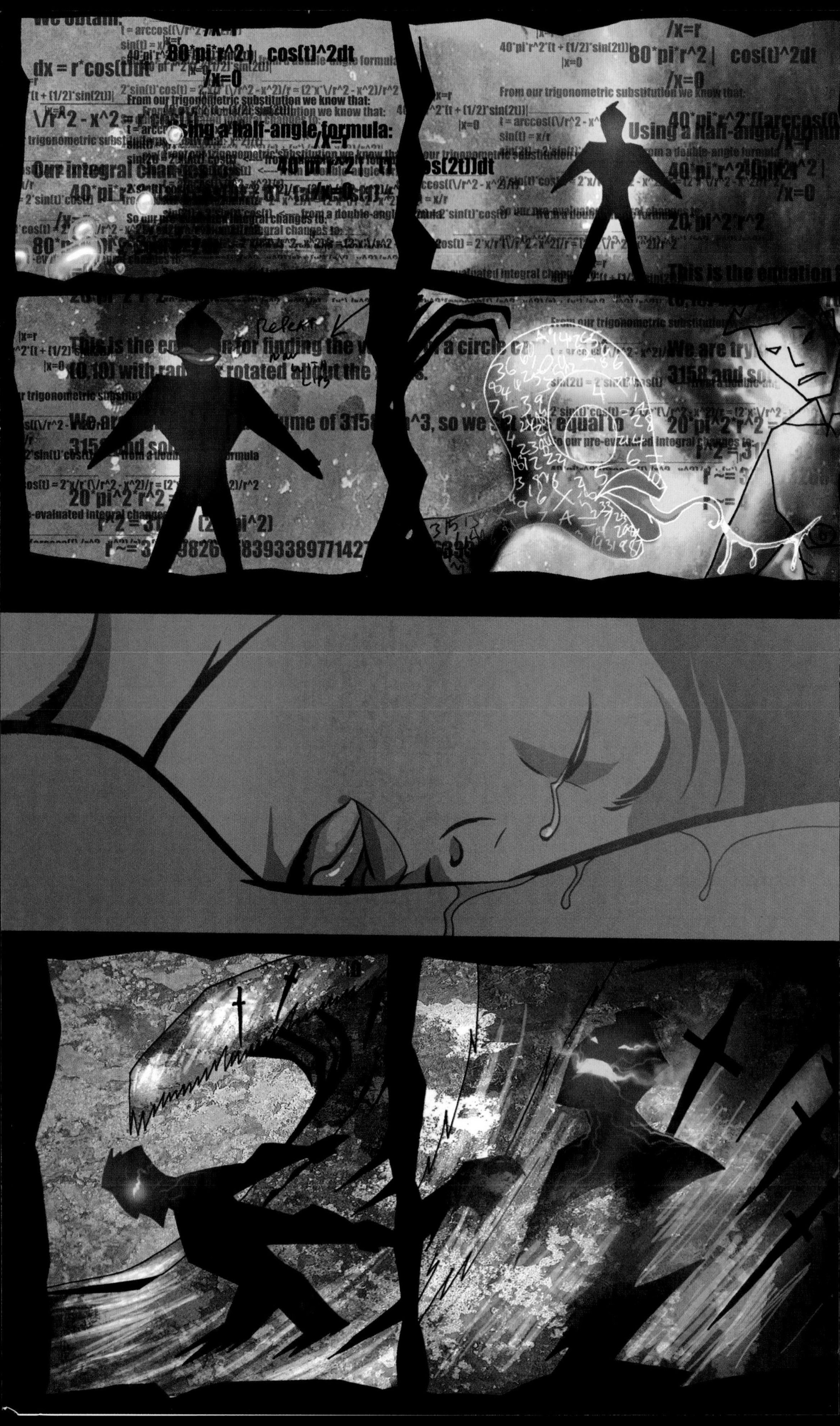

dx = r*cos(t)dt
80*pi*r^2 | cos(t)^2dt
/x=0
From our trigonometric substitution we know that:
Using a half-angle formula:
Our integral changes to:
20*pi^2*r^2

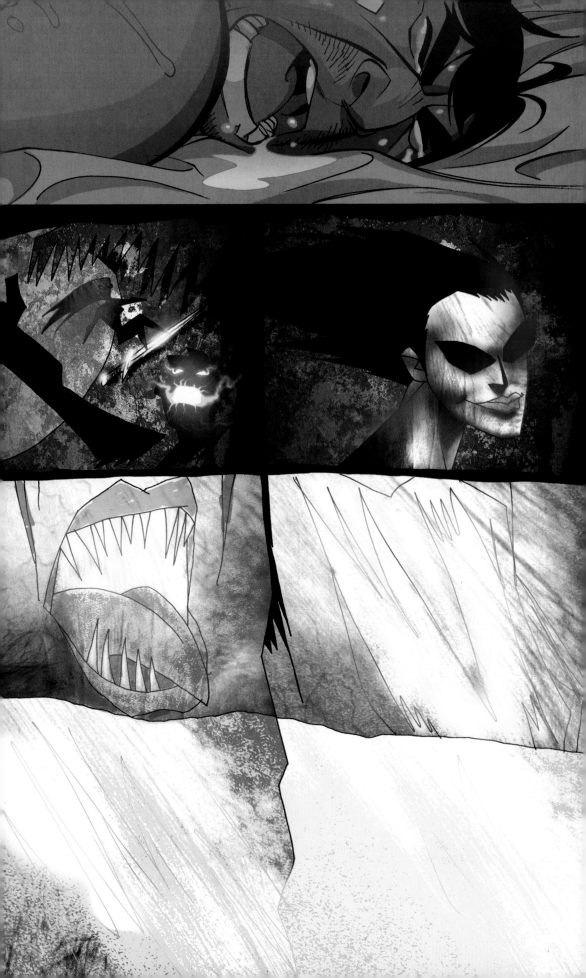

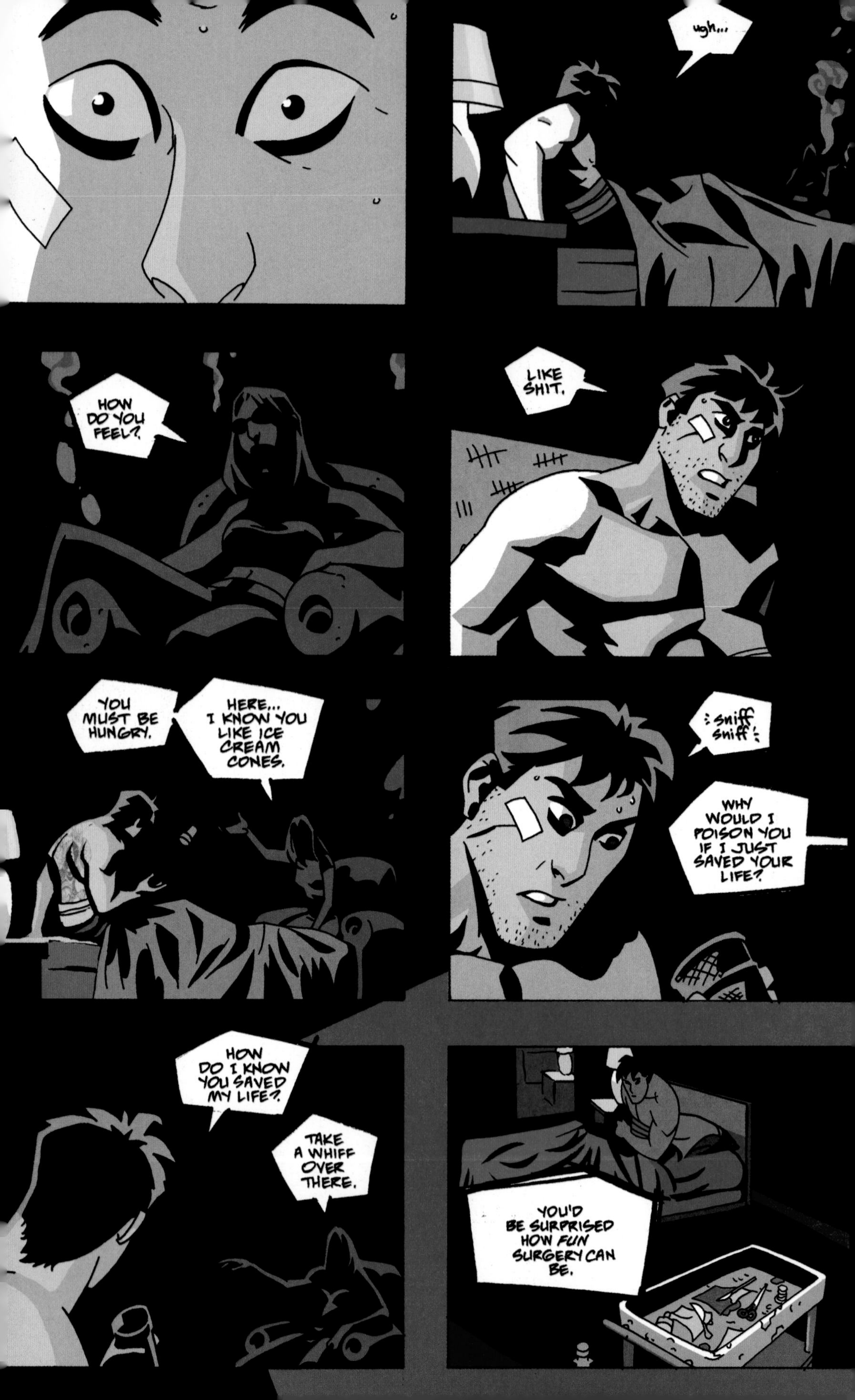
ugh...
HOW DO YOU FEEL?
LIKE SHIT.
YOU MUST BE HUNGRY.
HERE... I KNOW YOU LIKE ICE CREAM CONES.
sniff sniff
WHY WOULD I POISON YOU IF I JUST SAVED YOUR LIFE?
HOW DO I KNOW YOU SAVED MY LIFE?
TAKE A WHIFF OVER THERE.
YOU'D BE SURPRISED HOW *FUN* SURGERY CAN BE.

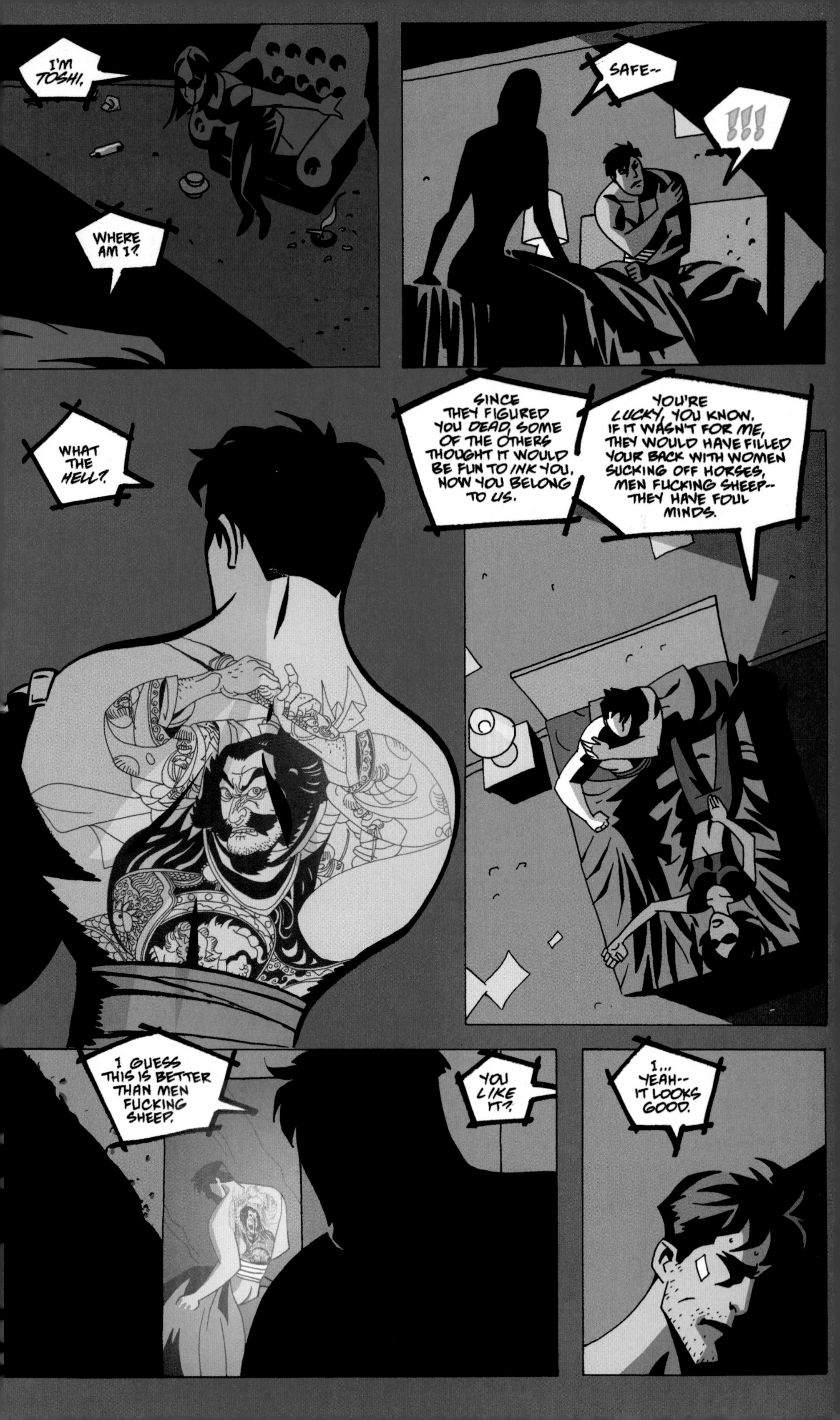
I'M TOSHI.
WHERE AM I?
SAFE--
!!!
WHAT THE HELL?
SINCE THEY FIGURED YOU DEAD, SOME OF THE OTHERS THOUGHT IT WOULD BE FUN TO INK YOU. NOW YOU BELONG TO US.
YOU'RE LUCKY, YOU KNOW. IF IT WASN'T FOR ME, THEY WOULD HAVE FILLED YOUR BACK WITH WOMEN SUCKING OFF HORSES, MEN FUCKING SHEEP-- THEY HAVE FOUL MINDS.
I GUESS THIS IS BETTER THAN MEN FUCKING SHEEP.
YOU LIKE IT?
I... YEAH-- IT LOOKS GOOD.

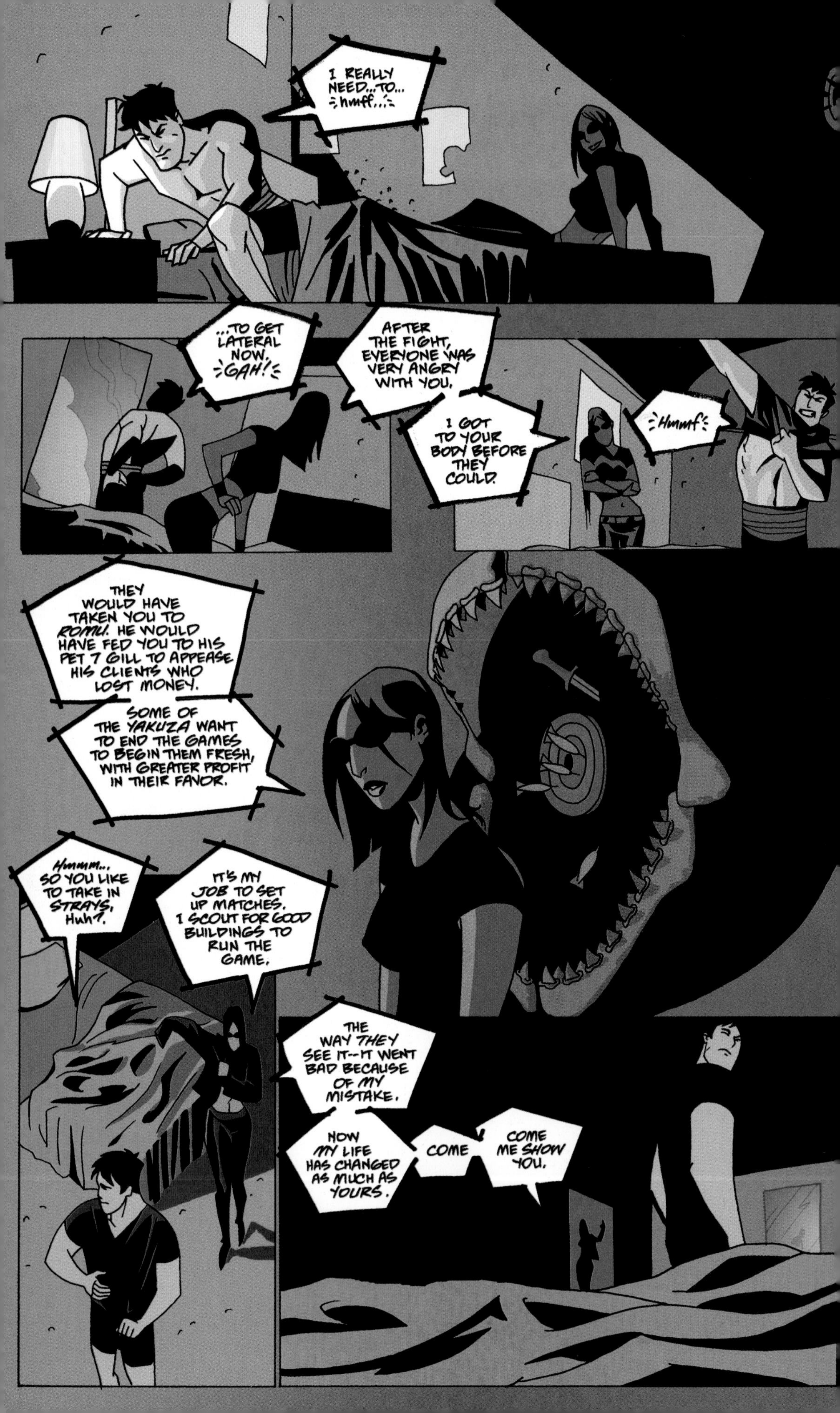
I REALLY NEED... TO... hmff...
...TO GET LATERAL NOW. GAH!
AFTER THE FIGHT, EVERYONE WAS VERY ANGRY WITH YOU.
I GOT TO YOUR BODY BEFORE THEY COULD.
Hmmf
THEY WOULD HAVE TAKEN YOU TO ROMU. HE WOULD HAVE FED YOU TO HIS PET 7 GILL TO APPEASE HIS CLIENTS WHO LOST MONEY.
SOME OF THE YAKUZA WANT TO END THE GAMES TO BEGIN THEM FRESH, WITH GREATER PROFIT IN THEIR FAVOR.
Hmmm... SO YOU LIKE TO TAKE IN STRAYS, Huh?.
IT'S MY JOB TO SET UP MATCHES. I SCOUT FOR GOOD BUILDINGS TO RUN THE GAME.
THE WAY THEY SEE IT-- IT WENT BAD BECAUSE OF MY MISTAKE.
NOW MY LIFE HAS CHANGED AS MUCH AS YOURS.
COME
COME ME SHOW YOU.

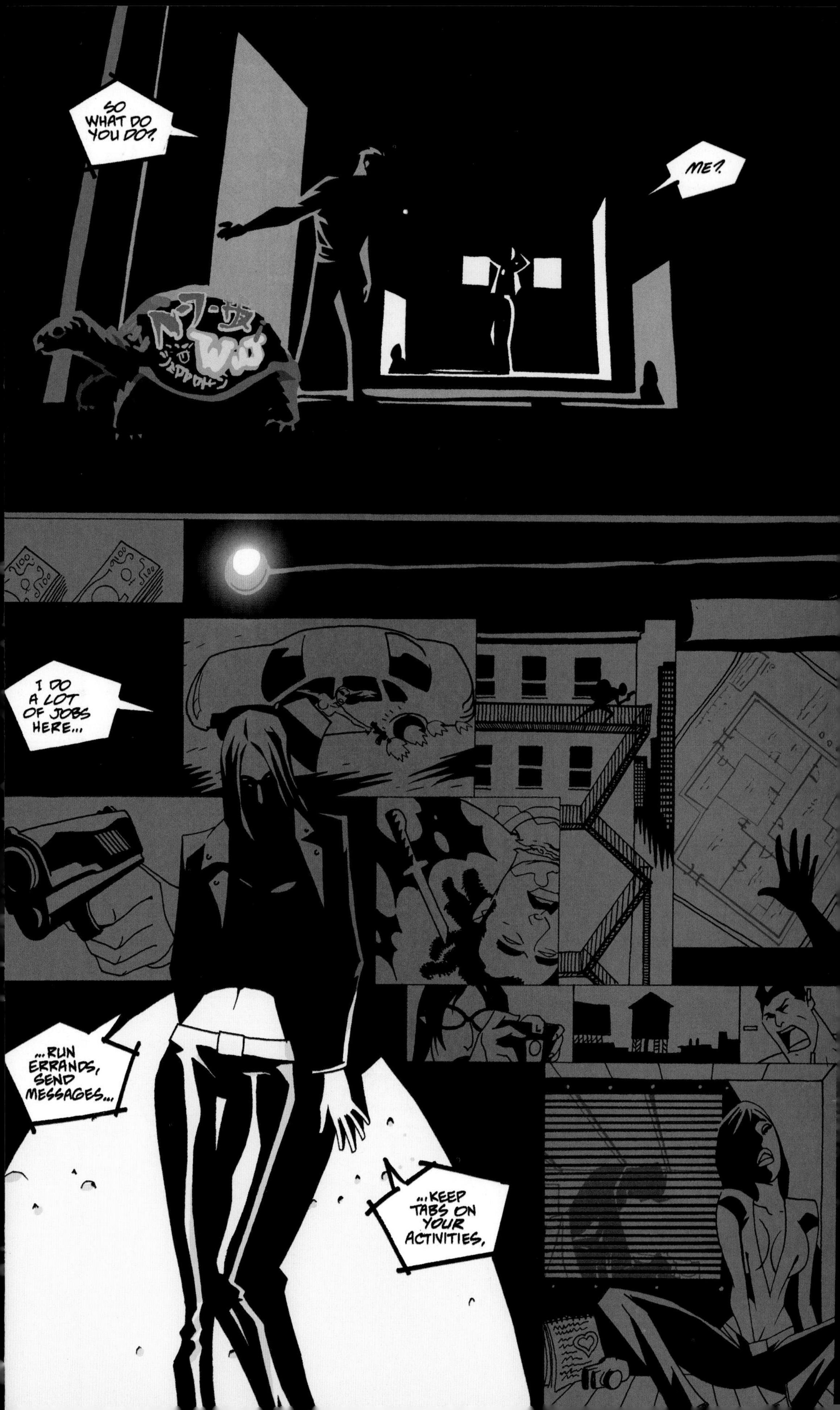

SO WHAT DO YOU DO?
ME?
I DO A LOT OF JOBS HERE...
...RUN ERRANDS, SEND MESSAGES...
...KEEP TABS ON YOUR ACTIVITIES.

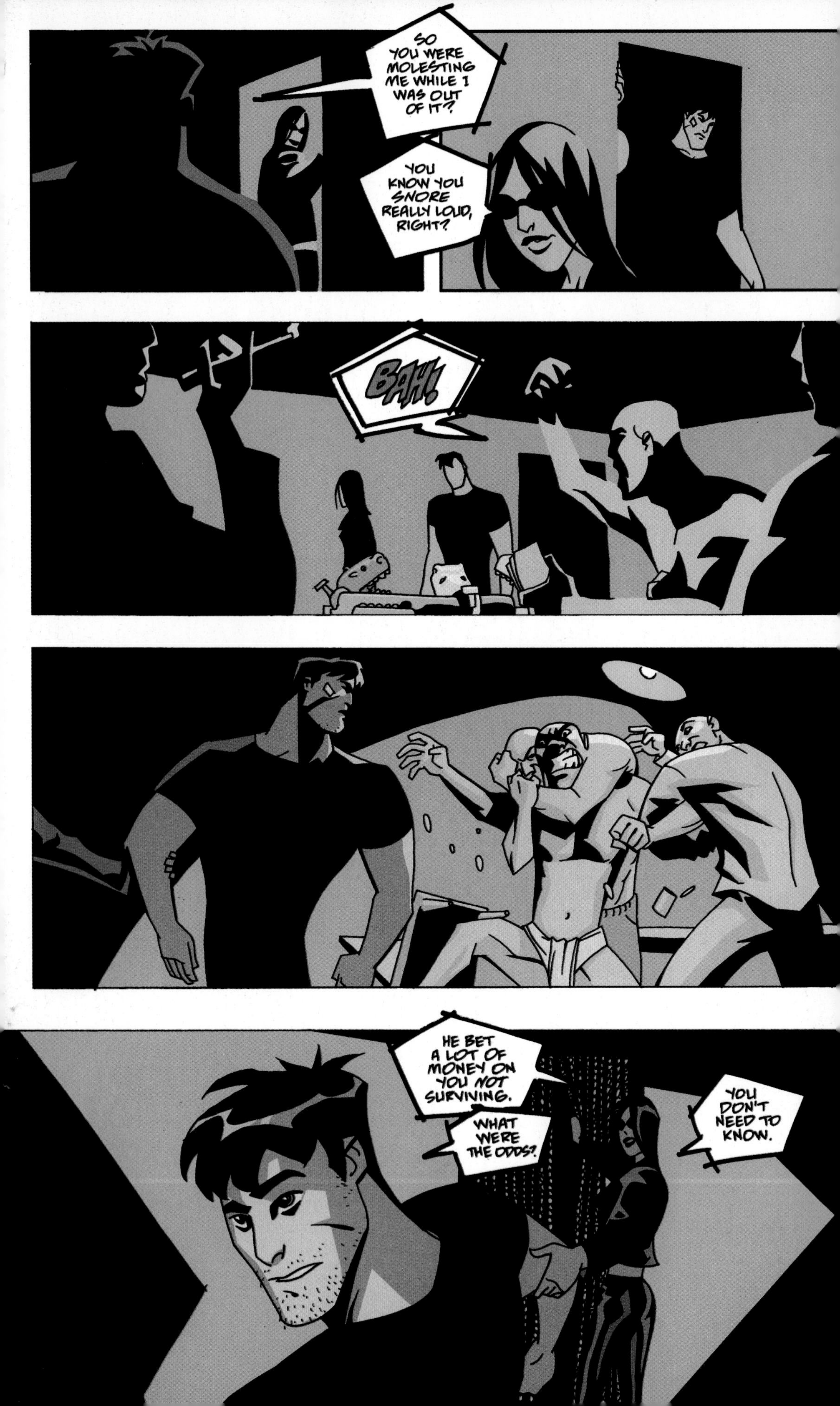

SO YOU WERE MOLESTING ME WHILE I WAS OUT OF IT?
YOU KNOW YOU SNORE REALLY LOUD, RIGHT?
BAH!
HE BET A LOT OF MONEY ON YOU *NOT* SURVIVING.
WHAT WERE THE ODDS?
YOU DON'T NEED TO KNOW.

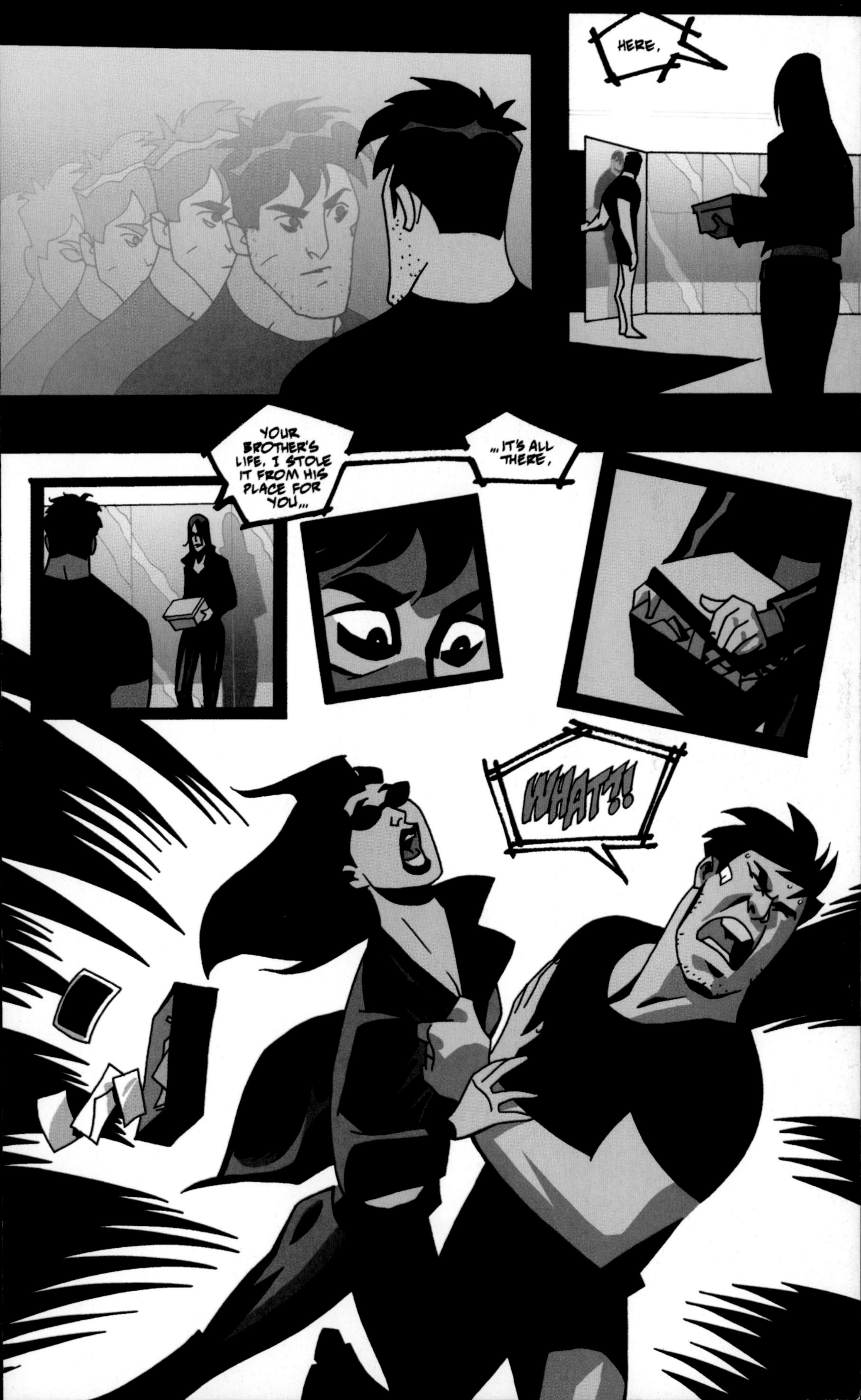
HERE.
YOUR BROTHER'S LIFE. I STOLE IT FROM HIS PLACE FOR YOU...
...IT'S ALL THERE.
WHAT?!

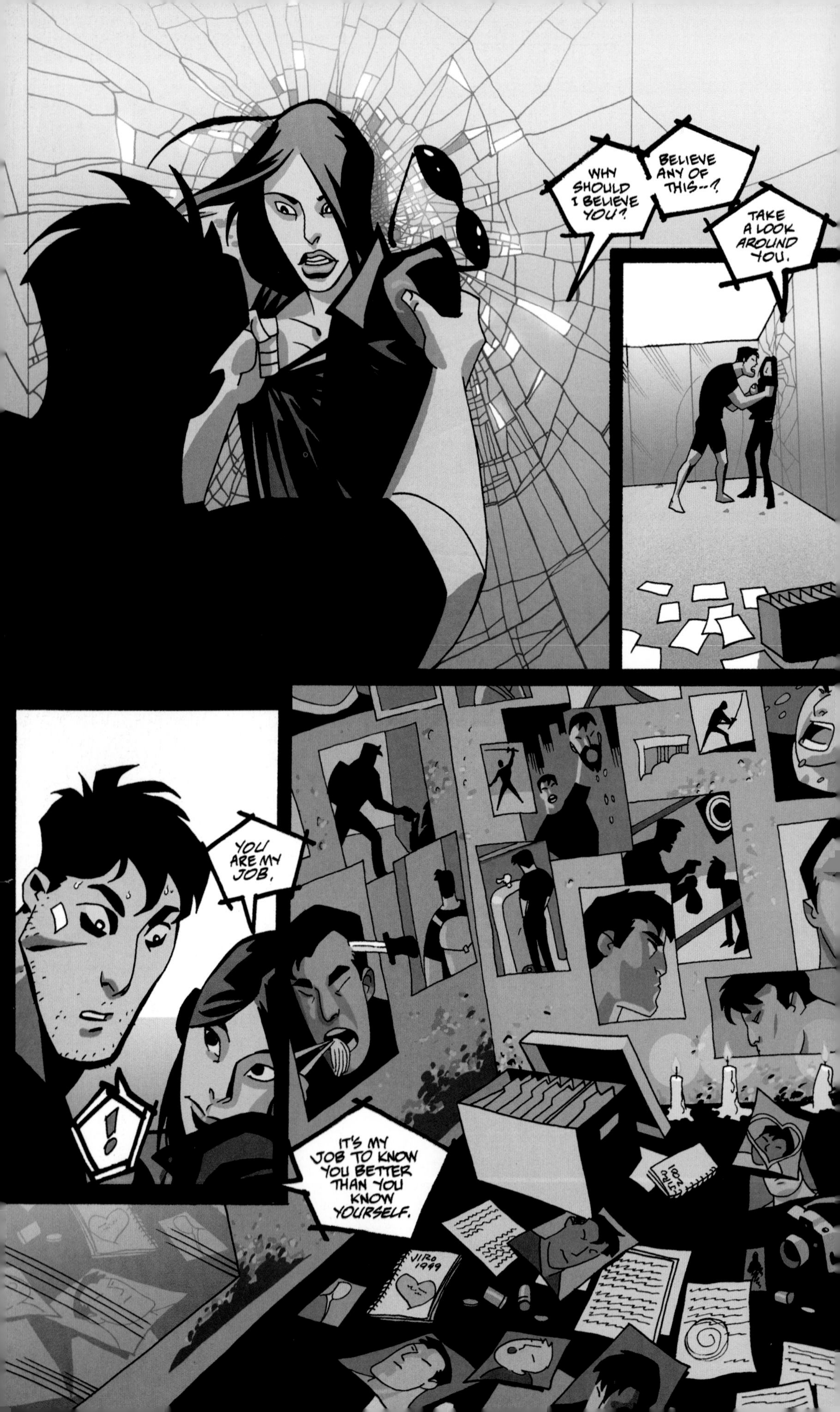

WHY SHOULD I BELIEVE YOU?
BELIEVE ANY OF THIS--?
TAKE A LOOK AROUND YOU.
YOU ARE MY JOB.
!
IT'S MY JOB TO KNOW YOU BETTER THAN YOU KNOW YOURSELF.

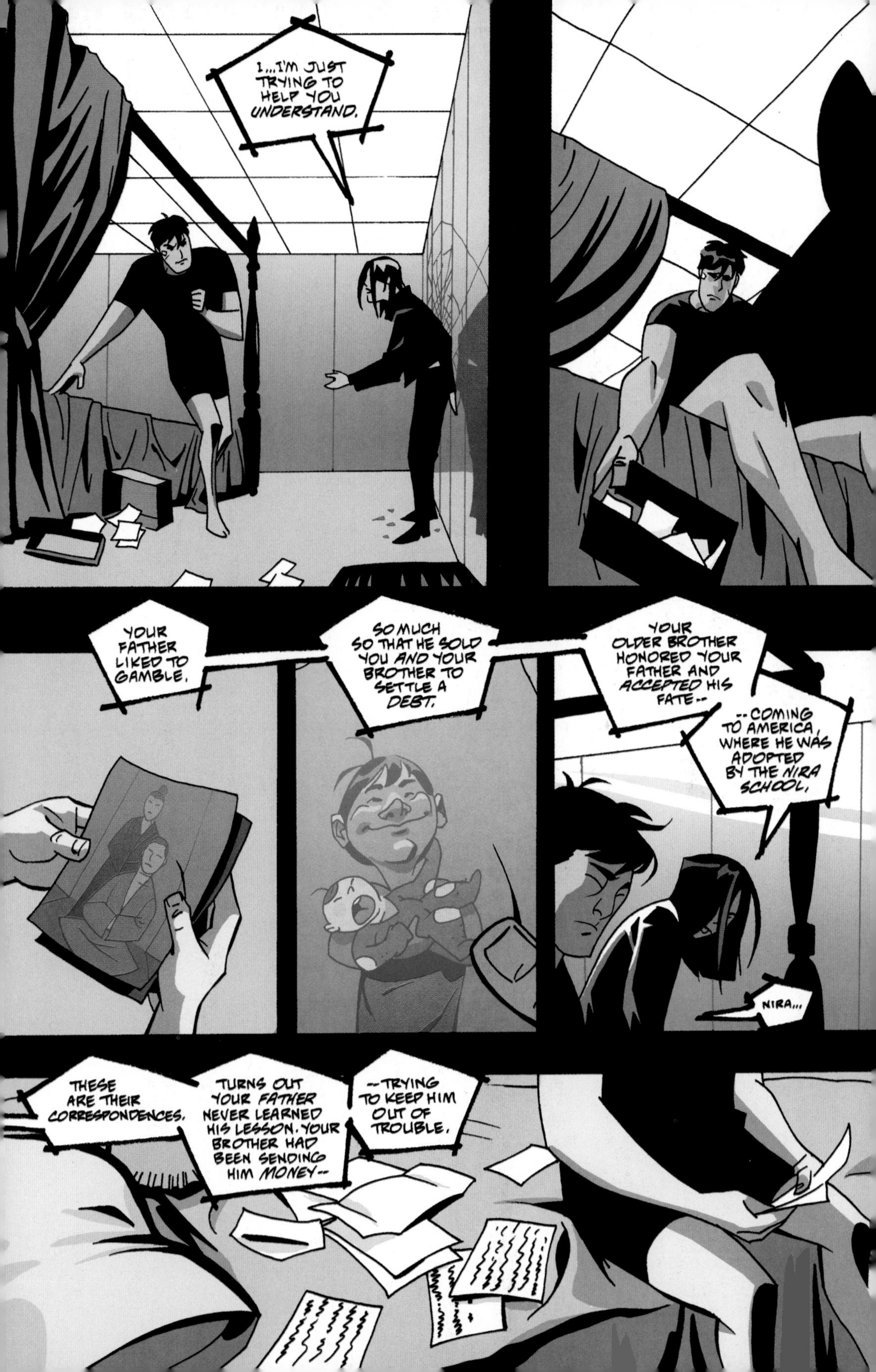

I...I'M JUST TRYING TO HELP YOU UNDERSTAND.
YOUR FATHER LIKED TO GAMBLE.
SO MUCH SO THAT HE SOLD YOU AND YOUR BROTHER TO SETTLE A DEBT.
YOUR OLDER BROTHER HONORED YOUR FATHER AND ACCEPTED HIS FATE--
--COMING TO AMERICA, WHERE HE WAS ADOPTED BY THE NIRA SCHOOL.
NIRA...
THESE ARE THEIR CORRESPONDENCES.
TURNS OUT YOUR FATHER NEVER LEARNED HIS LESSON. YOUR BROTHER HAD BEEN SENDING HIM MONEY--
--TRYING TO KEEP HIM OUT OF TROUBLE.

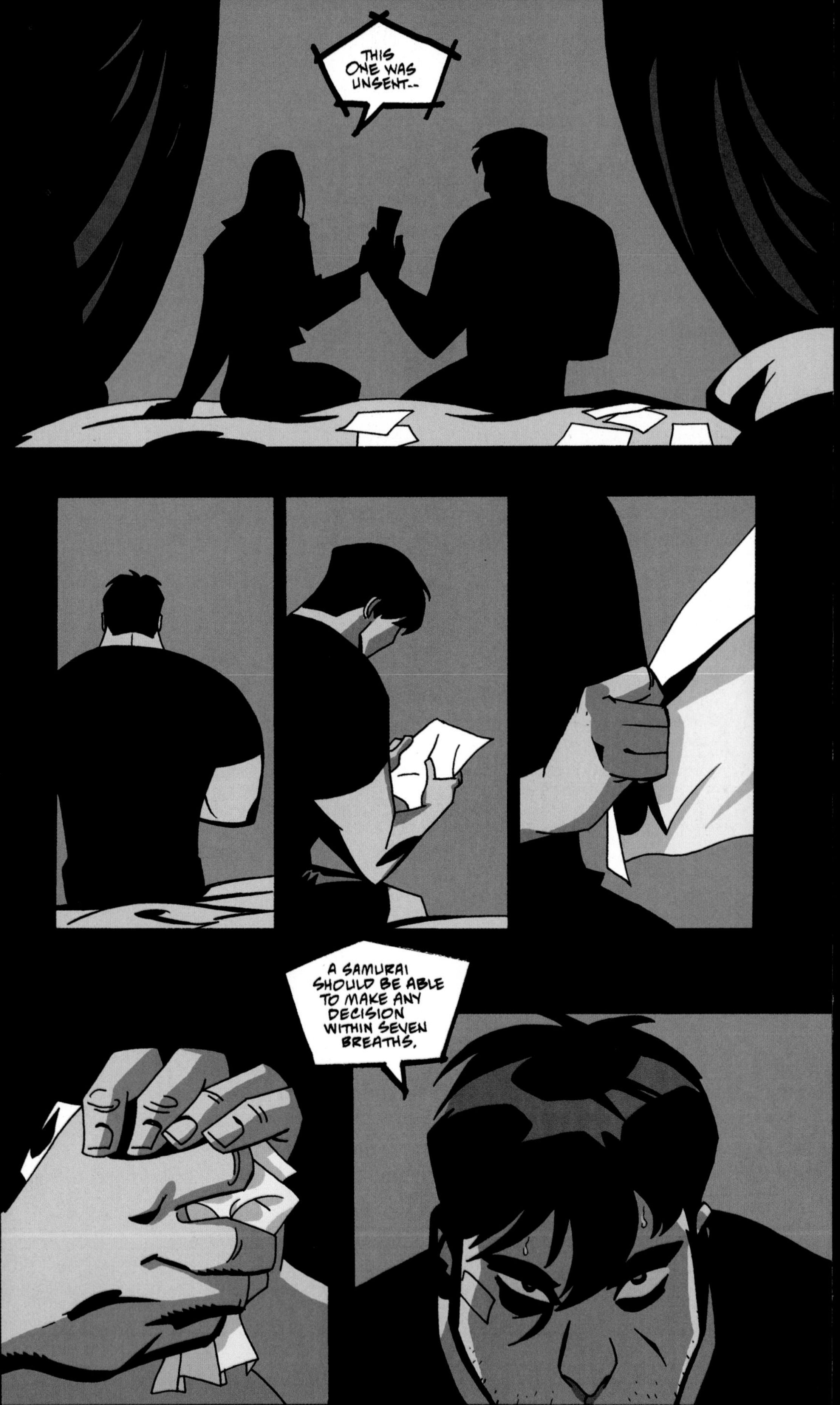
THIS ONE WAS UNSENT--
A SAMURAI SHOULD BE ABLE TO MAKE ANY DECISION WITHIN SEVEN BREATHS.

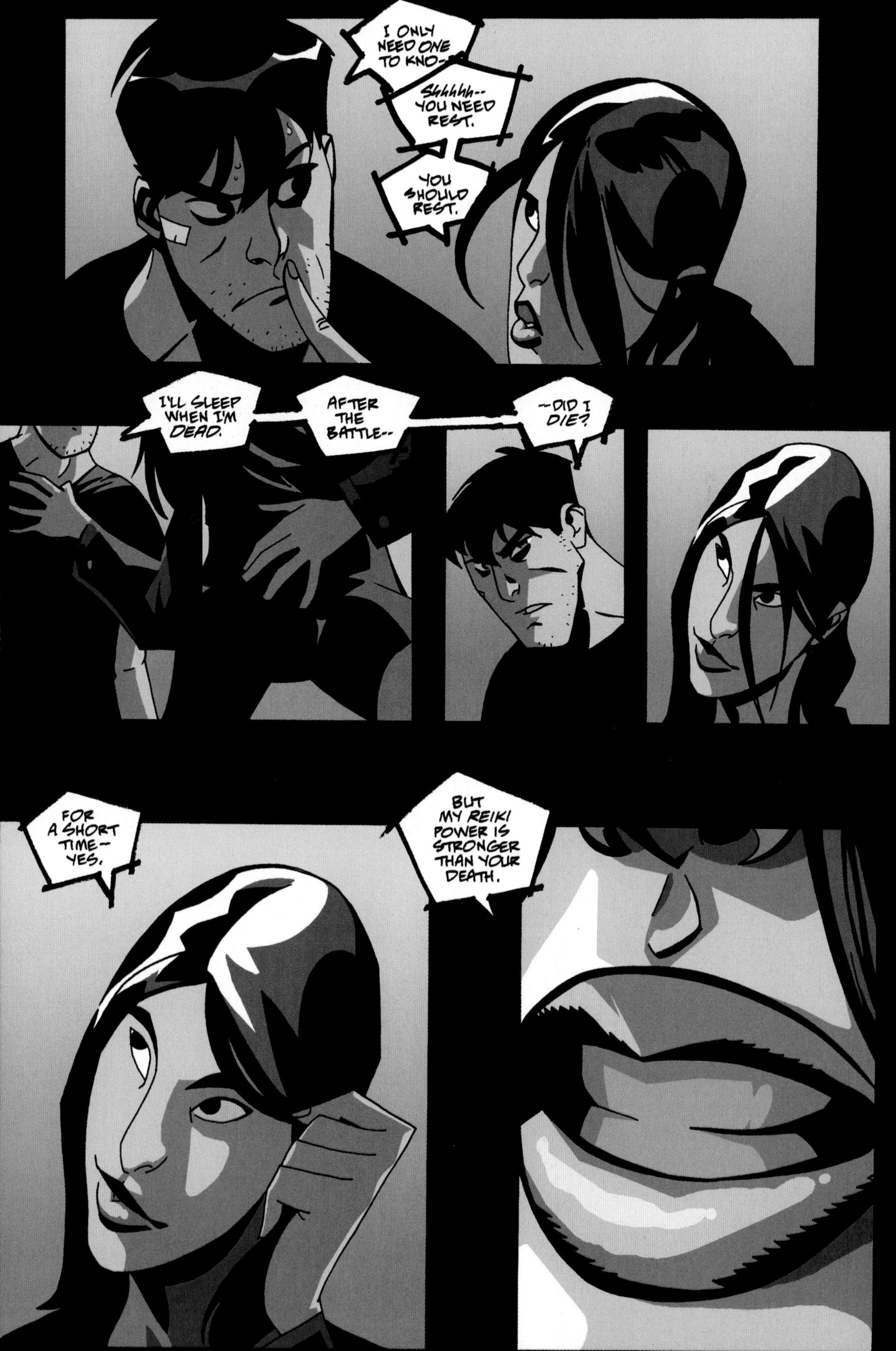
I ONLY NEED ONE TO KNO--
Shhhhh-- YOU NEED REST.
YOU SHOULD REST.
I'LL SLEEP WHEN I'M DEAD.
AFTER THE BATTLE--
--DID I DIE?
FOR A SHORT TIME-- YES.
BUT MY REIKI POWER IS STRONGER THAN YOUR DEATH.

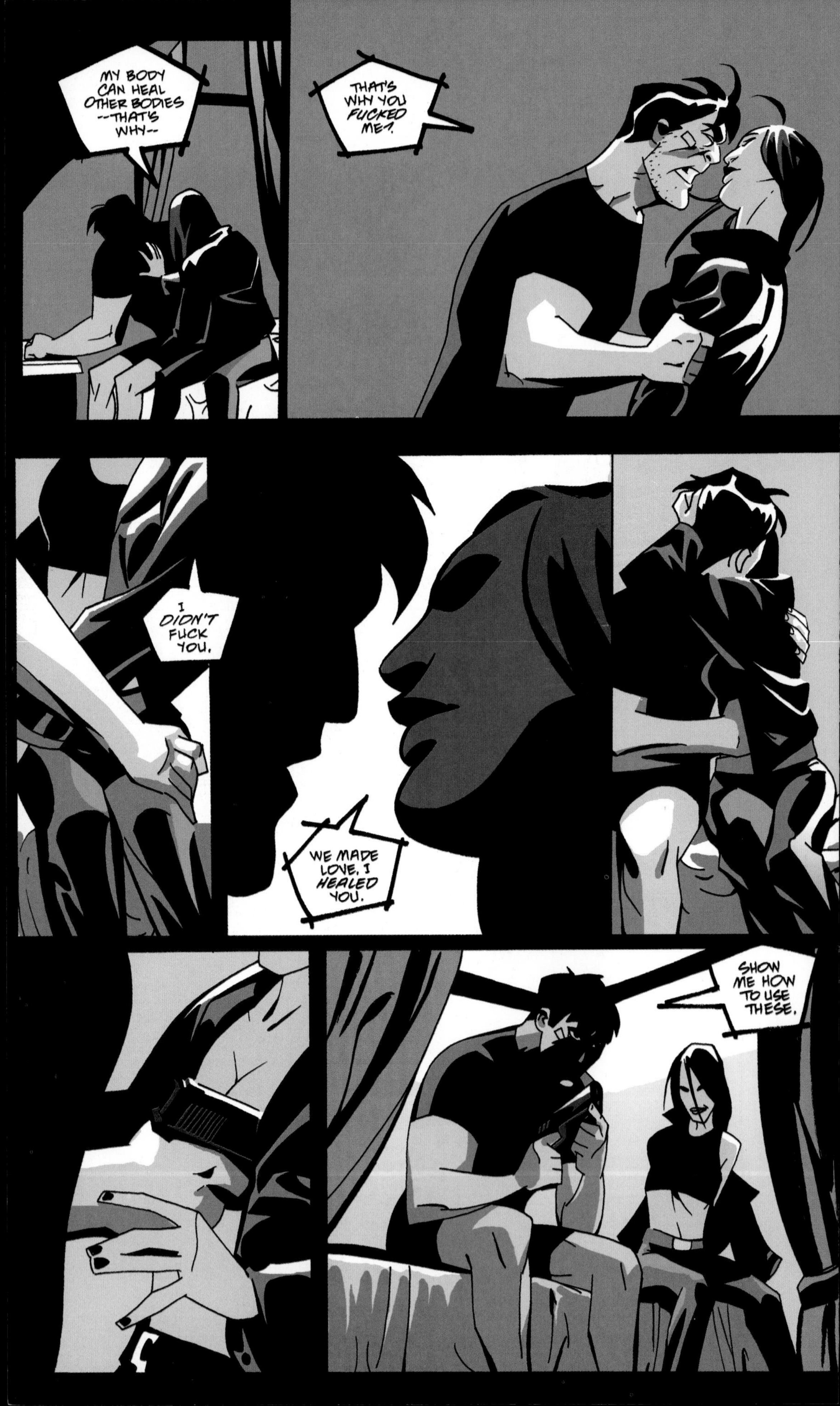
MY BODY CAN HEAL OTHER BODIES --THAT'S WHY--
THAT'S WHY YOU FUCKED ME?
I DIDN'T FUCK YOU.
WE MADE LOVE. I HEALED YOU.
SHOW ME HOW TO USE THESE.

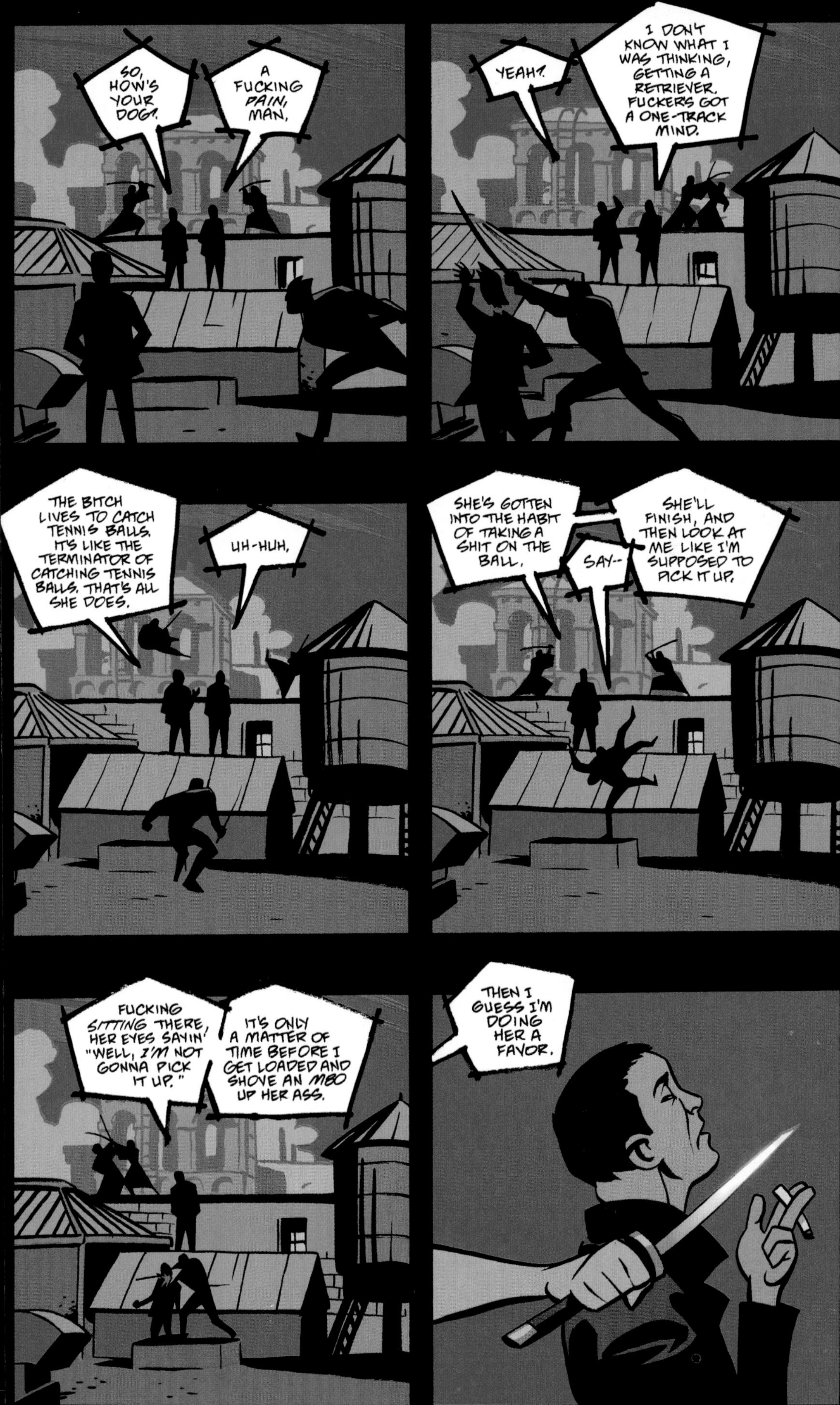

SO, HOW'S YOUR DOG?
A FUCKING PAIN, MAN.
YEAH?
I DON'T KNOW WHAT I WAS THINKING, GETTING A RETRIEVER. FUCKER'S GOT A ONE-TRACK MIND.
THE BITCH LIVES TO CATCH TENNIS BALLS. IT'S LIKE THE TERMINATOR OF CATCHING TENNIS BALLS. THAT'S ALL SHE DOES.
UH-HUH.
SHE'S GOTTEN INTO THE HABIT OF TAKING A SHIT ON THE BALL.
SAY--
SHE'LL FINISH, AND THEN LOOK AT ME LIKE I'M SUPPOSED TO PICK IT UP.
FUCKING SITTING THERE, HER EYES SAYIN' "WELL, I'M NOT GONNA PICK IT UP."
IT'S ONLY A MATTER OF TIME BEFORE I GET LOADED AND SHOVE AN M80 UP HER ASS.
THEN I GUESS I'M DOING HER A FAVOR.

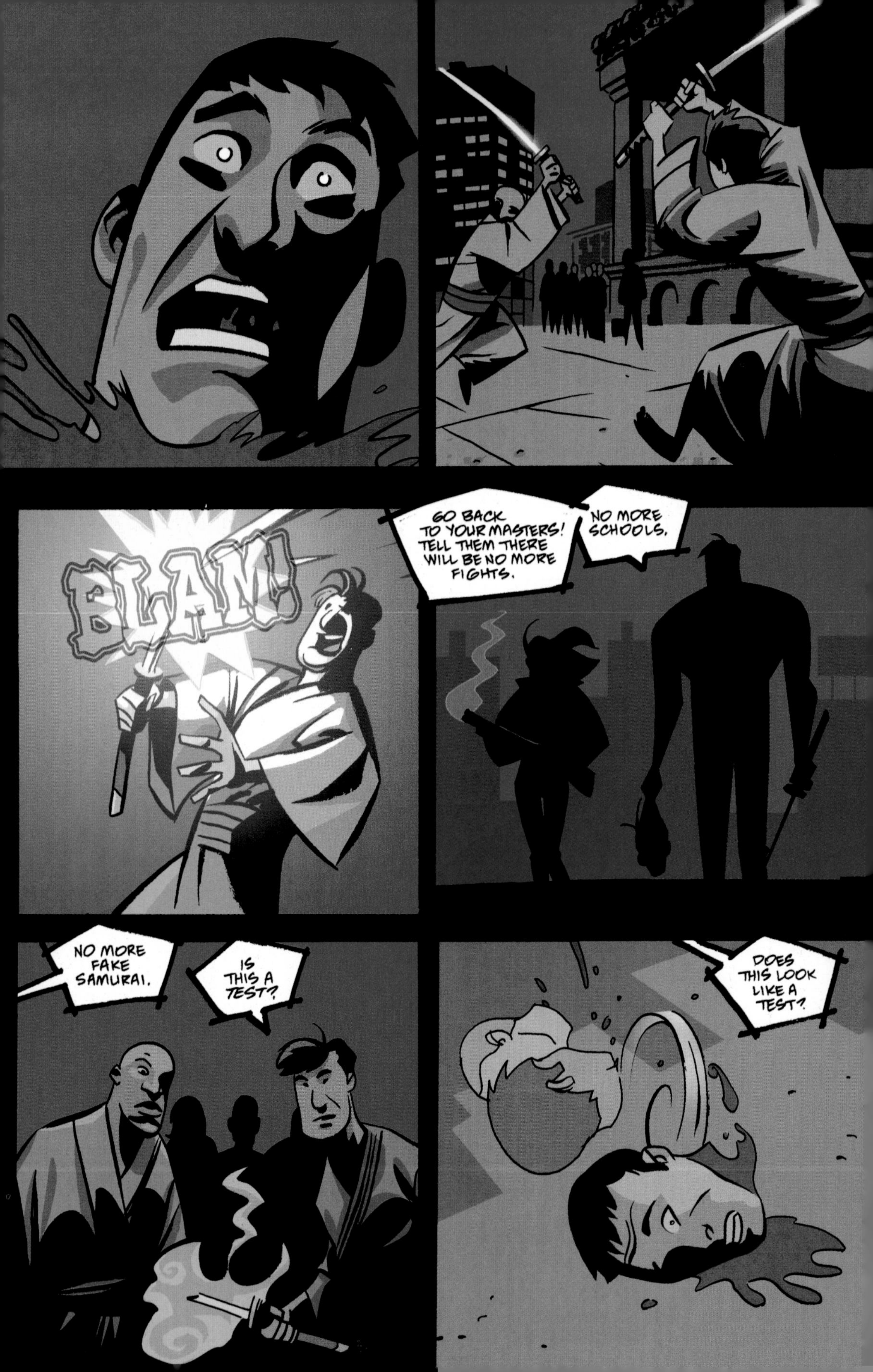
BLAM!
GO BACK TO YOUR MASTERS! TELL THEM THERE WILL BE NO MORE FIGHTS.
NO MORE SCHOOLS.
NO MORE FAKE SAMURAI.
IS THIS A TEST?
DOES THIS LOOK LIKE A TEST?

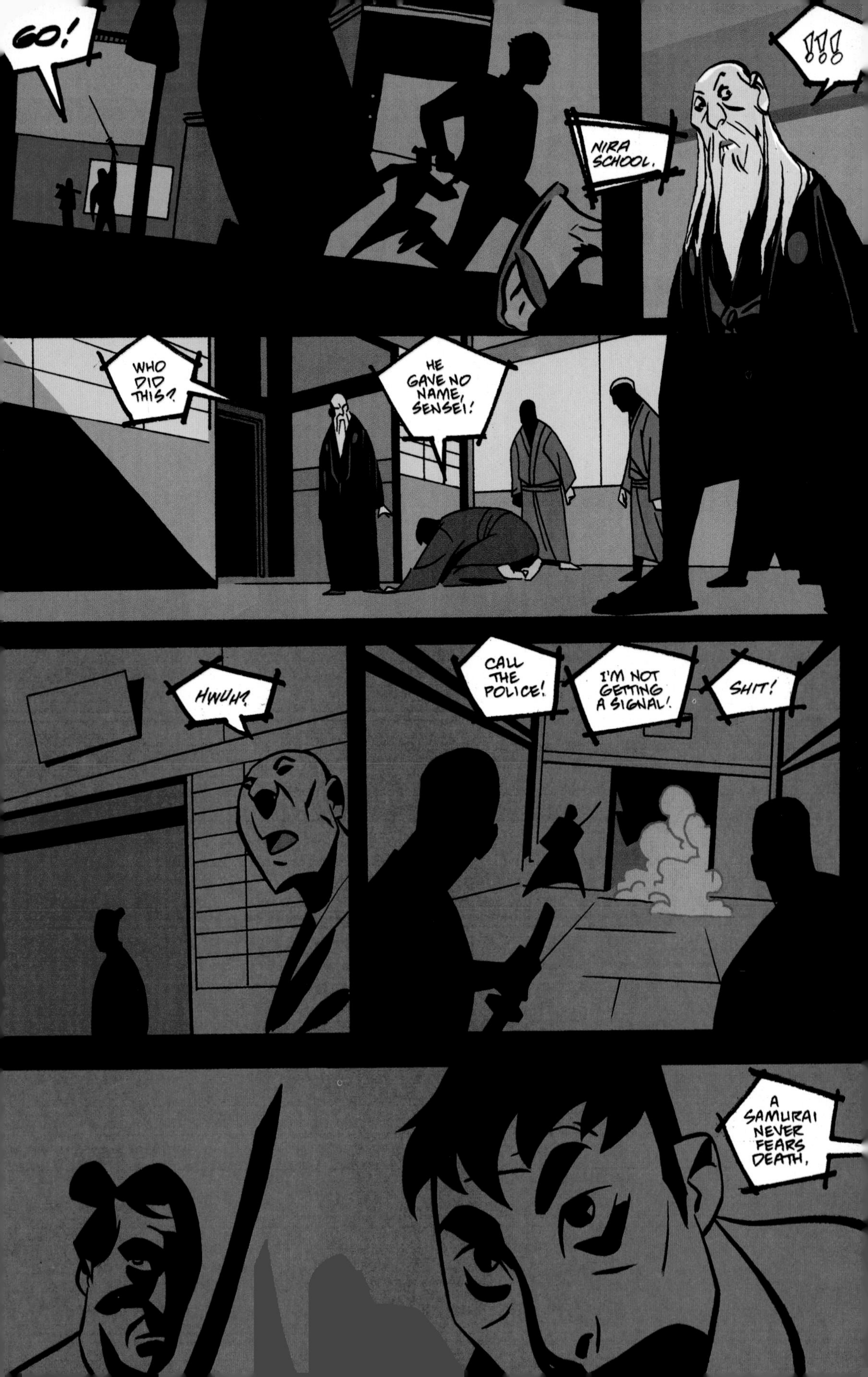
GO!
!!!
NIRA SCHOOL.
WHO DID THIS?
HE GAVE NO NAME, SENSEI!
HWUH?
CALL THE POLICE!
I'M NOT GETTING A SIGNAL!
SHIT!
A SAMURAI NEVER FEARS DEATH,

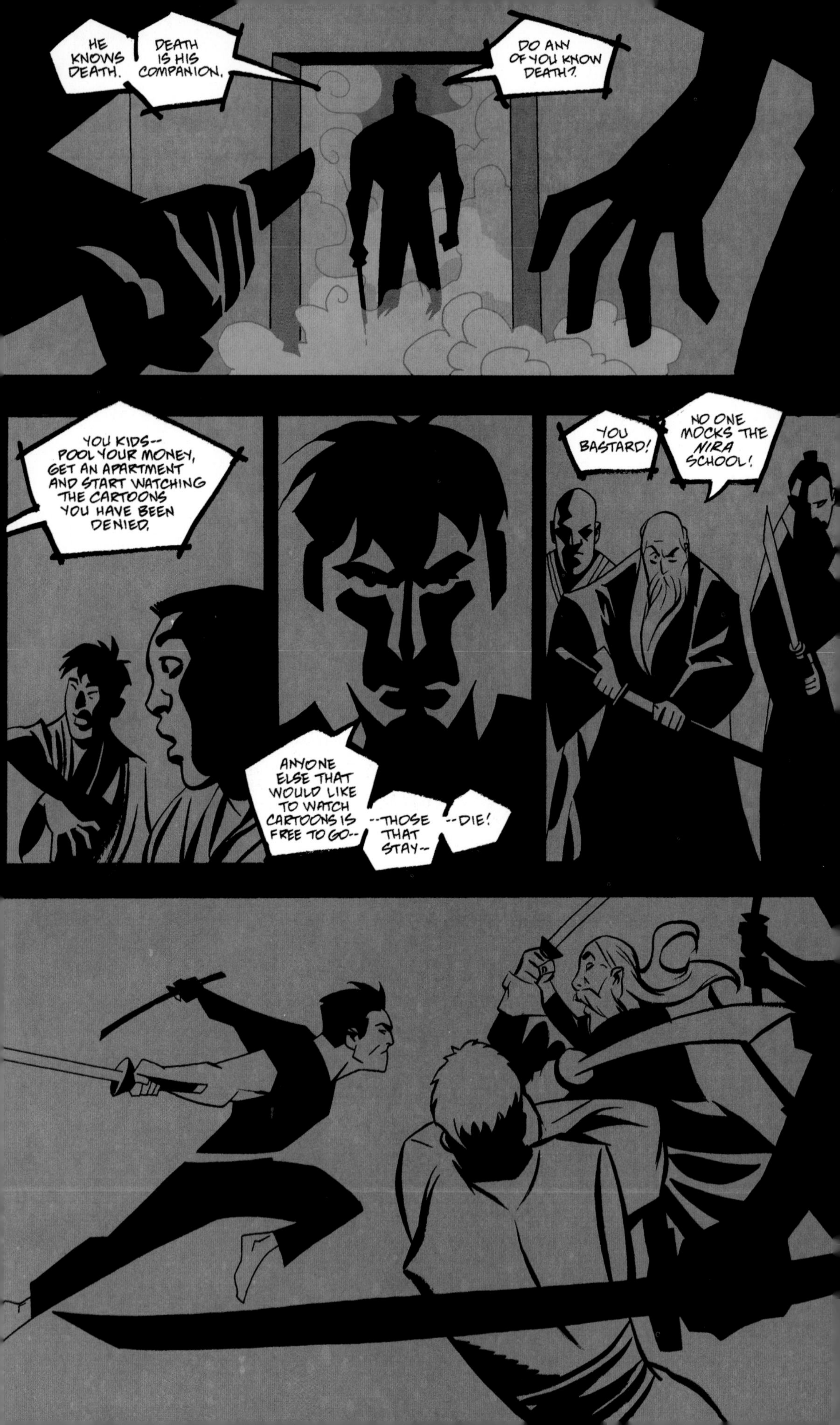
HE KNOWS DEATH.
DEATH IS HIS COMPANION.
DO ANY OF YOU KNOW DEATH?
YOU KIDS-- POOL YOUR MONEY, GET AN APARTMENT AND START WATCHING THE CARTOONS YOU HAVE BEEN DENIED.
ANYONE ELSE THAT WOULD LIKE TO WATCH CARTOONS IS FREE TO GO--
--THOSE THAT STAY--
--DIE!
YOU BASTARD!
NO ONE MOCKS THE NIRA SCHOOL!

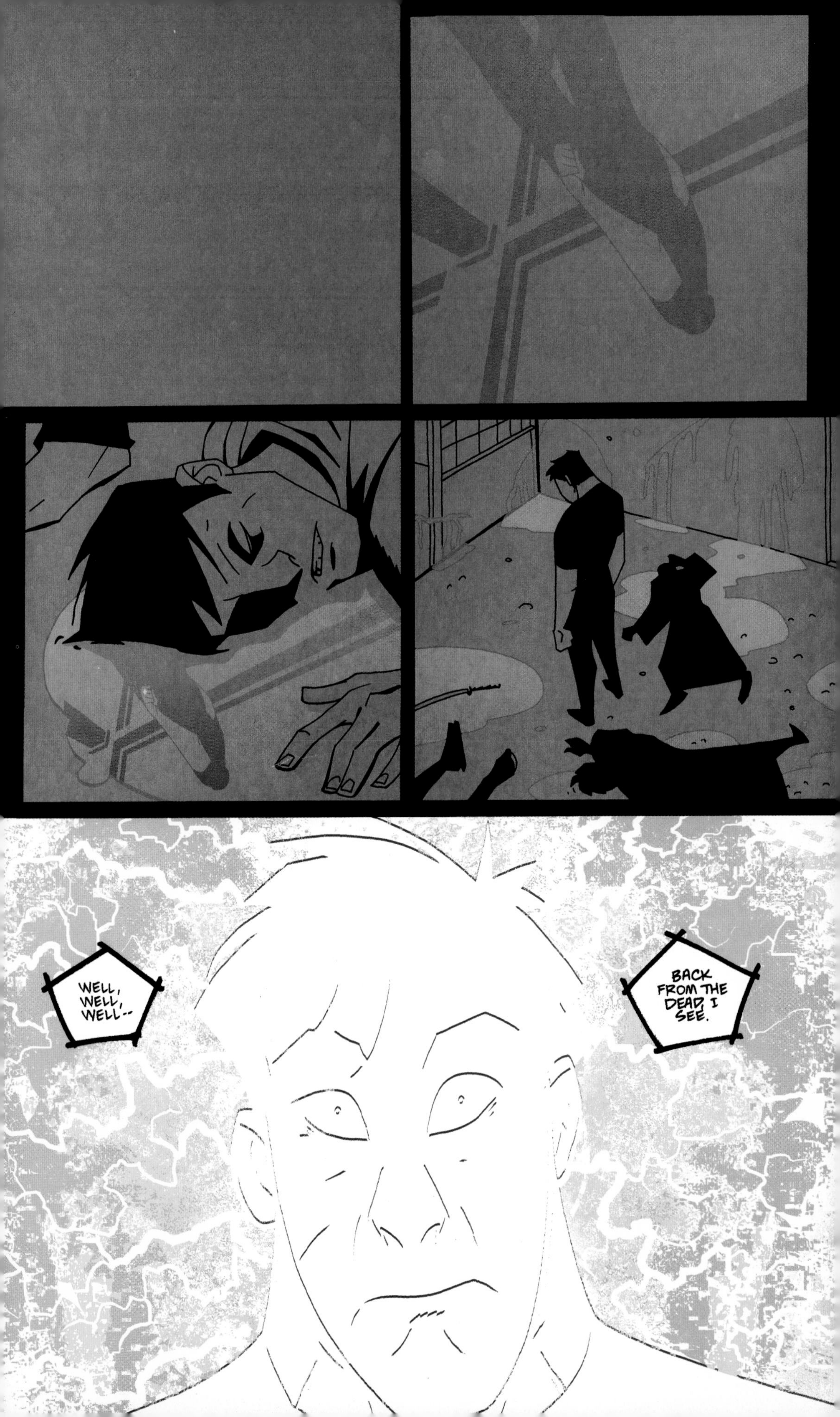
WELL, WELL, WELL--
BACK FROM THE DEAD, I SEE.

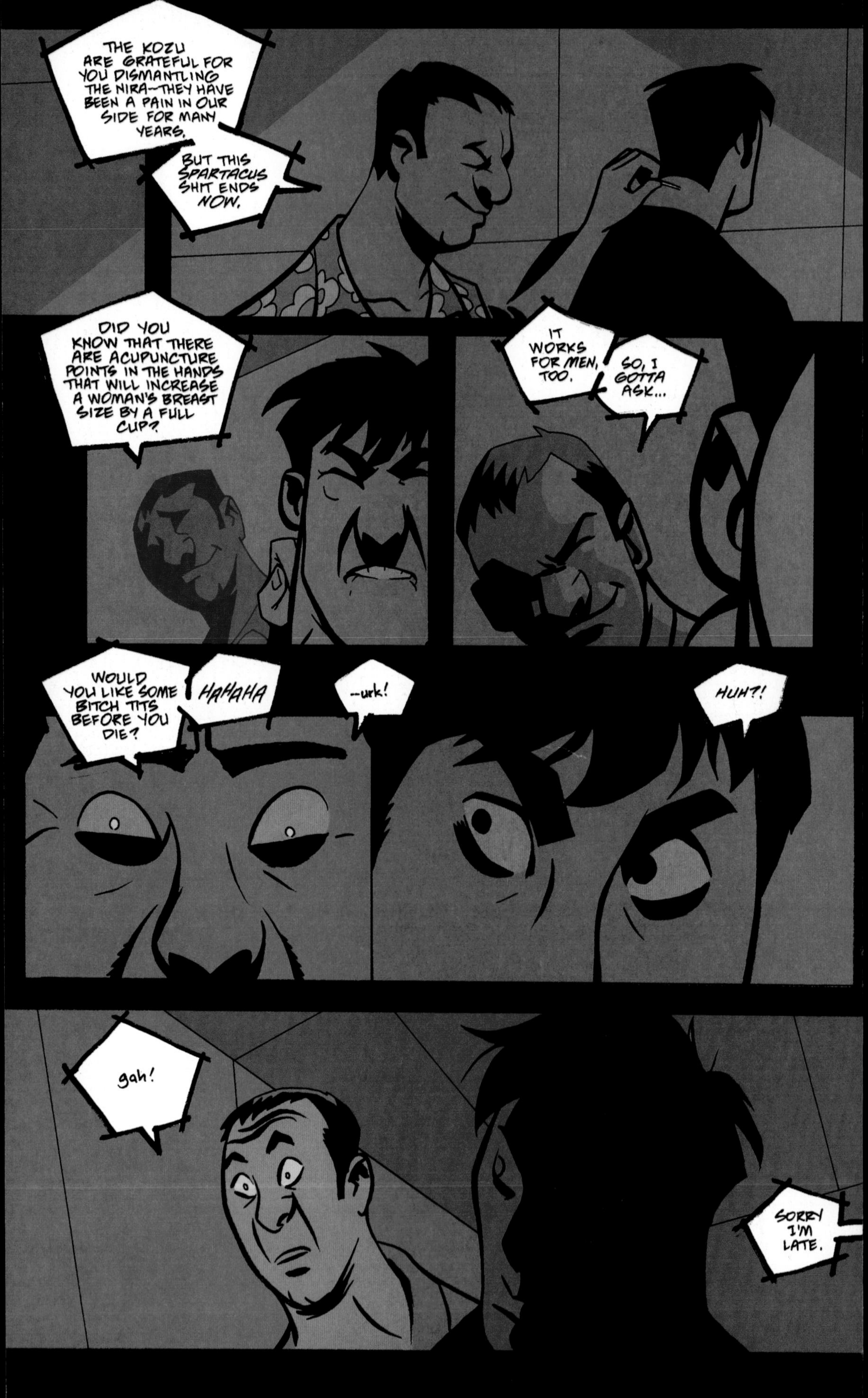
THE KOZU ARE GRATEFUL FOR YOU DISMANTLING THE NIRA--THEY HAVE BEEN A PAIN IN OUR SIDE FOR MANY YEARS.
BUT THIS SPARTACUS SHIT ENDS NOW.
DID YOU KNOW THAT THERE ARE ACUPUNCTURE POINTS IN THE HANDS THAT WILL INCREASE A WOMAN'S BREAST SIZE BY A FULL CUP?
IT WORKS FOR MEN, TOO.
SO, I GOTTA ASK...
WOULD YOU LIKE SOME BITCH TITS BEFORE YOU DIE?
HAHAHA
--urk!
HUH?!
gah!
SORRY I'M LATE.

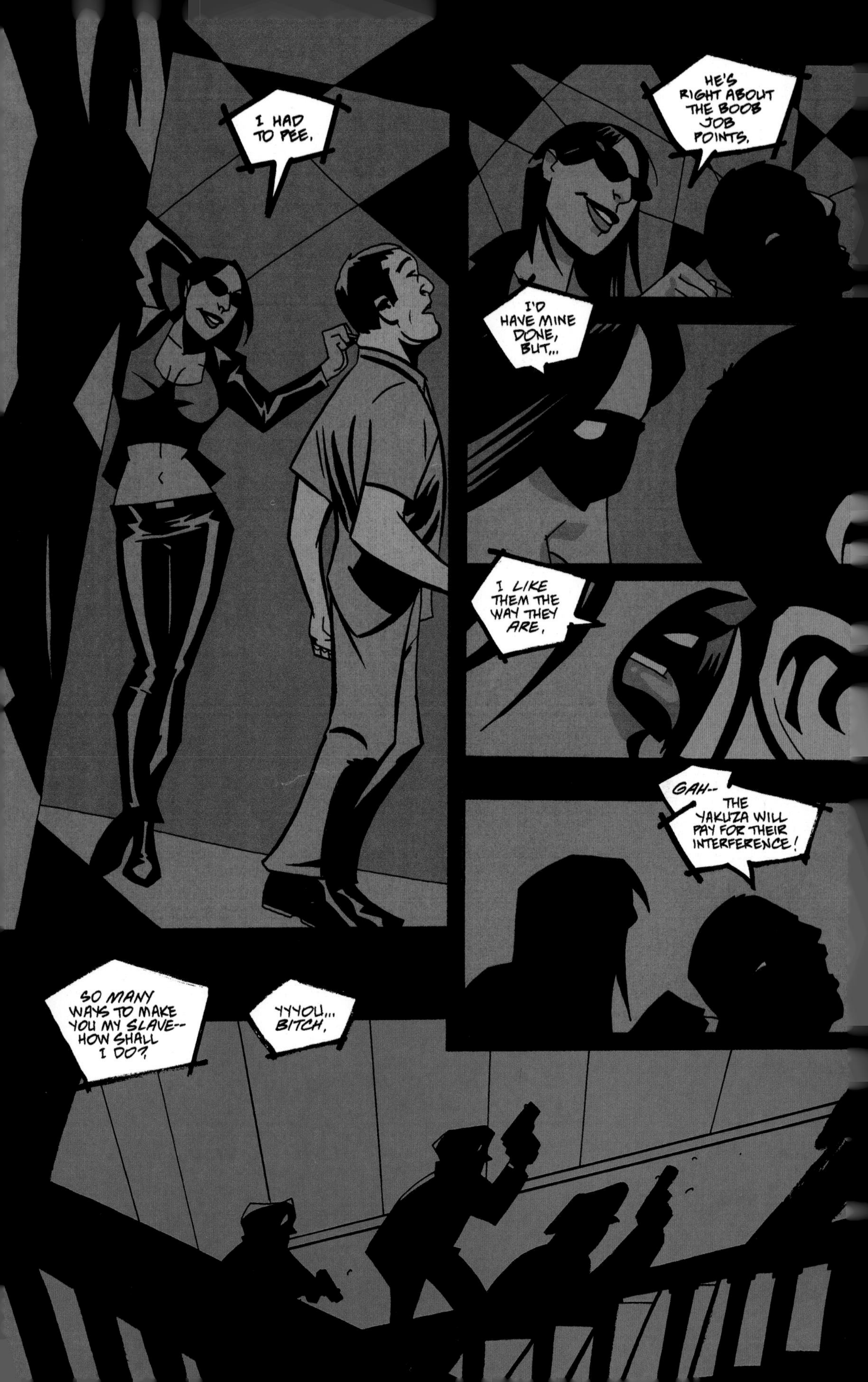
I HAD TO PEE.
HE'S RIGHT ABOUT THE BOOB JOB POINTS.
I'D HAVE MINE DONE, BUT...
I LIKE THEM THE WAY THEY ARE.
GAH-- THE YAKUZA WILL PAY FOR THEIR INTERFERENCE!
SO MANY WAYS TO MAKE YOU MY SLAVE-- HOW SHALL I DO?
YYYOU... BITCH.

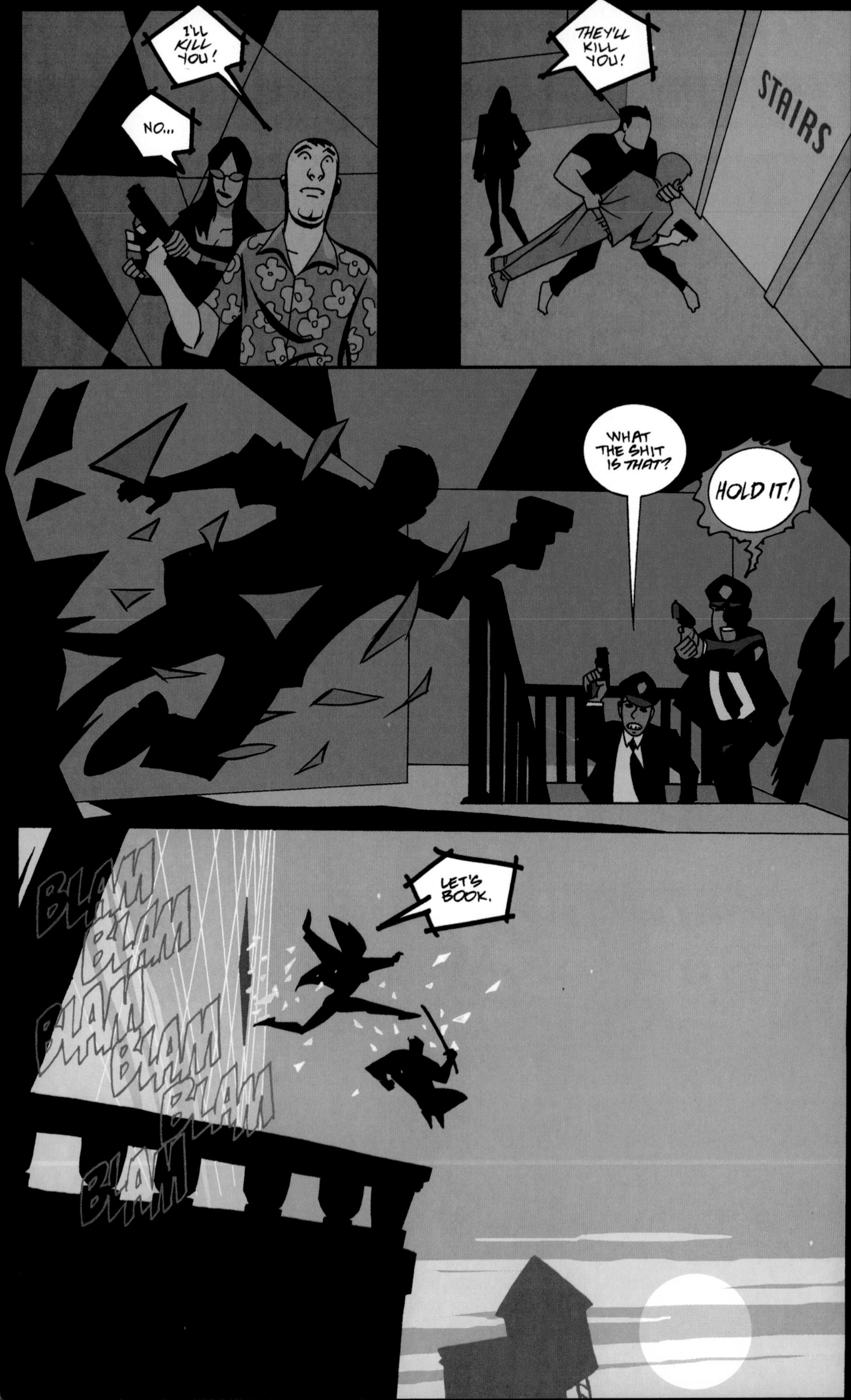
I'LL KILL YOU!
NO...
THEY'LL KILL YOU!
STAIRS
WHAT THE SHIT IS THAT?
HOLD IT!
LET'S BOOK.
BLAM BLAM BLAM BLAM BLAM BLAM BLAM BLAM

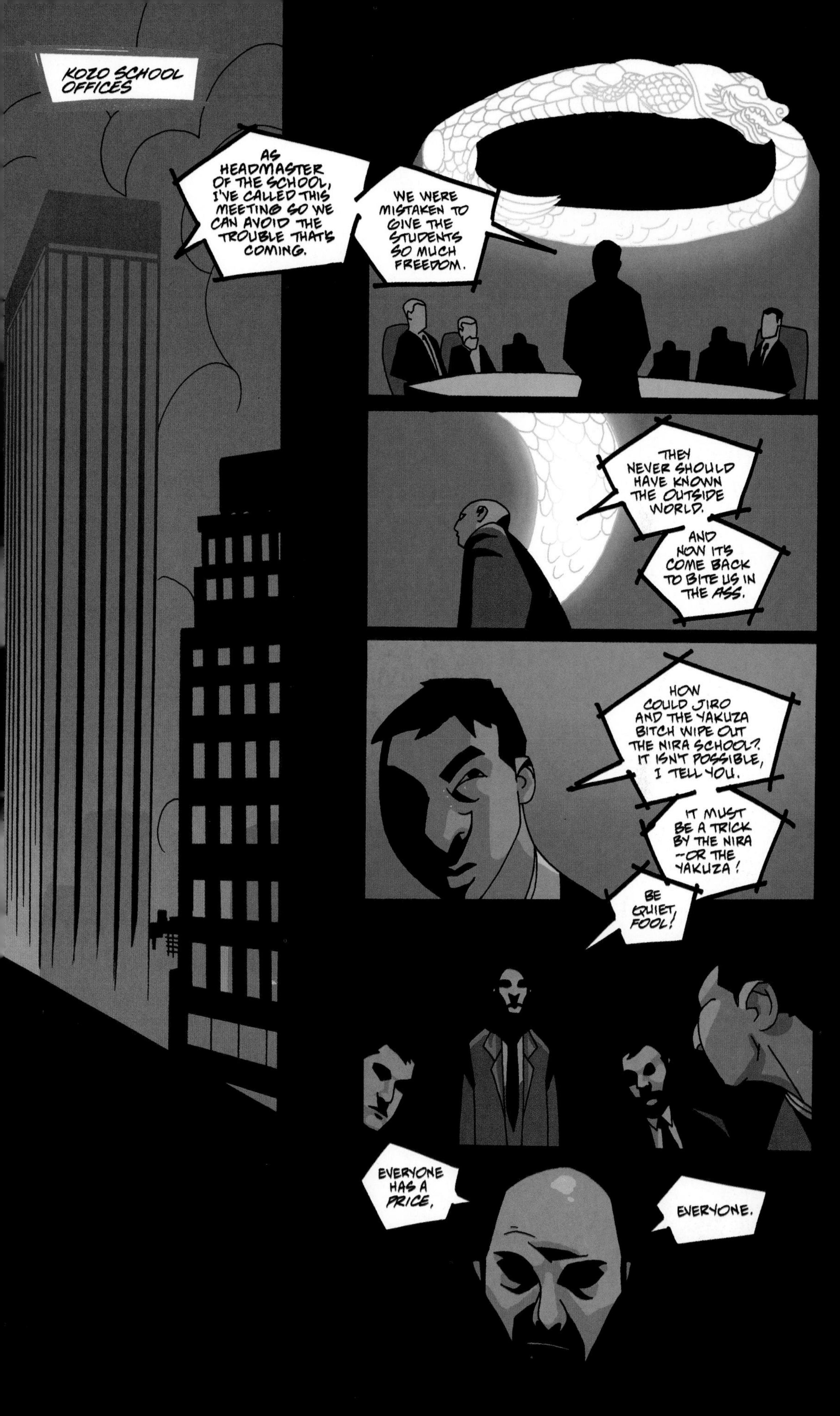
KOZO SCHOOL OFFICES
AS HEADMASTER OF THE SCHOOL, I'VE CALLED THIS MEETING SO WE CAN AVOID THE TROUBLE THAT'S COMING.
WE WERE MISTAKEN TO GIVE THE STUDENTS SO MUCH FREEDOM.
THEY NEVER SHOULD HAVE KNOWN THE OUTSIDE WORLD.
AND NOW IT'S COME BACK TO BITE US IN THE ASS.
HOW COULD JIRO AND THE YAKUZA BITCH WIPE OUT THE NIRA SCHOOL? IT ISN'T POSSIBLE, I TELL YOU.
IT MUST BE A TRICK BY THE NIRA --OR THE YAKUZA!
BE QUIET, FOOL!
EVERYONE HAS A PRICE.
EVERYONE.

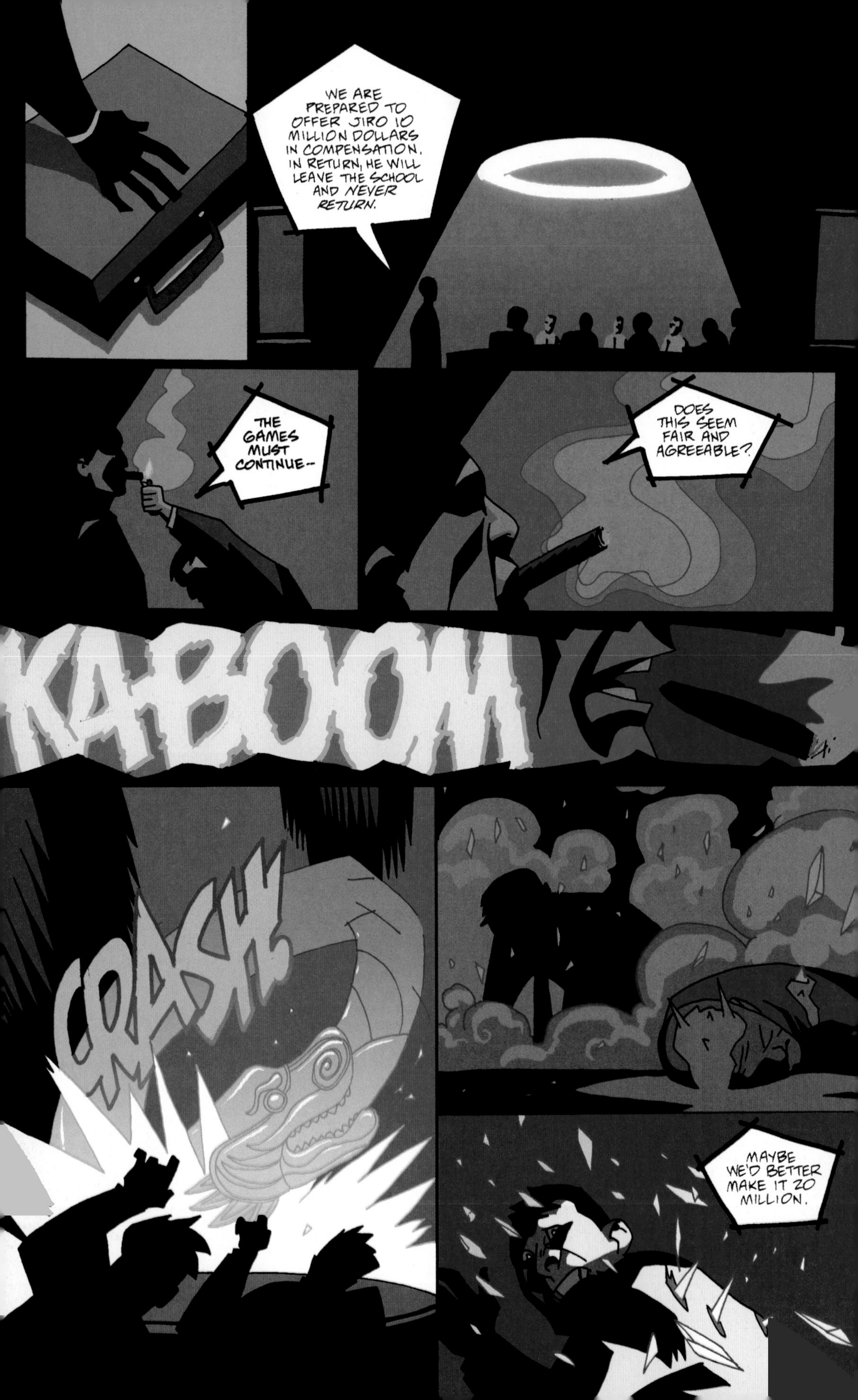
WE ARE PREPARED TO OFFER JIRO 10 MILLION DOLLARS IN COMPENSATION. IN RETURN, HE WILL LEAVE THE SCHOOL AND *NEVER* RETURN.
THE GAMES MUST CONTINUE--
DOES THIS SEEM FAIR AND AGREEABLE?
KABOOM
CRASH
MAYBE WE'D BETTER MAKE IT 20 MILLION.

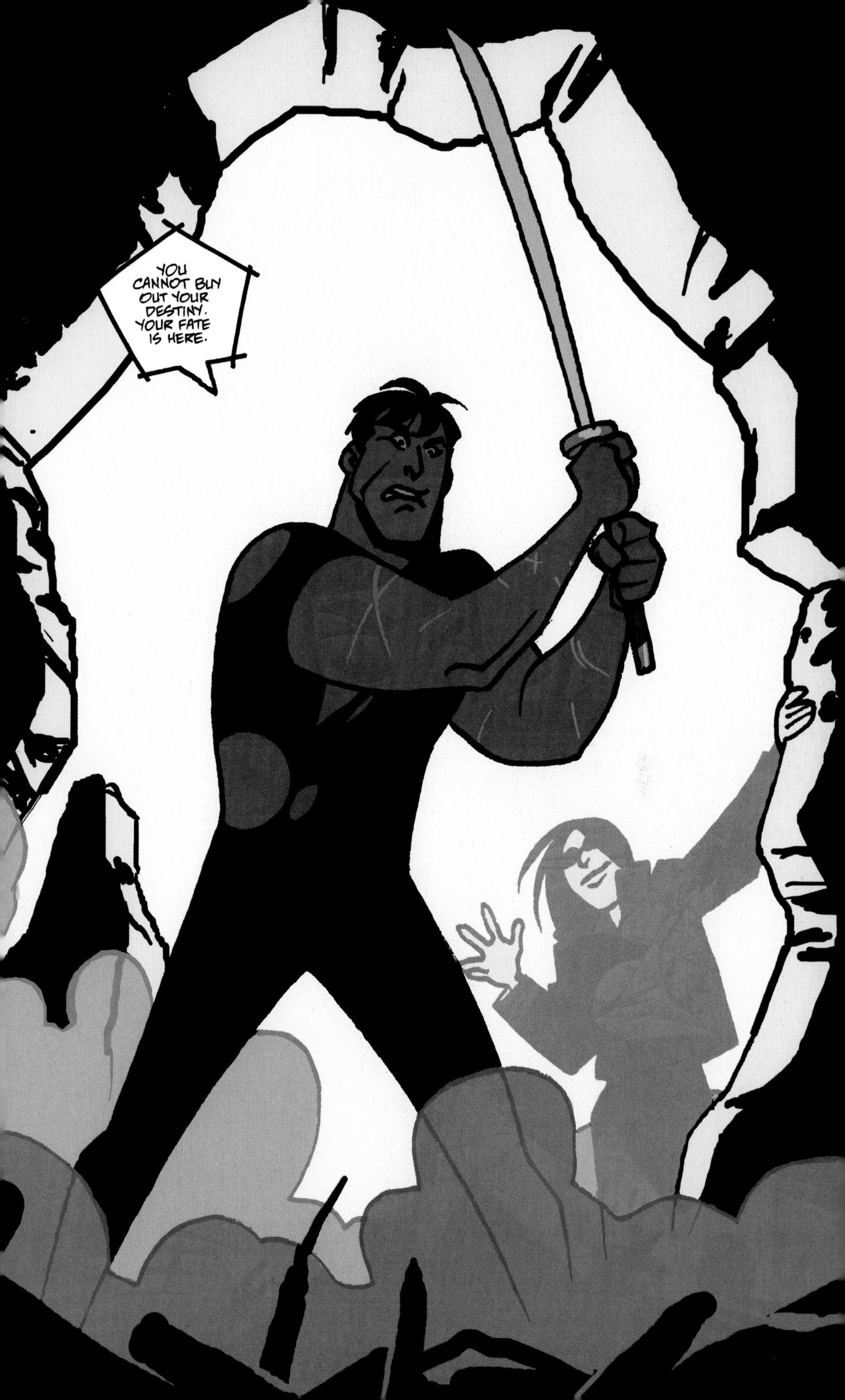
YOU CANNOT BUY OUT YOUR DESTINY. YOUR FATE IS HERE.

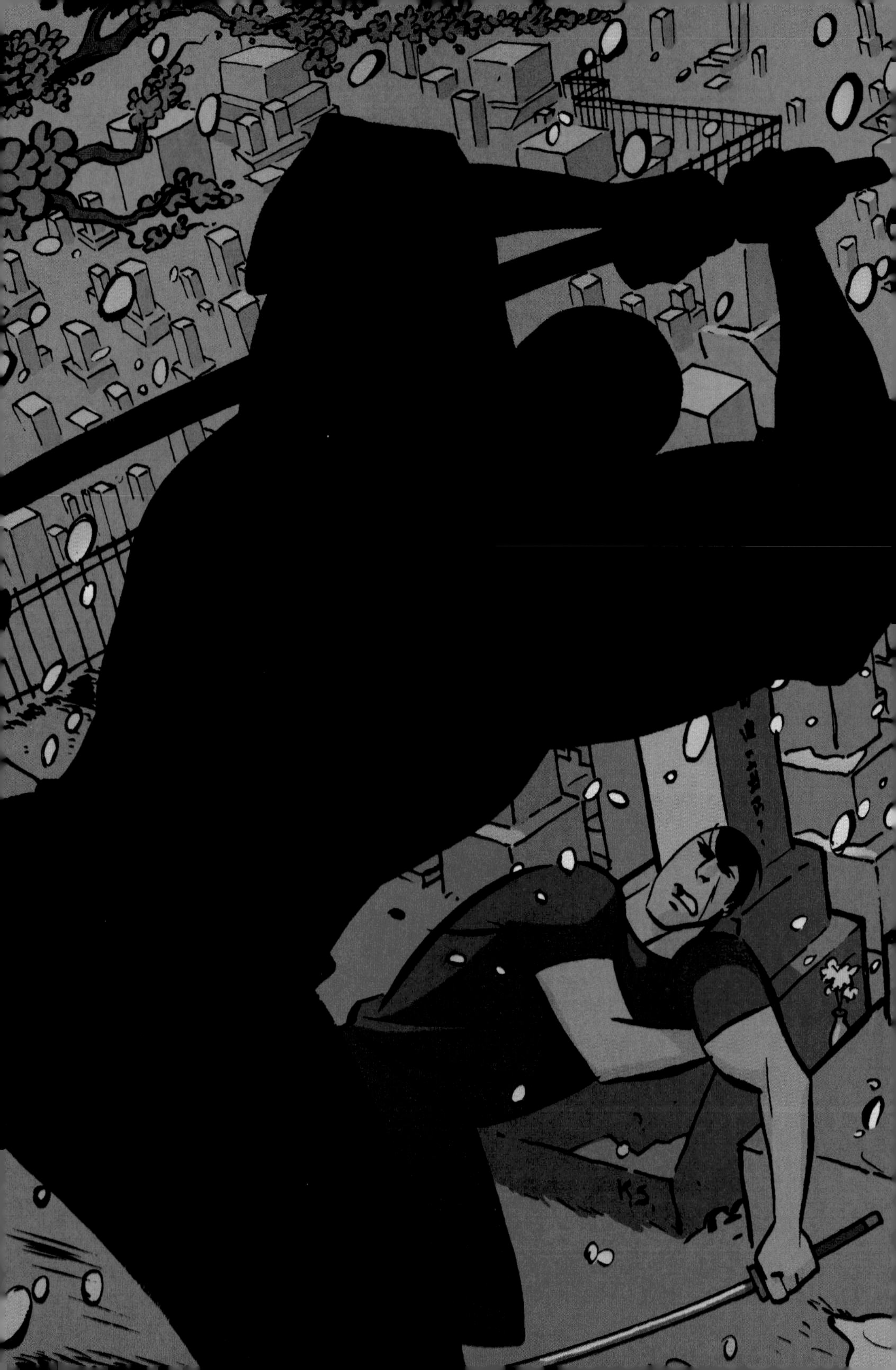

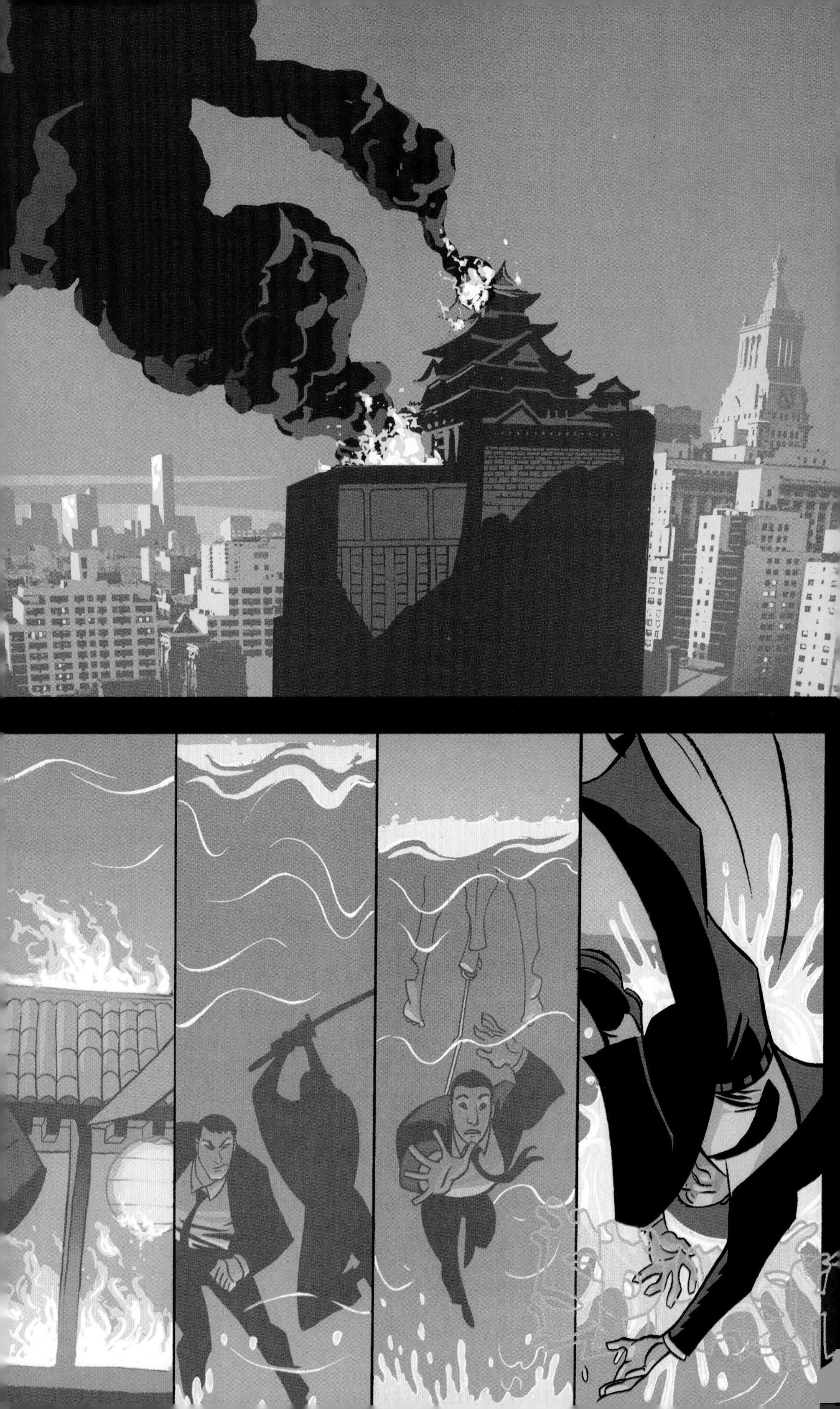

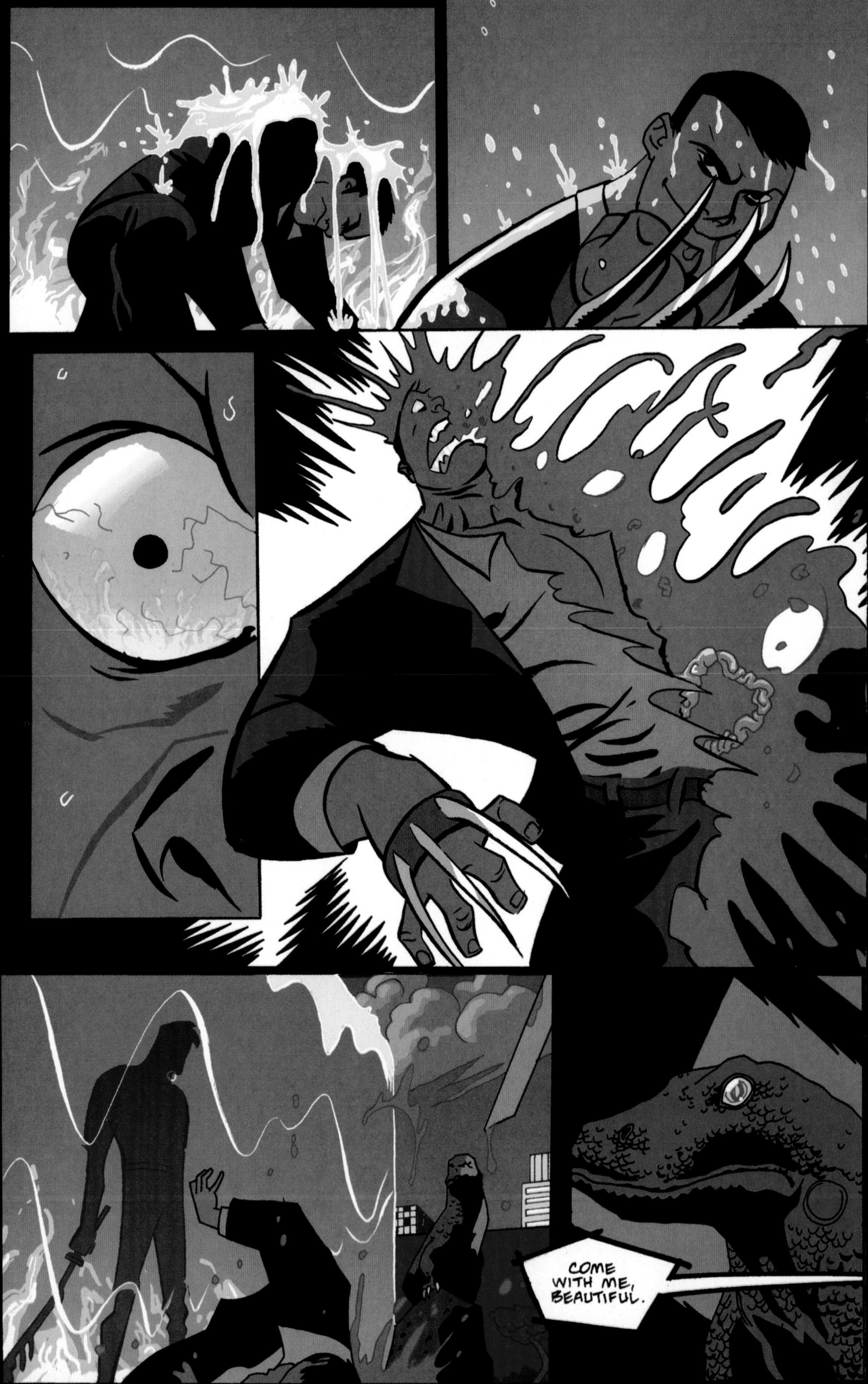
COME WITH ME, BEAUTIFUL.

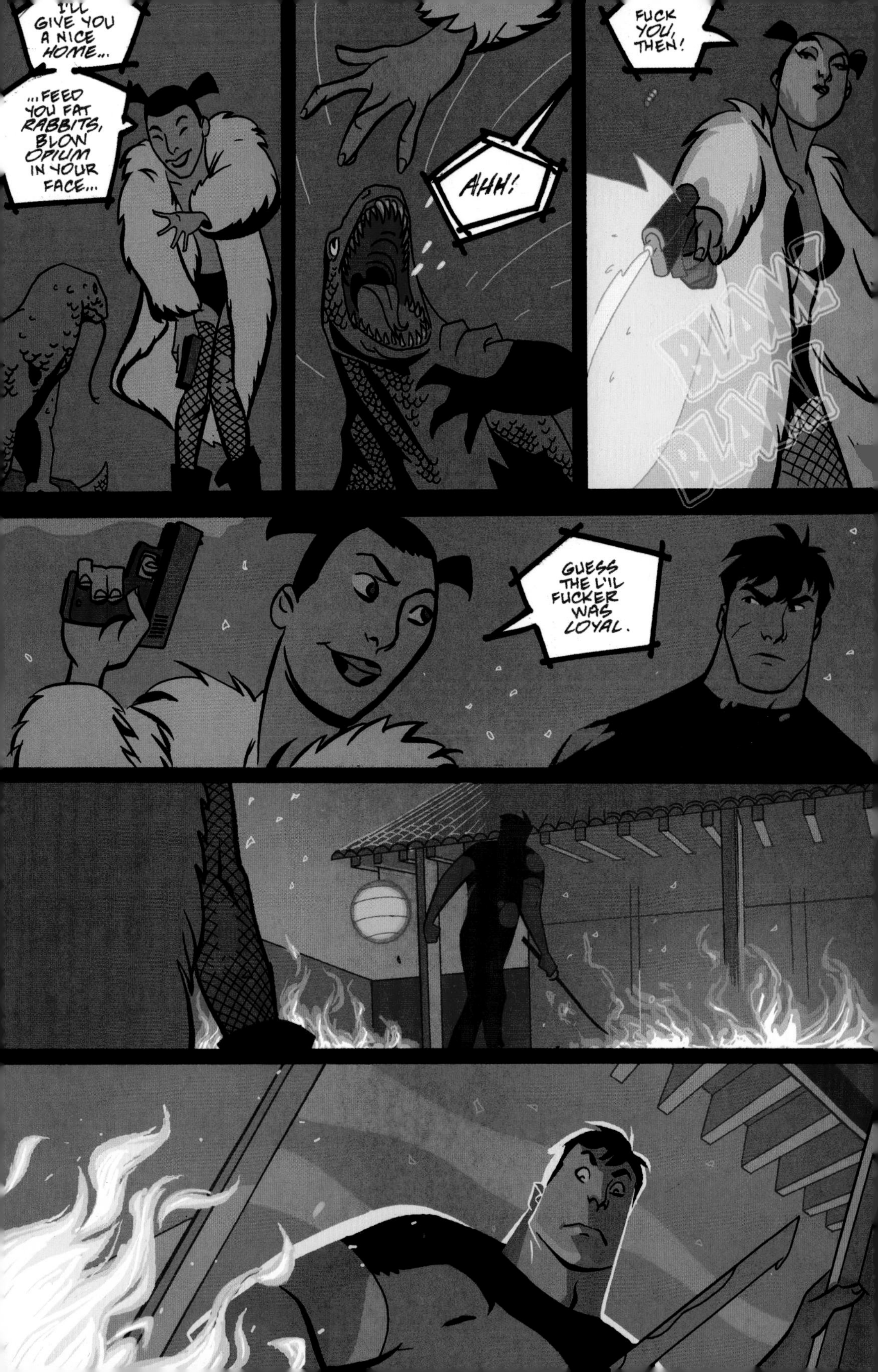
I'LL GIVE YOU A NICE HOME...
...FEED YOU FAT RABBITS, BLOW OPIUM IN YOUR FACE...
AHH!
FUCK YOU, THEN!
BLAM! BLAM!
GUESS THE L'IL FUCKER WAS LOYAL.

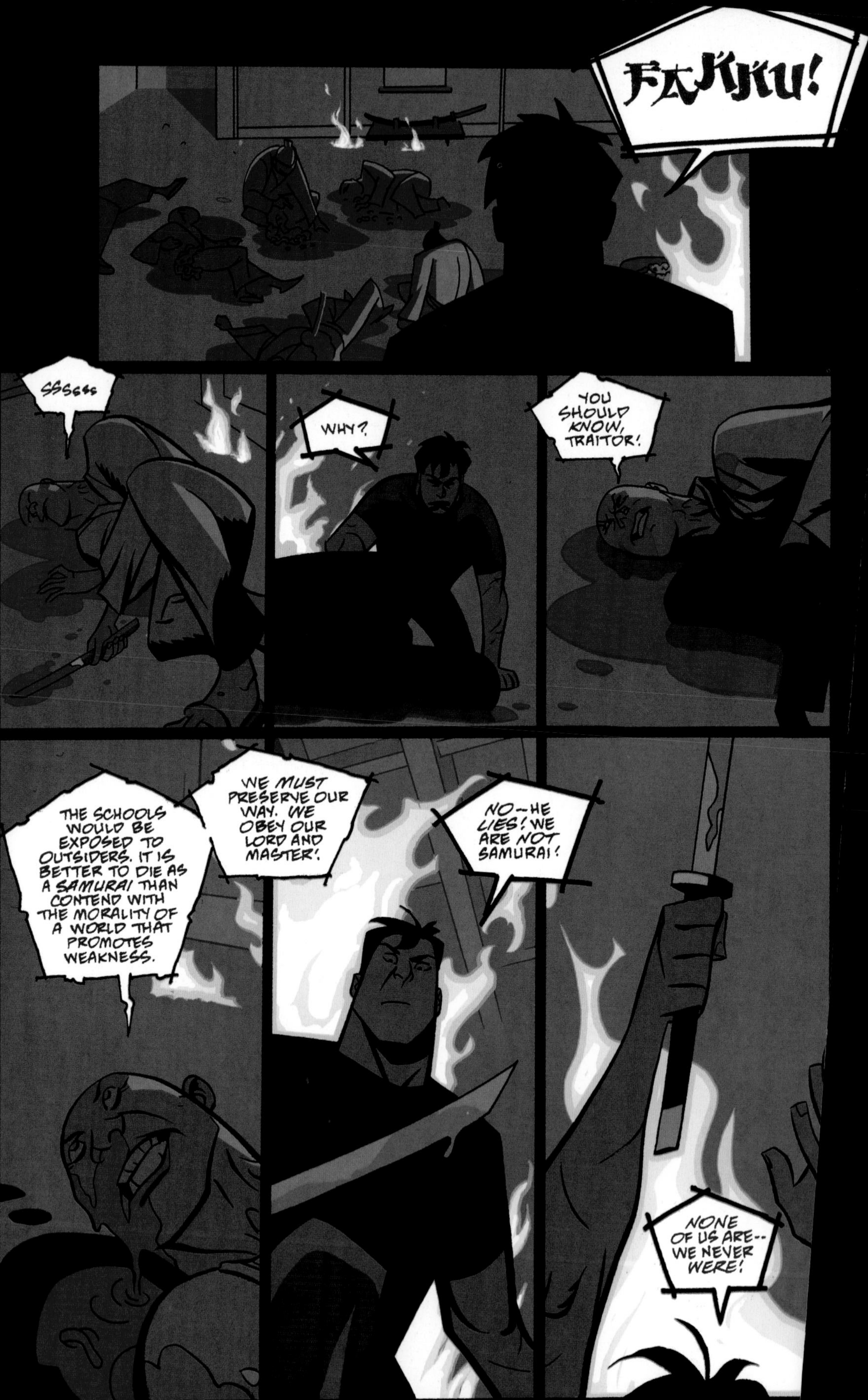
FUKU!
SSSsss
WHY?
YOU SHOULD KNOW, TRAITOR!
THE SCHOOLS WOULD BE EXPOSED TO OUTSIDERS. IT IS BETTER TO DIE AS A SAMURAI THAN CONTEND WITH THE MORALITY OF A WORLD THAT PROMOTES WEAKNESS.
WE MUST PRESERVE OUR WAY. WE OBEY OUR LORD AND MASTER!
NO--HE LIES! WE ARE NOT SAMURAI!
NONE OF US ARE-- WE NEVER WERE!

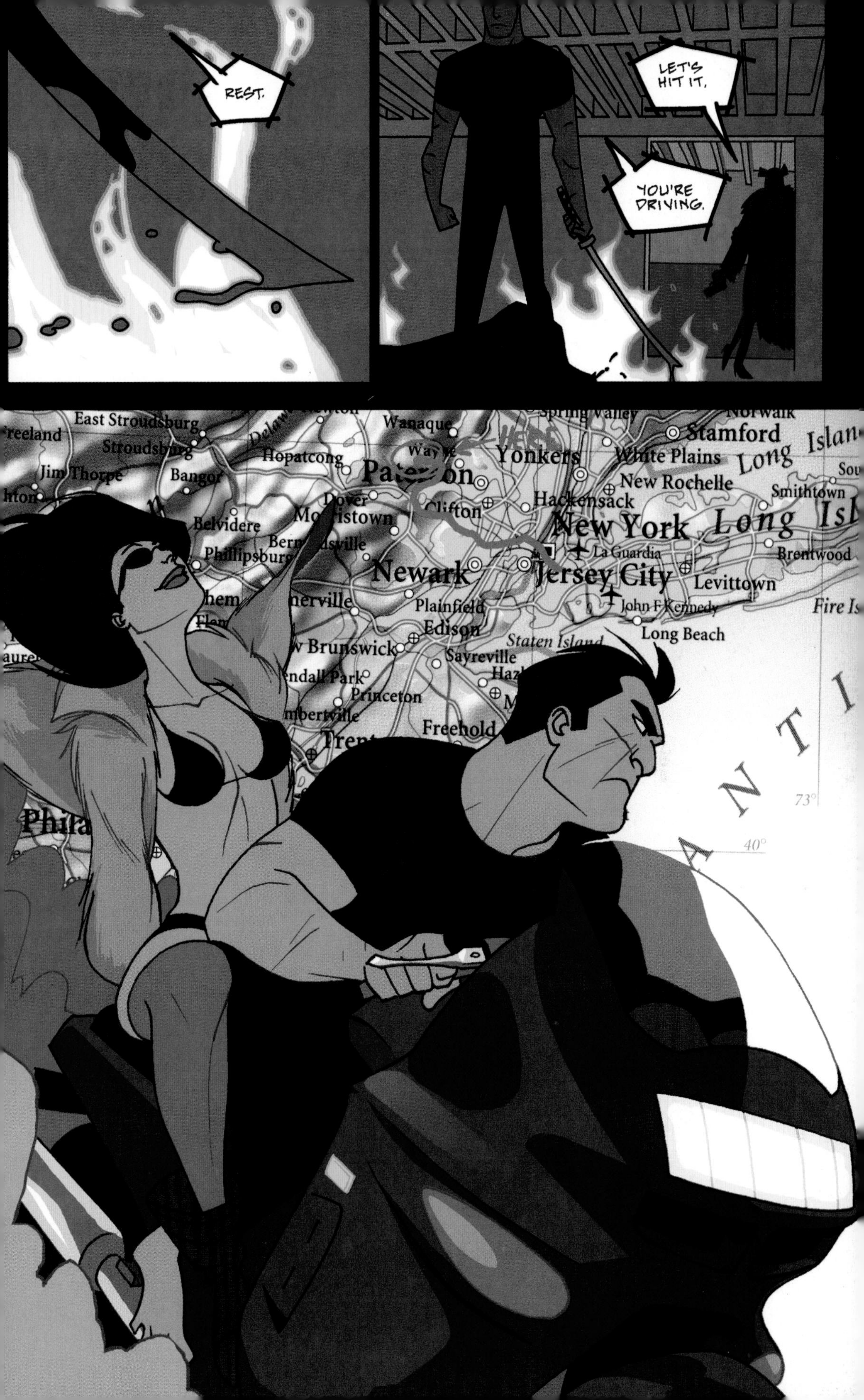
REST.
LET'S HIT IT.
YOU'RE DRIVING.
East Stroudsburg
Stroudsburg
Jim Thorpe
Bangor
Belvidere
Phillipsburg
Wanaque
Hopatcong
Dover
Clifton
Newark
Plainfield
Edison
Sayreville
Princeton
Freehold
Staten Island
Yonkers
Hackensack
New York
La Guardia
Jersey City
John F Kennedy
Long Beach
Levittown
Stamford
White Plains
New Rochelle
Long
Smithtown
Brentwood
73°
40°

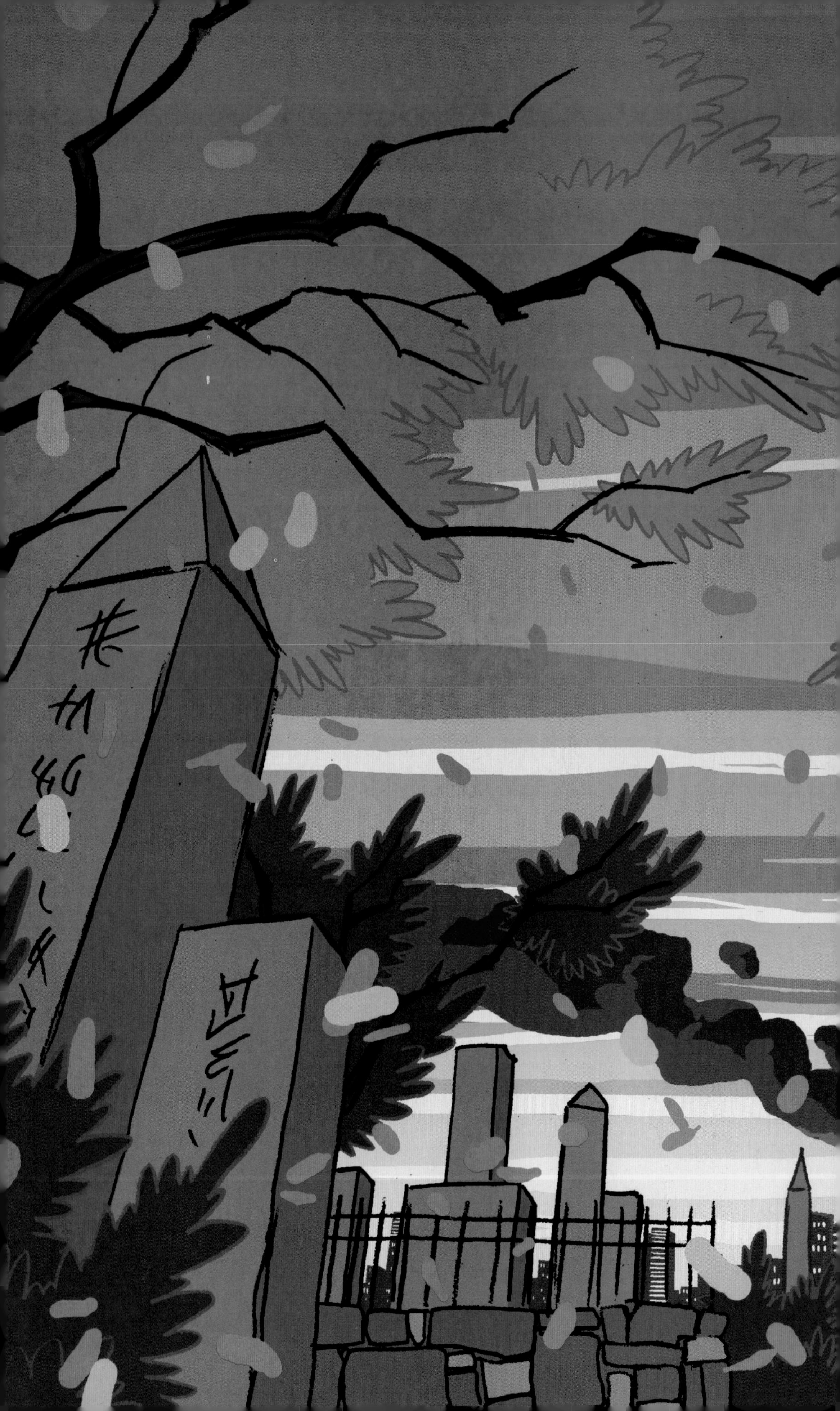

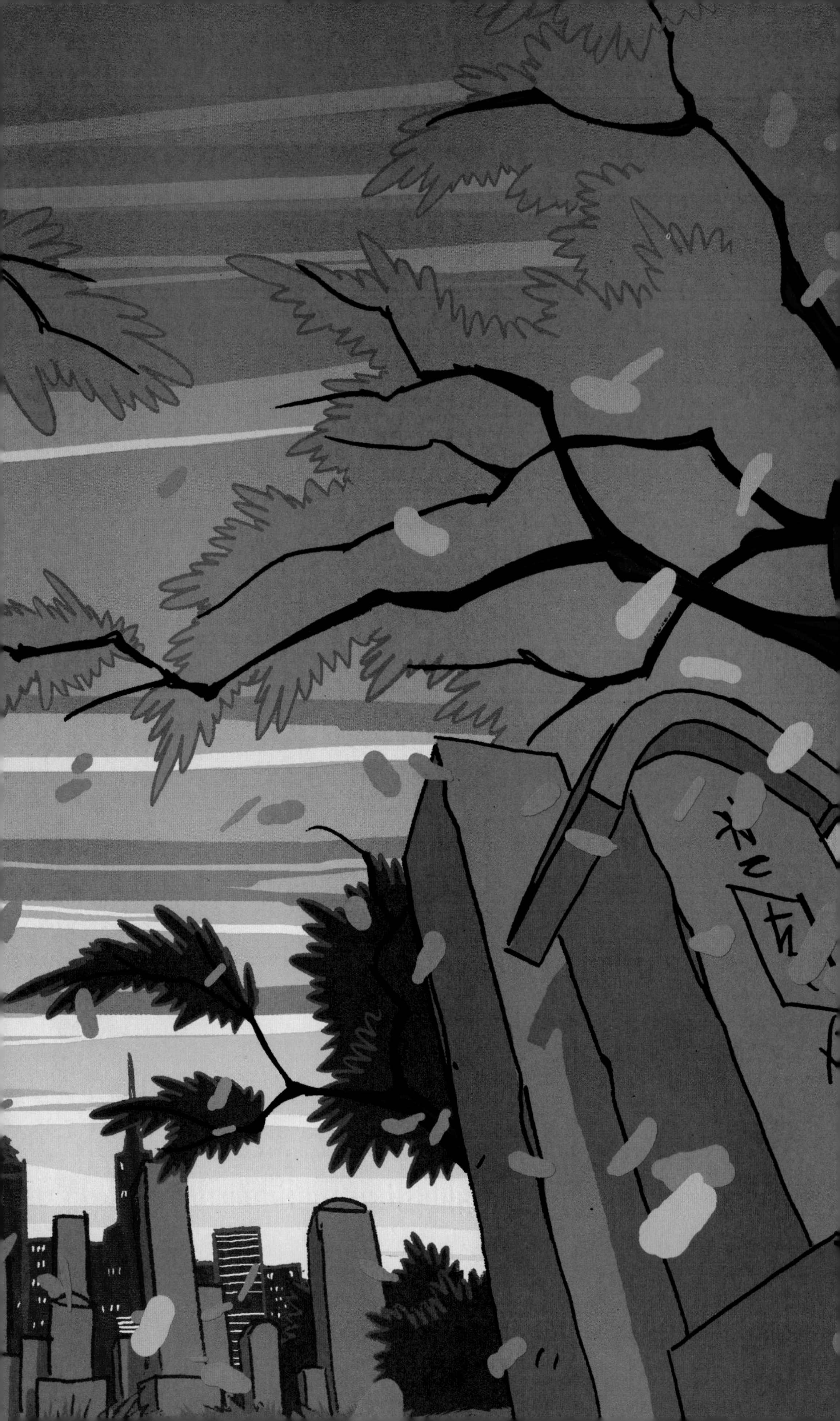

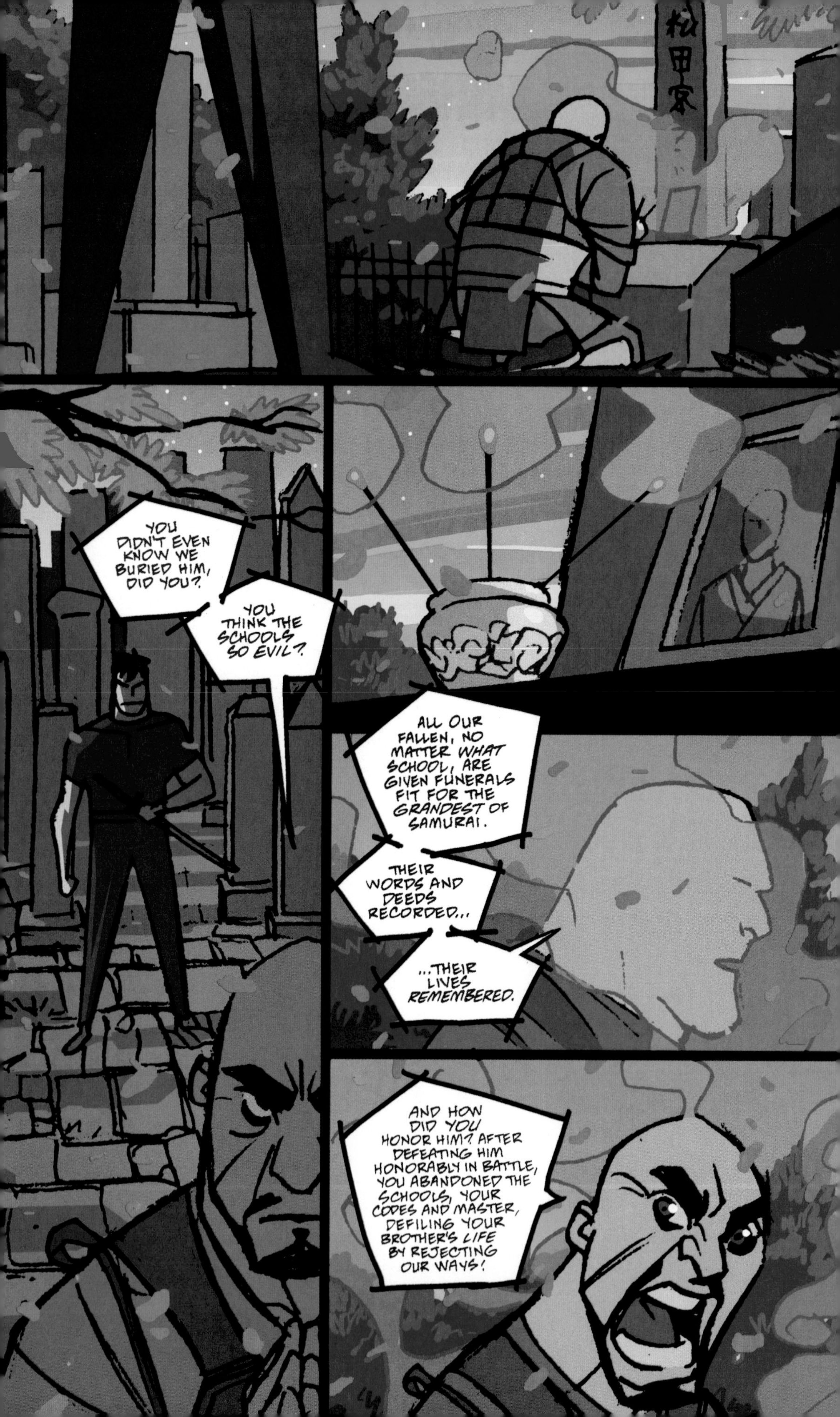
松田家
YOU DIDN'T EVEN KNOW WE BURIED HIM, DID YOU?
YOU THINK THE SCHOOLS SO EVIL?
ALL OUR FALLEN, NO MATTER WHAT SCHOOL, ARE GIVEN FUNERALS FIT FOR THE GRANDEST OF SAMURAI.
THEIR WORDS AND DEEDS RECORDED...
...THEIR LIVES REMEMBERED.
AND HOW DID YOU HONOR HIM? AFTER DEFEATING HIM HONORABLY IN BATTLE, YOU ABANDONED THE SCHOOLS, YOUR CODES AND MASTER, DEFILING YOUR BROTHER'S LIFE BY REJECTING OUR WAYS!

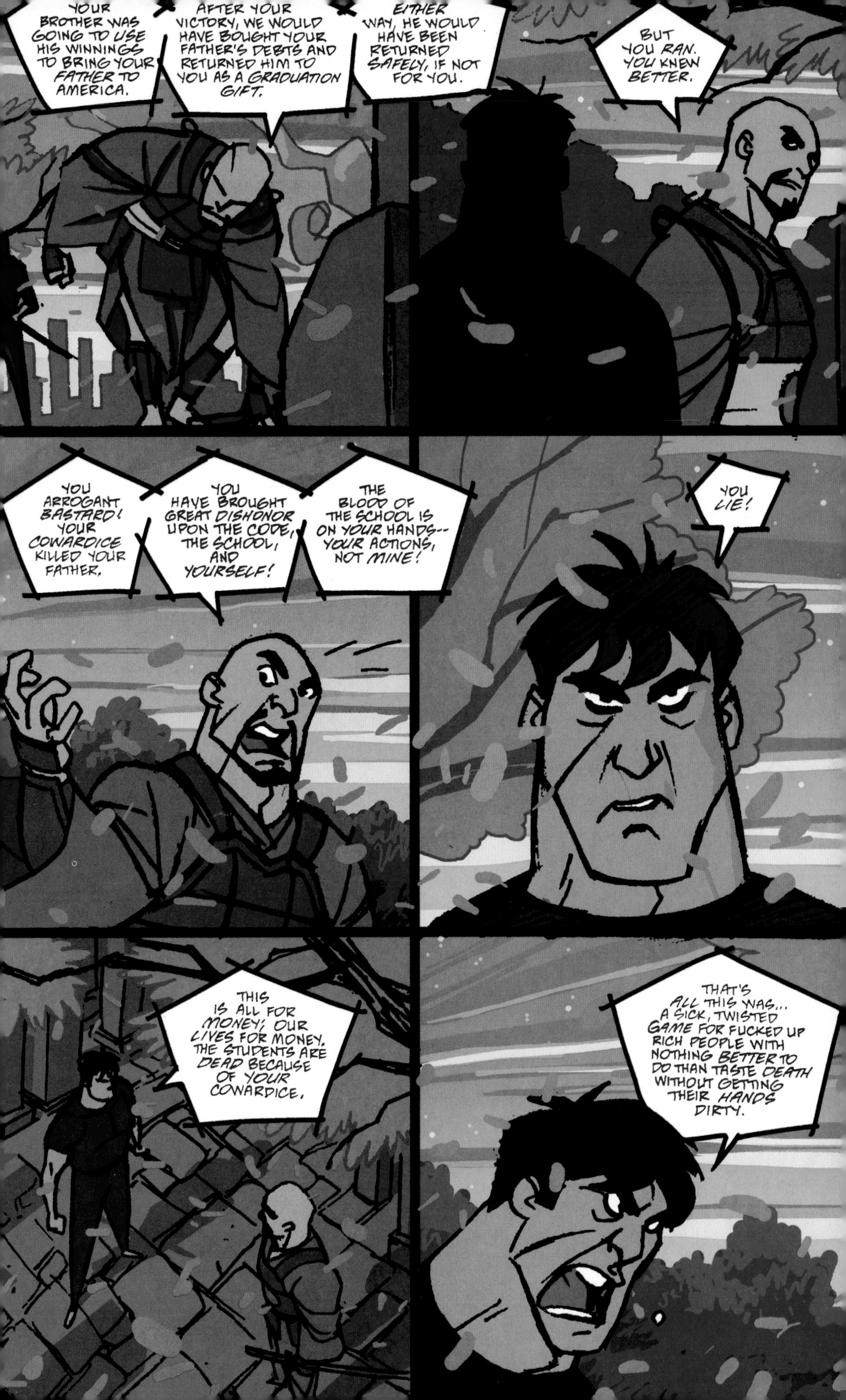
YOUR BROTHER WAS GOING TO USE HIS WINNINGS TO BRING YOUR FATHER TO AMERICA.
AFTER YOUR VICTORY, WE WOULD HAVE BOUGHT YOUR FATHER'S DEBTS AND RETURNED HIM TO YOU AS A GRADUATION GIFT.
EITHER WAY, HE WOULD HAVE BEEN RETURNED SAFELY, IF NOT FOR YOU.
BUT YOU RAN. YOU KNEW BETTER.
YOU ARROGANT BASTARD! YOUR COWARDICE KILLED YOUR FATHER.
YOU HAVE BROUGHT GREAT DISHONOR UPON THE CODE, THE SCHOOL, AND YOURSELF!
THE BLOOD OF THE SCHOOL IS ON YOUR HANDS-- YOUR ACTIONS, NOT MINE!
YOU LIE!
THIS IS ALL FOR MONEY; OUR LIVES FOR MONEY. THE STUDENTS ARE DEAD BECAUSE OF YOUR COWARDICE.
THAT'S ALL THIS WAS... A SICK, TWISTED GAME FOR FUCKED UP RICH PEOPLE WITH NOTHING BETTER TO DO THAN TASTE DEATH WITHOUT GETTING THEIR HANDS DIRTY.

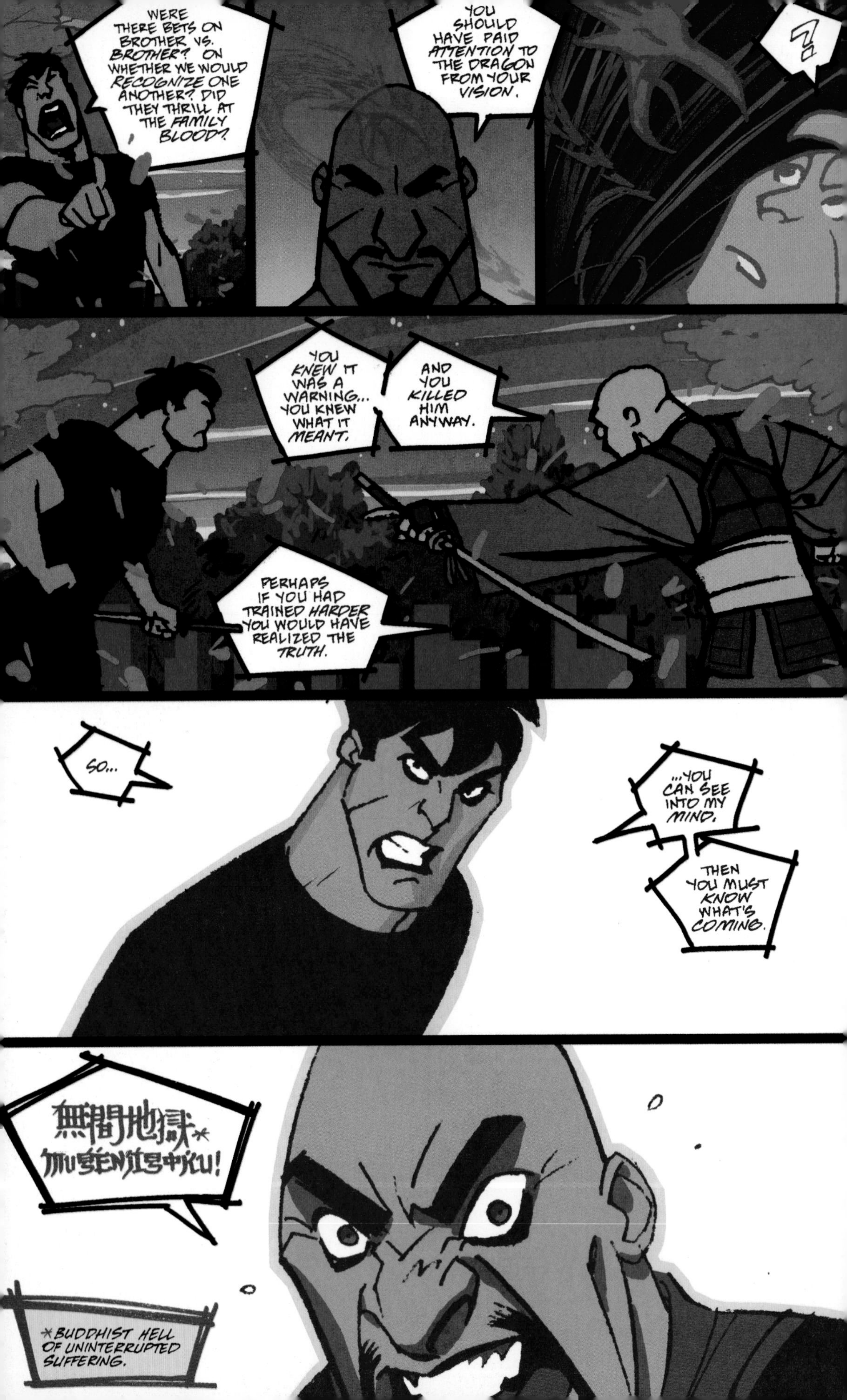
WERE THERE BETS ON BROTHER VS. BROTHER? ON WHETHER WE WOULD RECOGNIZE ONE ANOTHER? DID THEY THRILL AT THE FAMILY BLOOD?
YOU SHOULD HAVE PAID ATTENTION TO THE DRAGON FROM YOUR VISION.
?
YOU KNEW IT WAS A WARNING... YOU KNEW WHAT IT MEANT.
AND YOU KILLED HIM ANYWAY.
PERHAPS IF YOU HAD TRAINED HARDER YOU WOULD HAVE REALIZED THE TRUTH.
SO...
...YOU CAN SEE INTO MY MIND.
THEN YOU MUST KNOW WHAT'S COMING.
無間地獄* MUGENJIGOKU!
*BUDDHIST HELL OF UNINTERRUPTED SUFFERING.

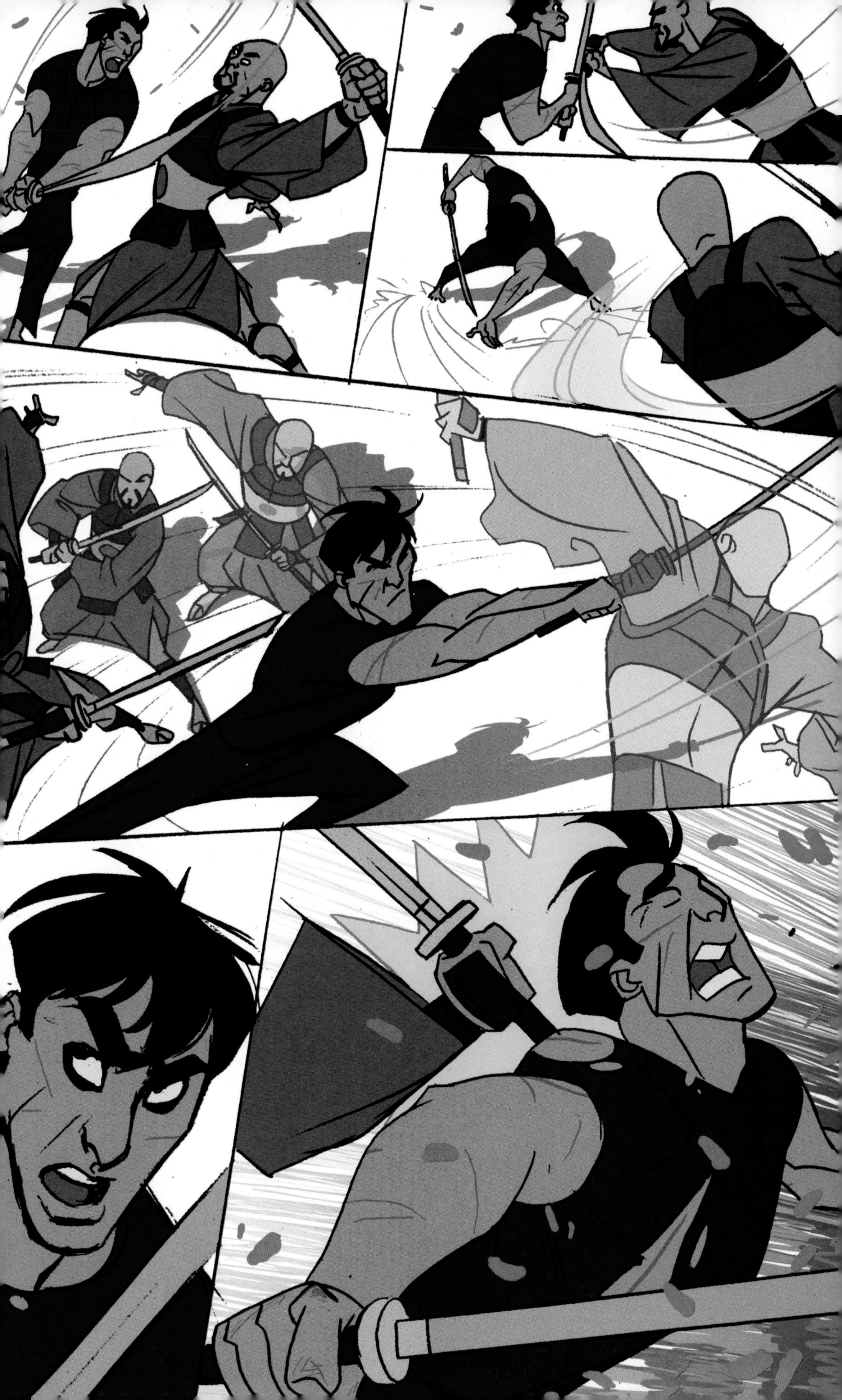

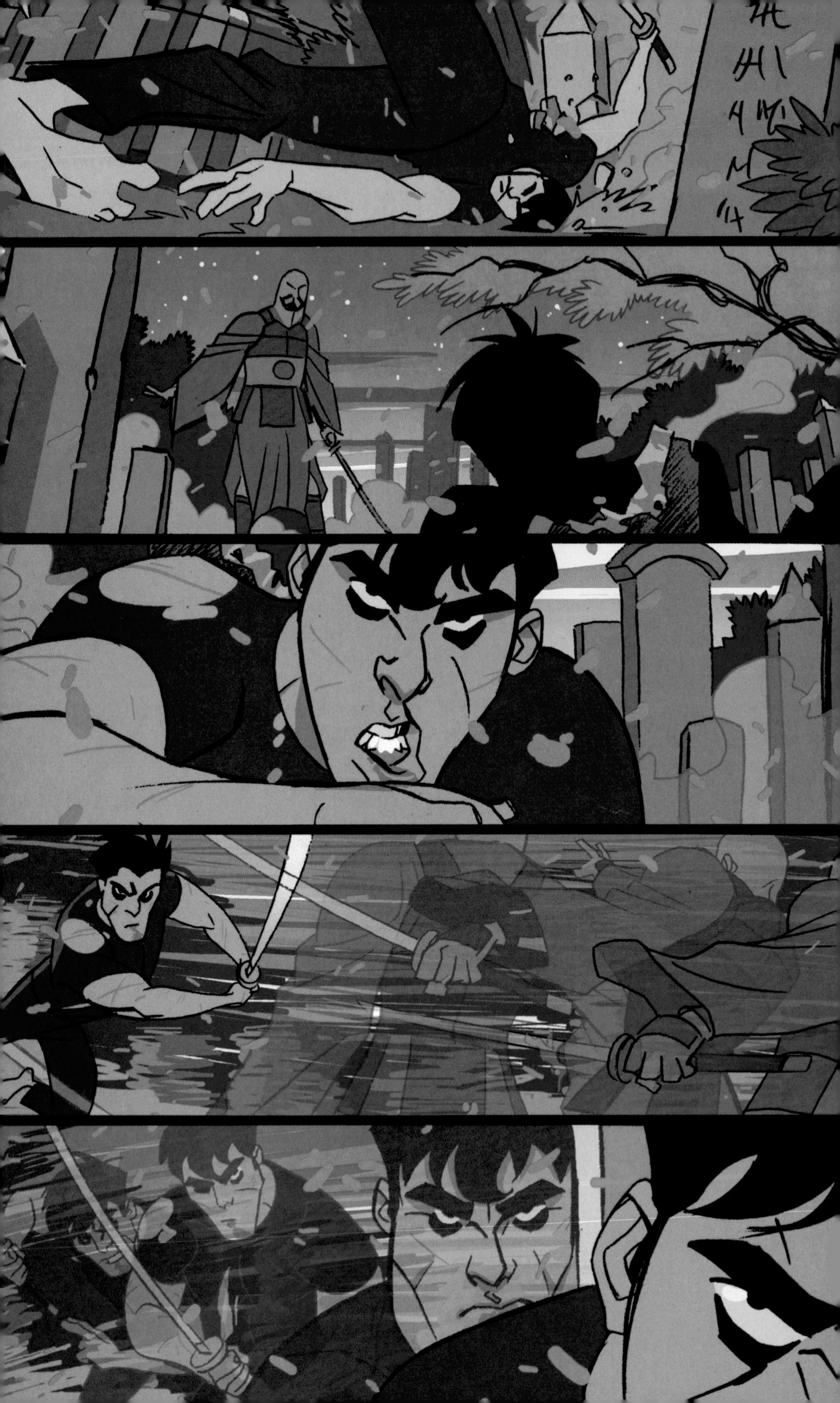

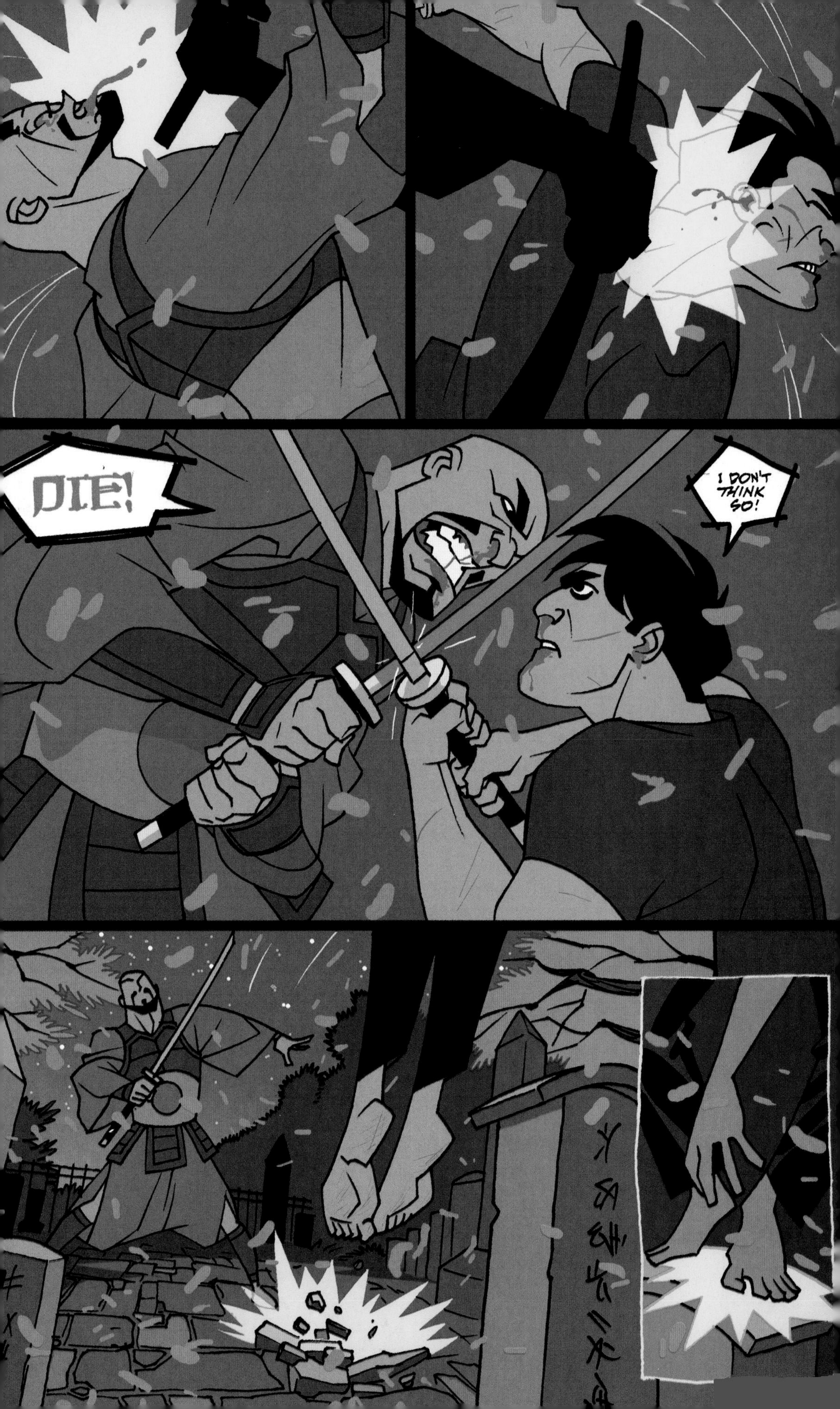
DIE!
I DON'T THINK SO!

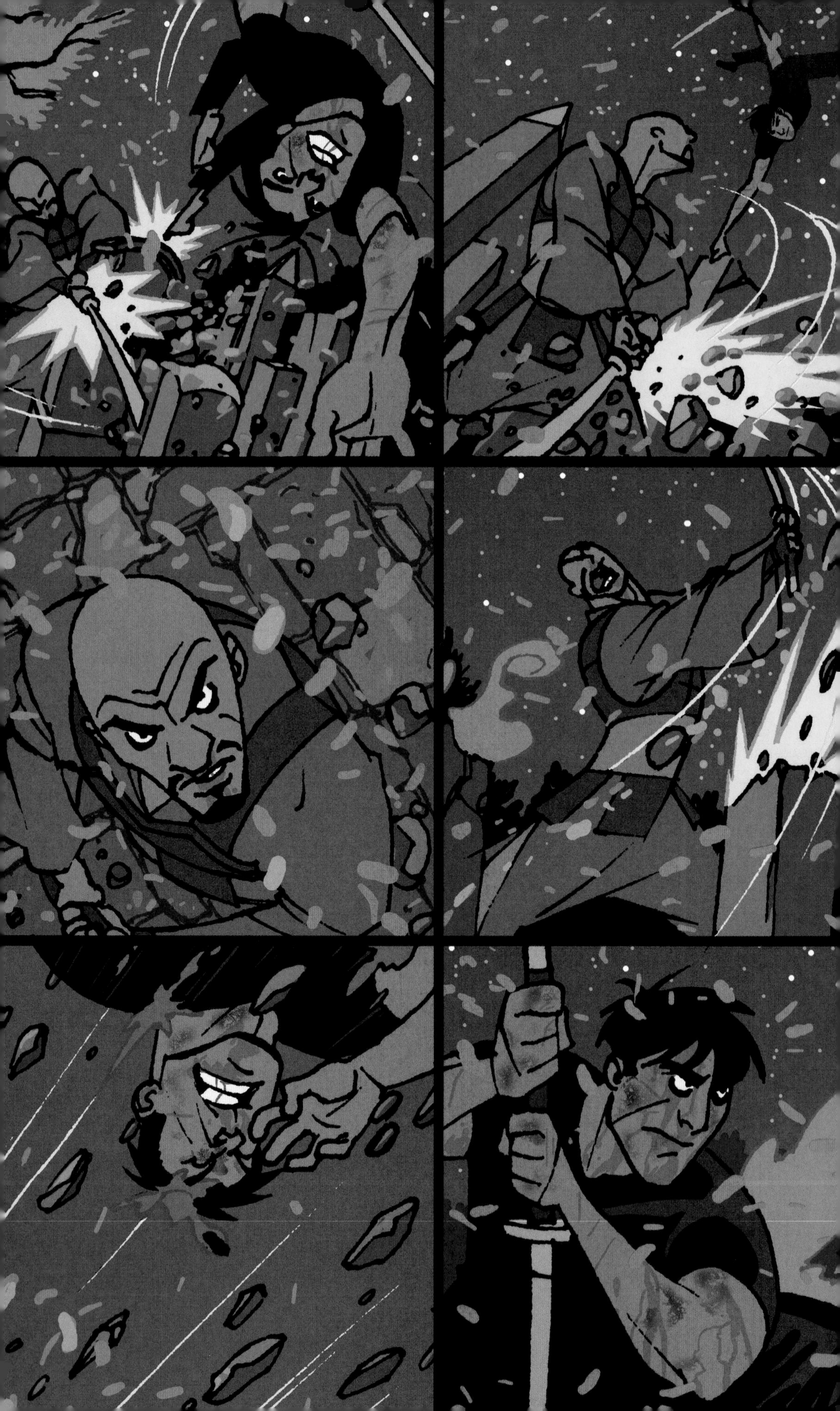

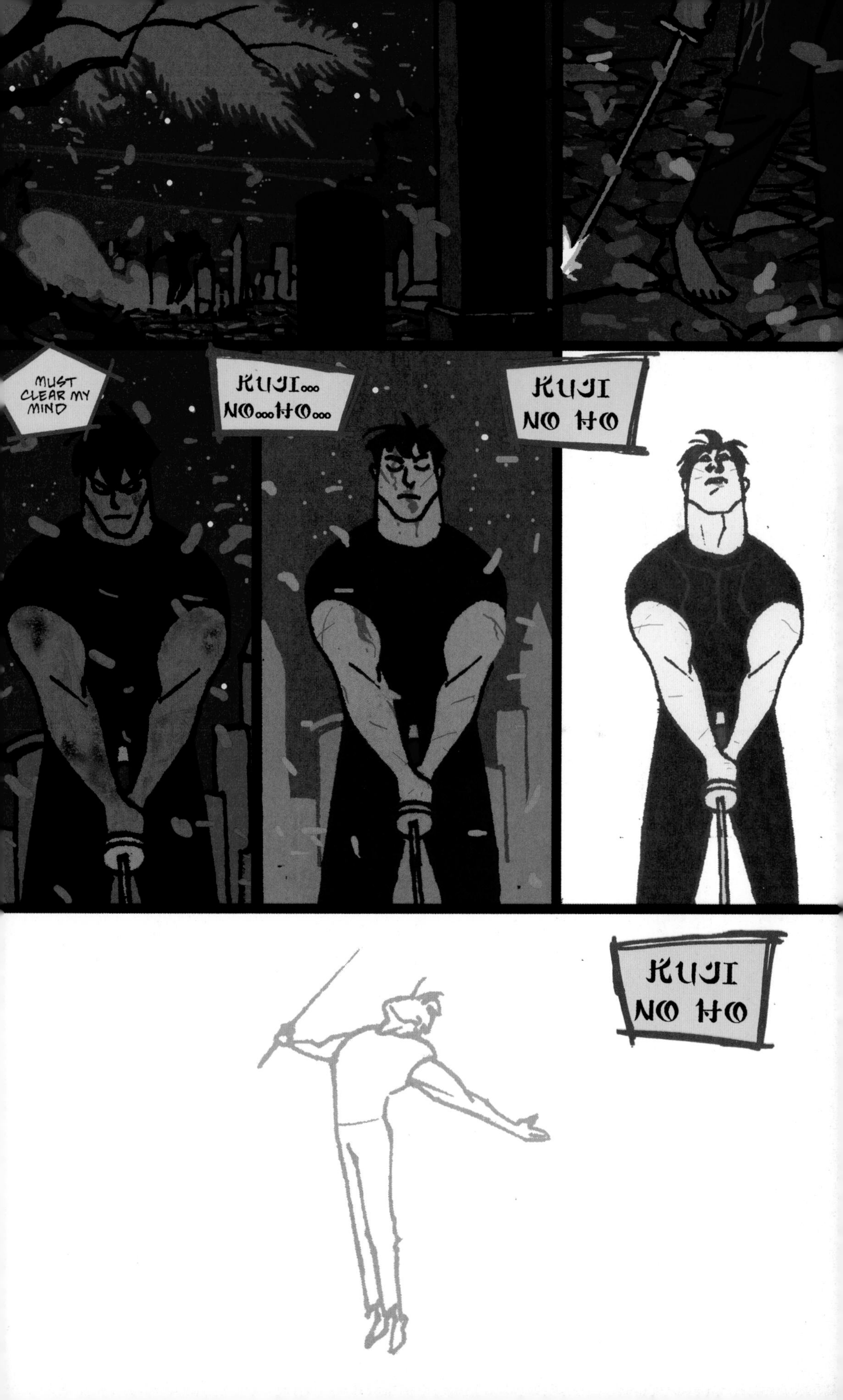
MUST CLEAR MY MIND
KUJI... NO...HO...
KUJI NO HO
KUJI NO HO

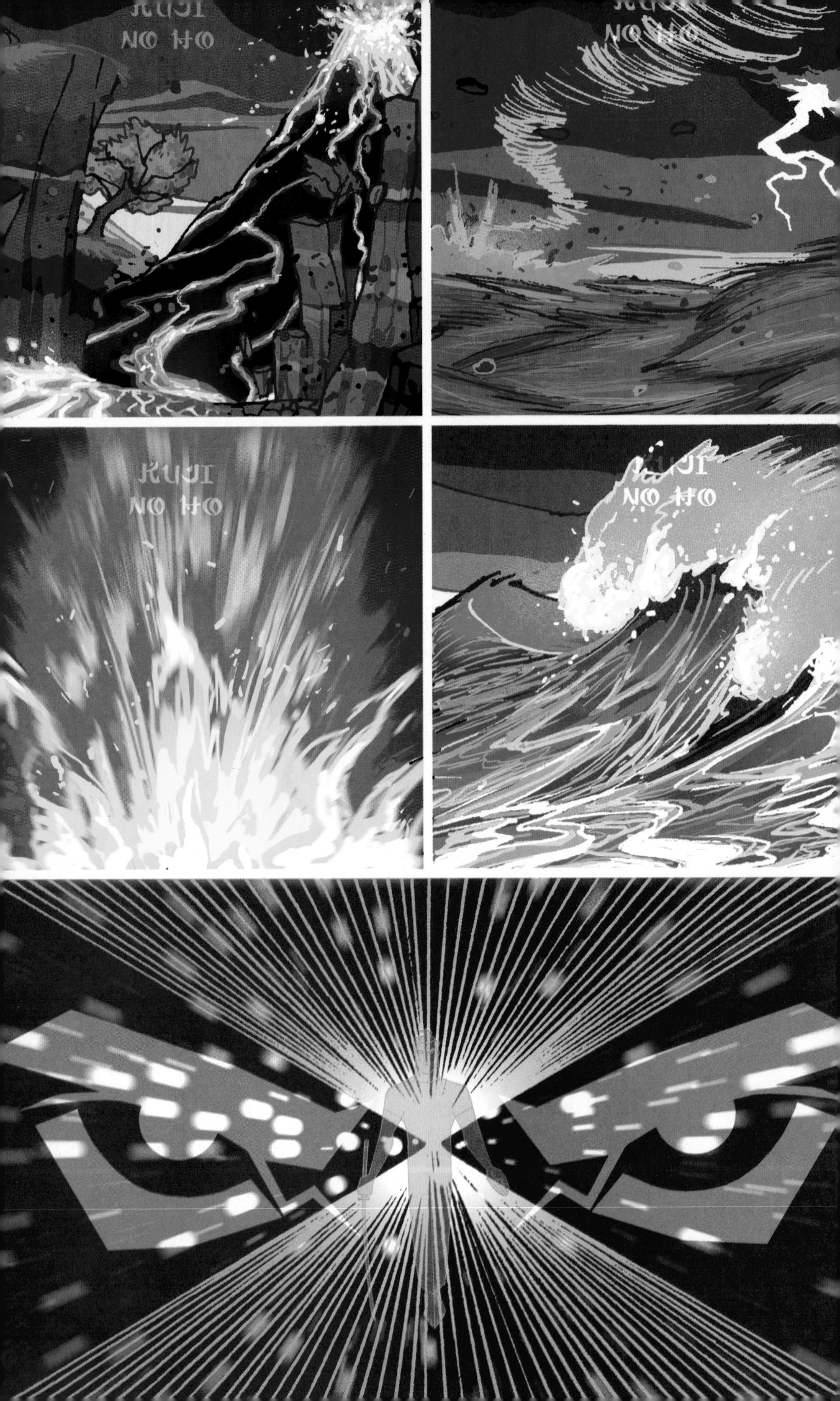

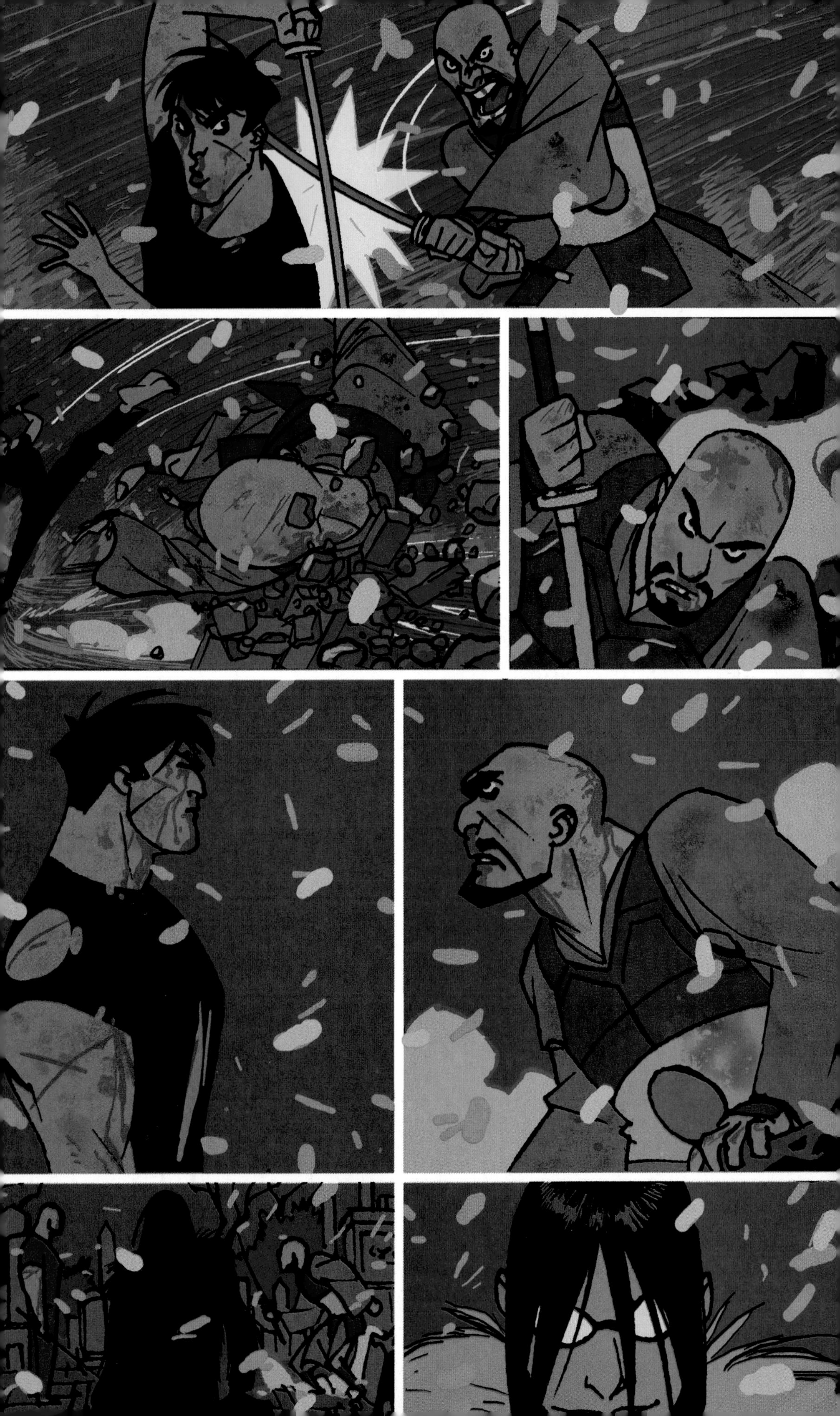

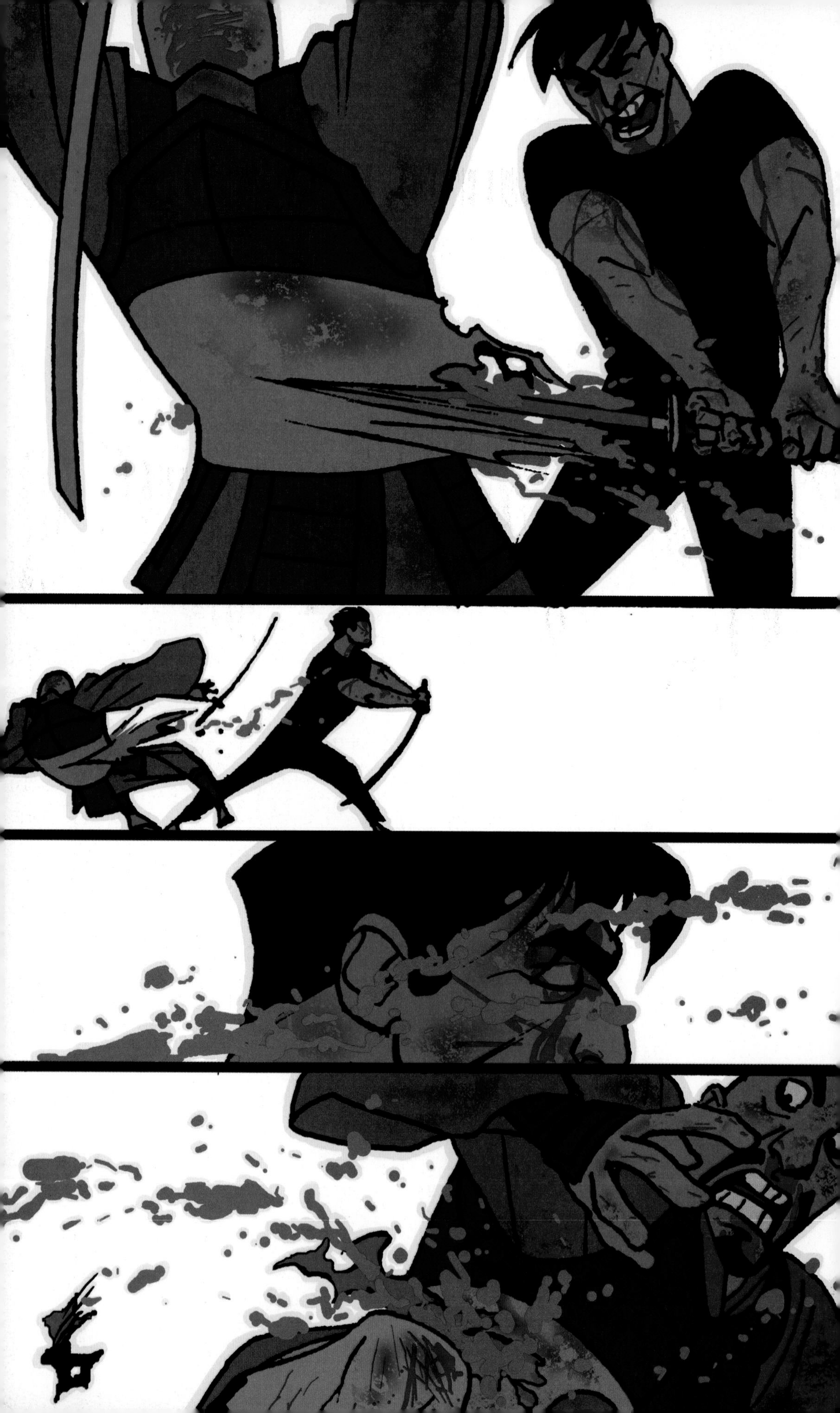

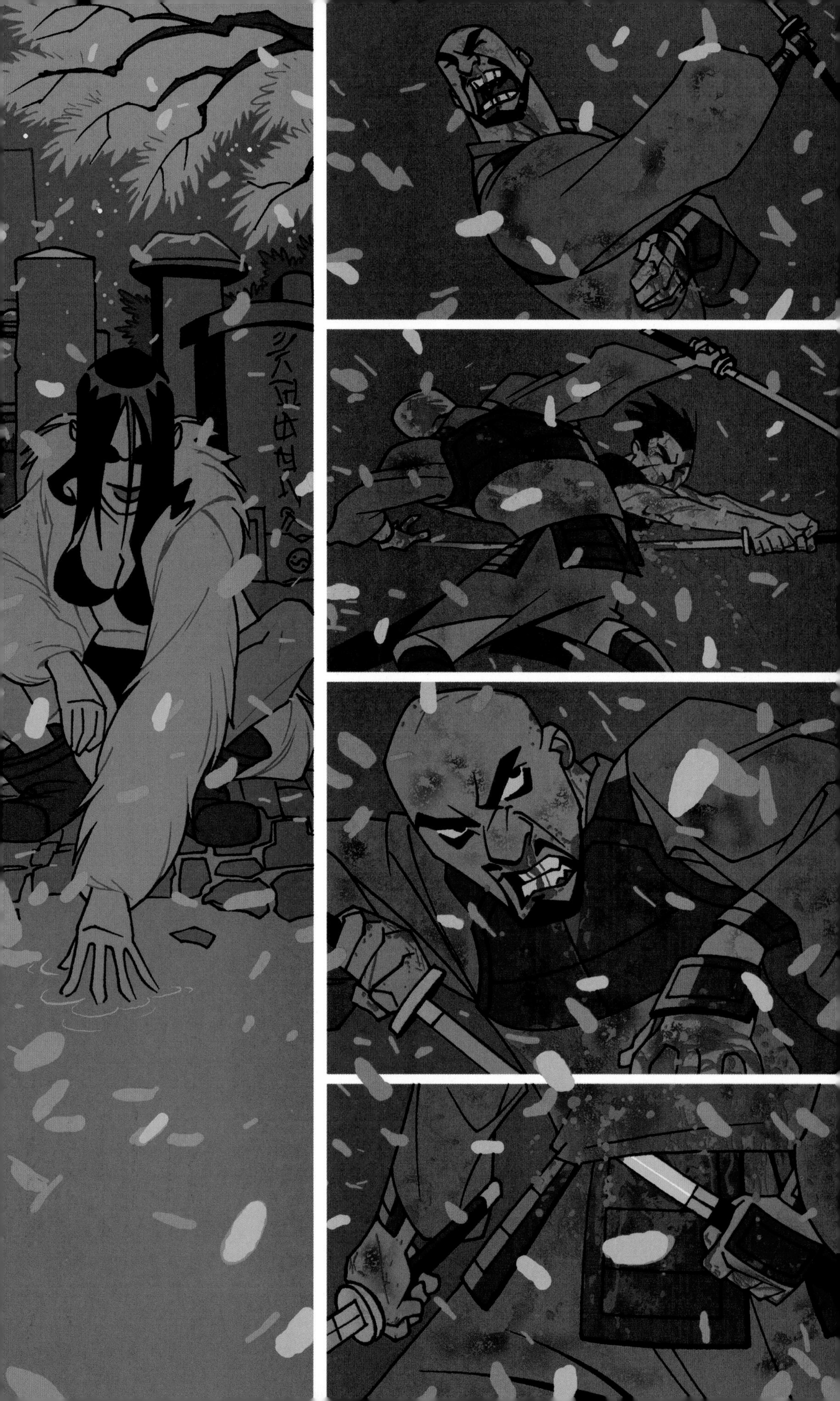

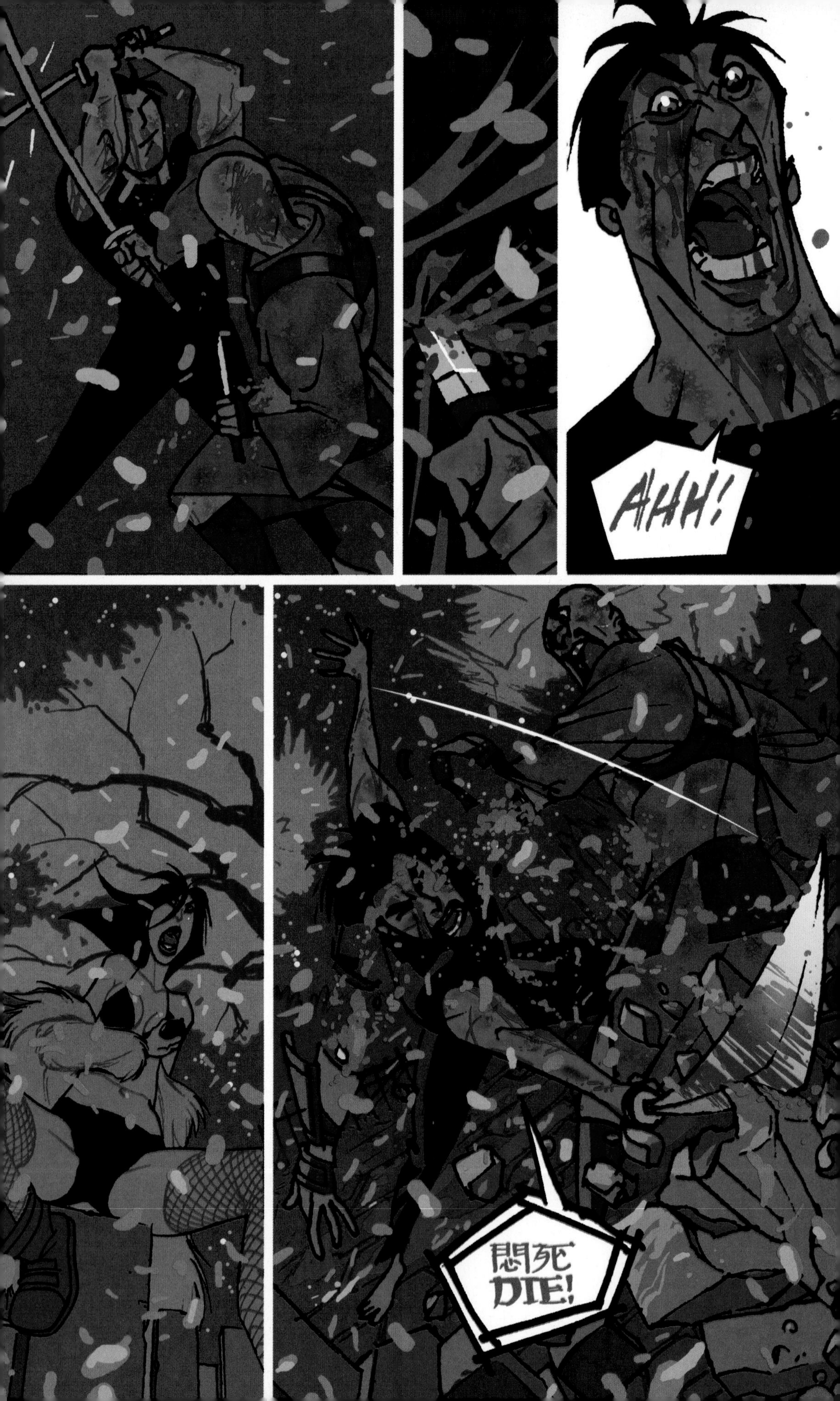
AHH!
悶死
DIE!

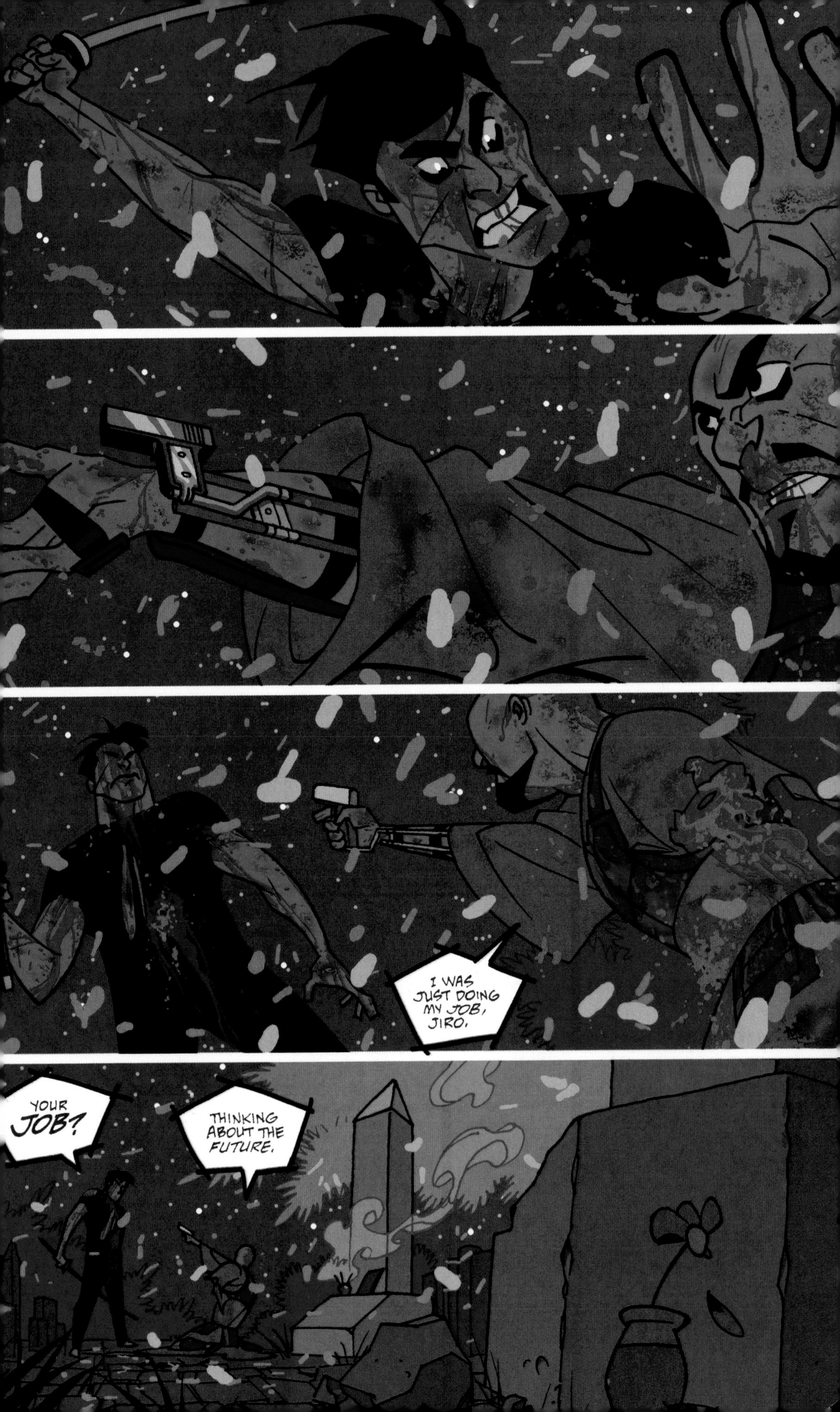
I WAS JUST DOING MY JOB, JIRO.
YOUR JOB?
THINKING ABOUT THE FUTURE.

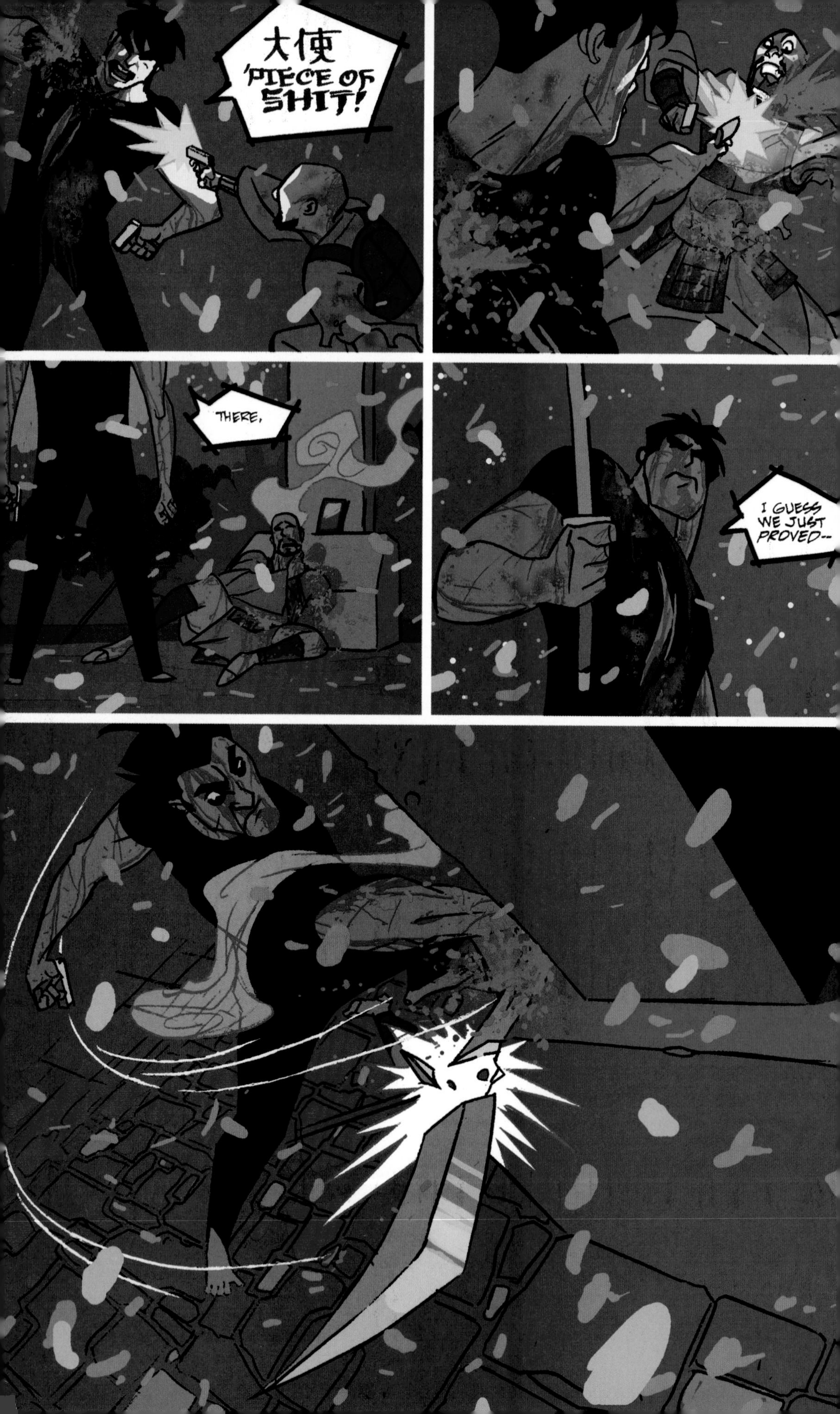

大使 'PIECE OF SHIT!
THERE,
I GUESS WE JUST PROVED--

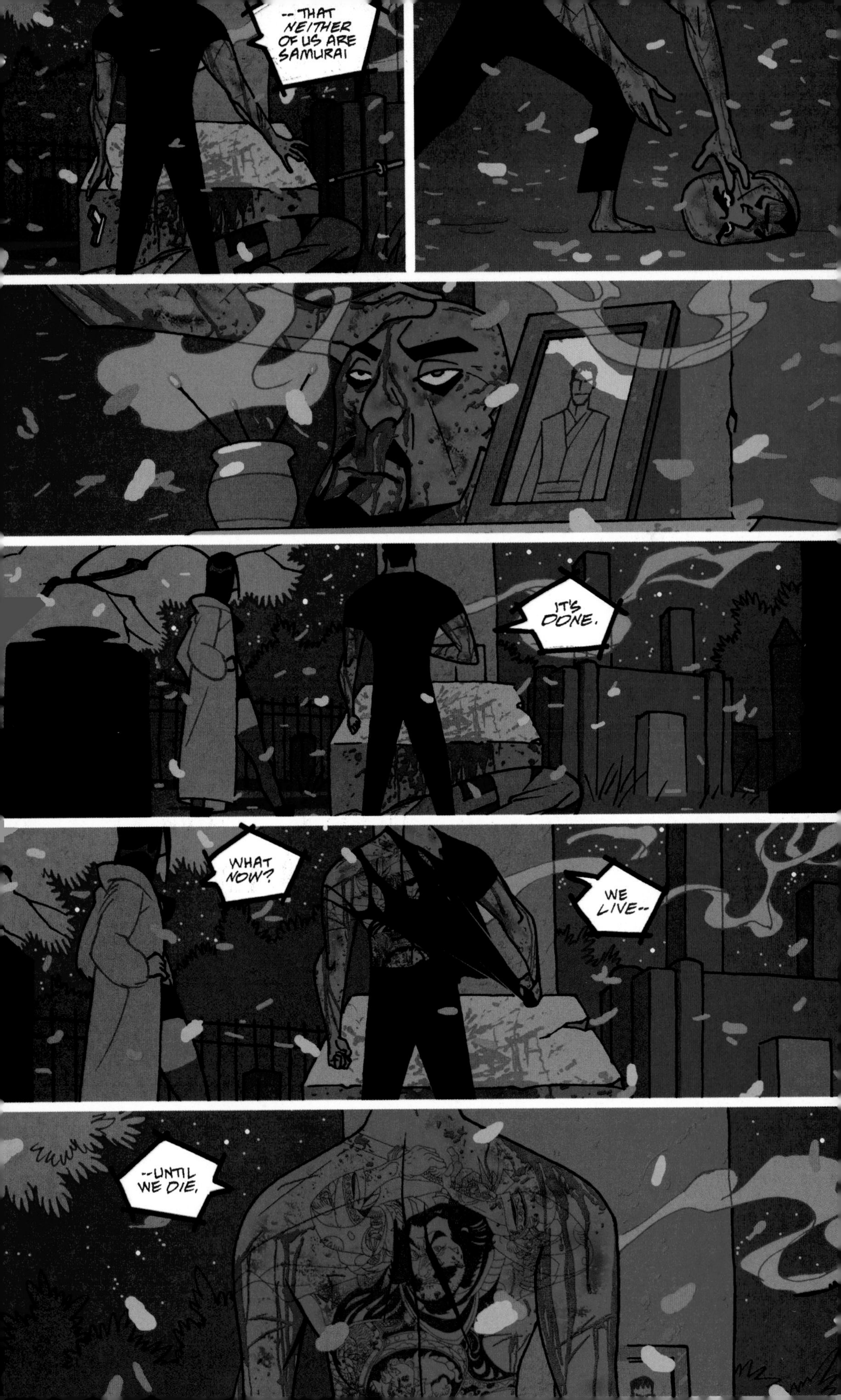
--THAT NEITHER OF US ARE SAMURAI
IT'S DONE.
WHAT NOW?
WE LIVE--
--UNTIL WE DIE.

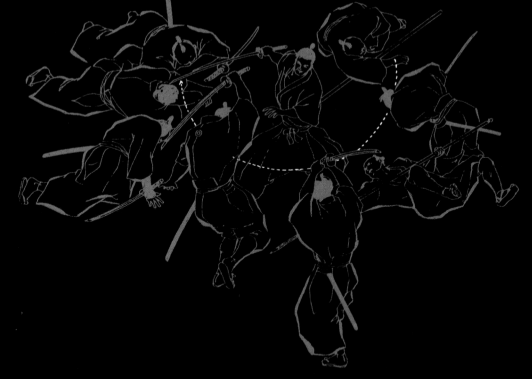

Bastard Short Stories

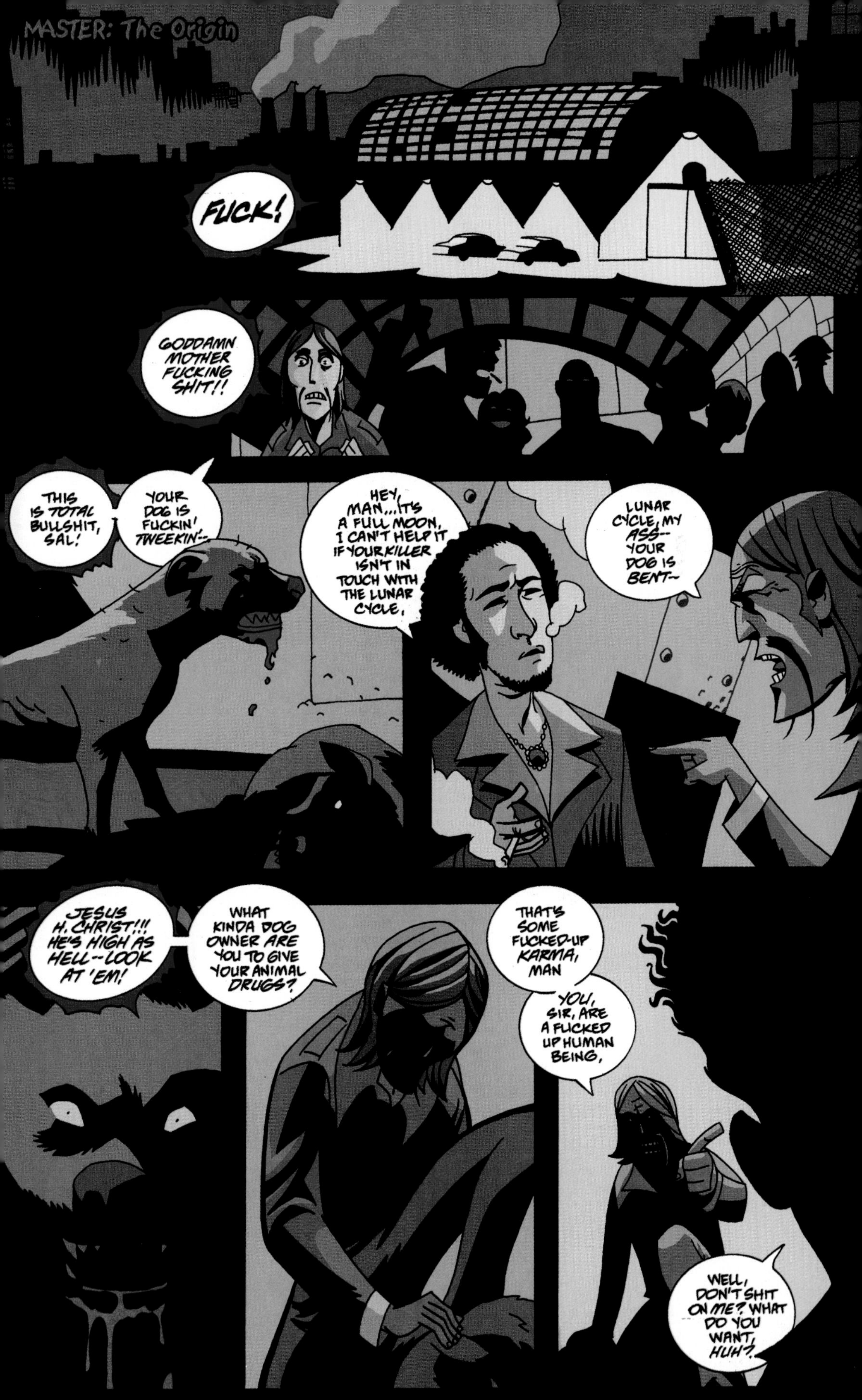
MASTER: The Origin
FUCK!
GODDAMN MOTHER FUCKING SHIT!!
THIS IS TOTAL BULLSHIT, SAL!
YOUR DOG IS FUCKIN' TWEEKIN'--
HEY, MAN... IT'S A FULL MOON, I CAN'T HELP IT IF YOUR KILLER ISN'T IN TOUCH WITH THE LUNAR CYCLE,
LUNAR CYCLE, MY ASS-- YOUR DOG IS BENT-
JESUS H. CHRIST!!! HE'S HIGH AS HELL--LOOK AT 'EM!
WHAT KINDA DOG OWNER ARE YOU TO GIVE YOUR ANIMAL DRUGS?
THAT'S SOME FUCKED-UP KARMA, MAN
YOU, SIR, ARE A FUCKED UP HUMAN BEING,
WELL, DON'T SHIT ON ME? WHAT DO YOU WANT, HUH?

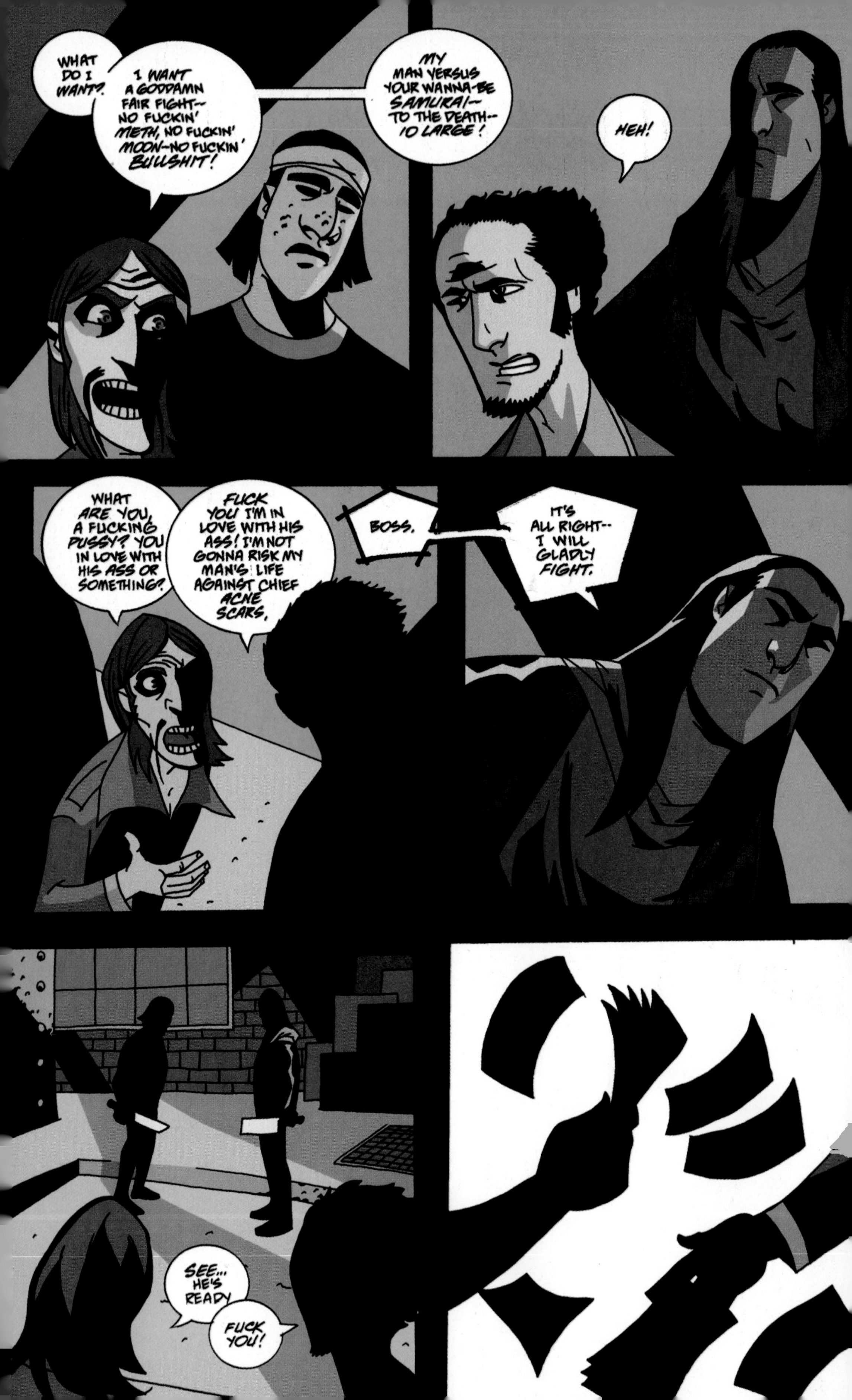
WHAT DO I WANT?
I WANT A GODDAMN FAIR FIGHT-- NO FUCKIN' METH, NO FUCKIN' MOON--NO FUCKIN' BULLSHIT!
MY MAN VERSUS YOUR WANNA-BE SAMURAI-- TO THE DEATH-- 10 LARGE!
HEH!
WHAT ARE YOU, A FUCKING PUSSY? YOU IN LOVE WITH HIS ASS OR SOMETHING?
FUCK YOU! I'M IN LOVE WITH HIS ASS! I'M NOT GONNA RISK MY MAN'S LIFE AGAINST CHIEF ACNE SCARS.
BOSS.
IT'S ALL RIGHT-- I WILL GLADLY FIGHT.
SEE... HE'S READY
FUCK YOU!

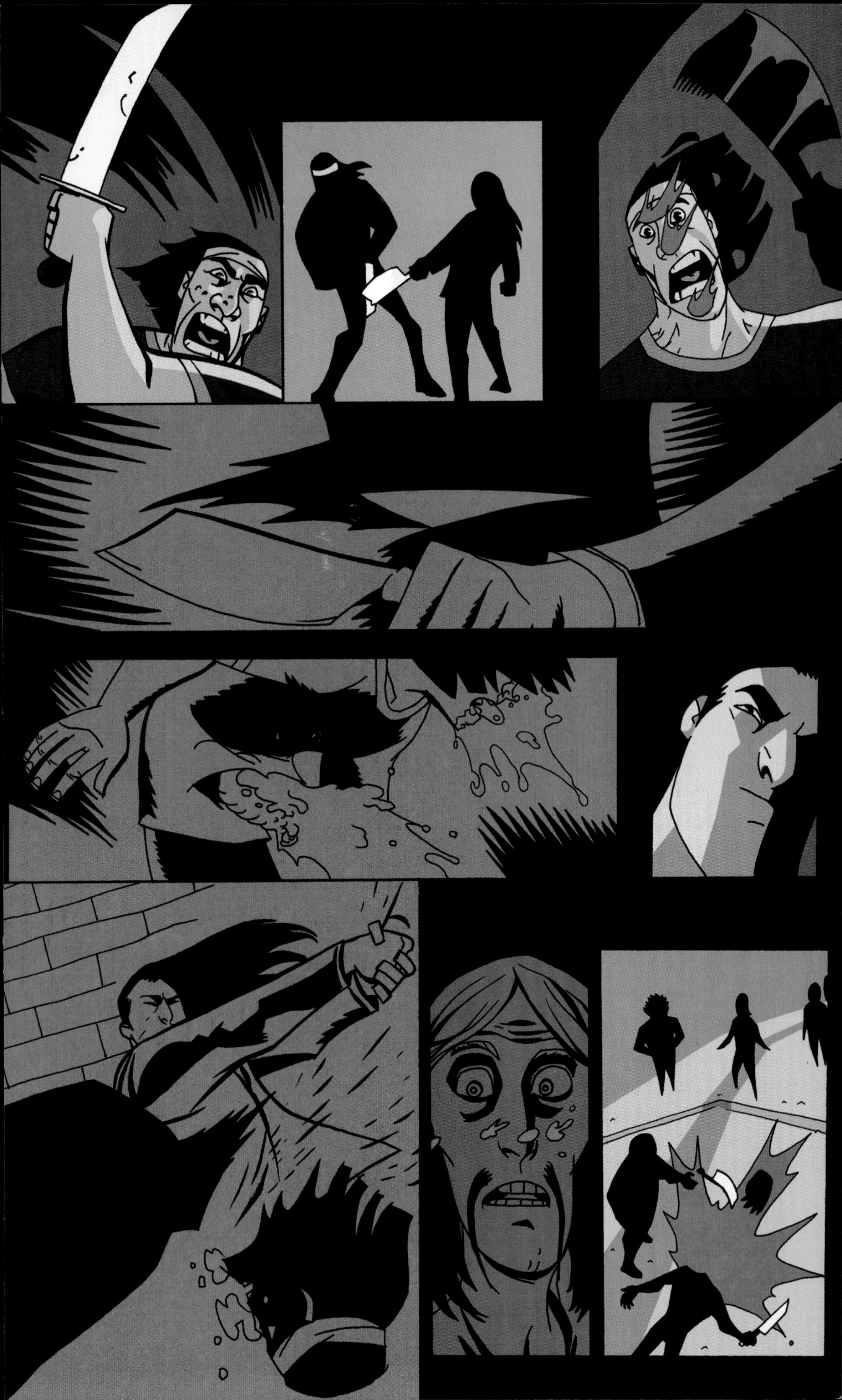

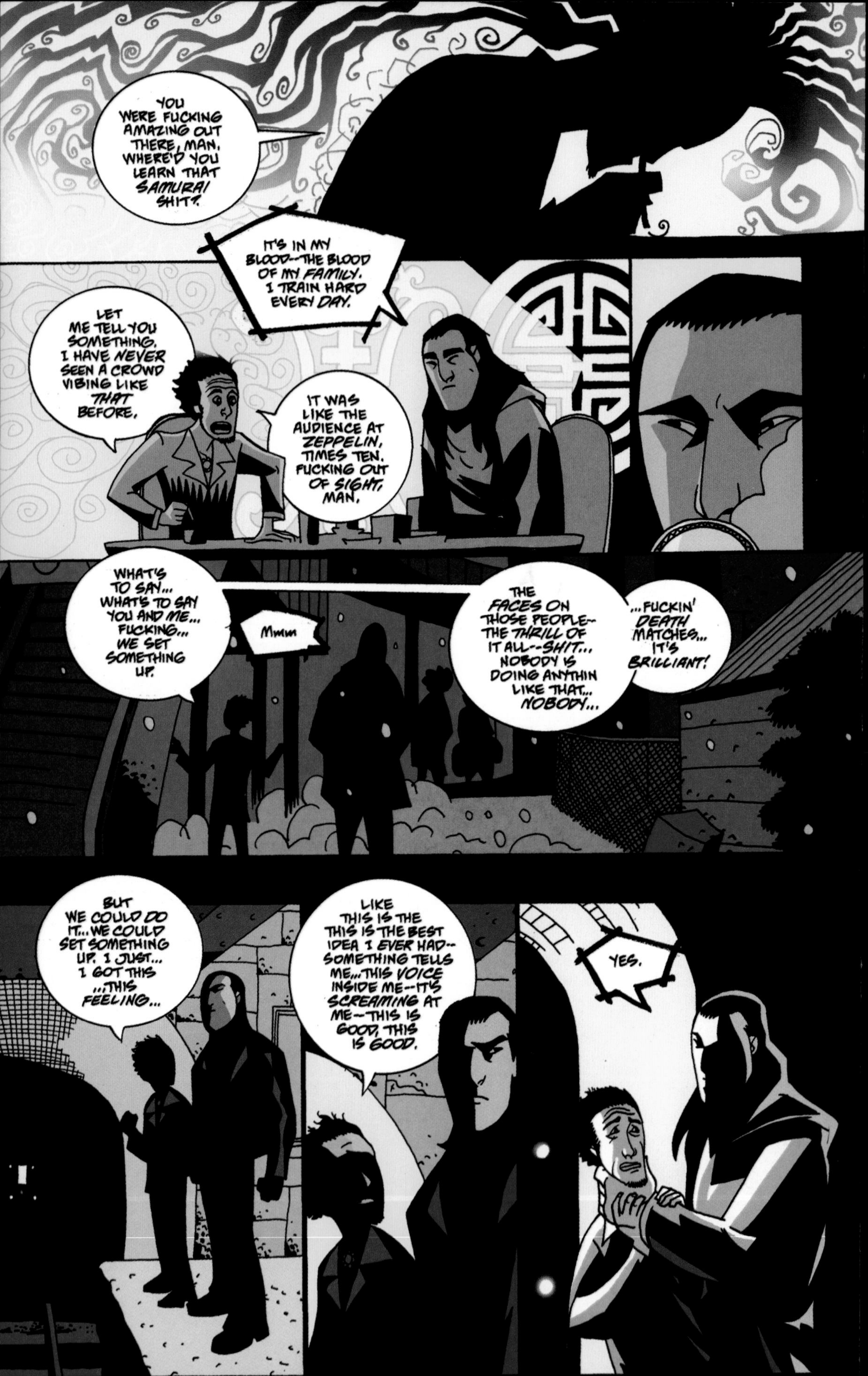
YOU WERE FUCKING AMAZING OUT THERE, MAN. WHERE'D YOU LEARN THAT SAMURAI SHIT?
IT'S IN MY BLOOD--THE BLOOD OF MY FAMILY. I TRAIN HARD EVERY DAY.
LET ME TELL YOU SOMETHING. I HAVE NEVER SEEN A CROWD VIBING LIKE THAT BEFORE.
IT WAS LIKE THE AUDIENCE AT ZEPPELIN, TIMES TEN. FUCKING OUT OF SIGHT, MAN.
WHAT'S TO SAY... WHAT'S TO SAY YOU AND ME... FUCKING... WE SET SOMETHING UP.
Mmm
THE FACES ON THOSE PEOPLE-- THE THRILL OF IT ALL--SHIT... NOBODY IS DOING ANYTHIN LIKE THAT... NOBODY...
...FUCKIN' DEATH MATCHES... IT'S BRILLIANT!
BUT WE COULD DO IT... WE COULD SET SOMETHING UP. I JUST... I GOT THIS ...THIS FEELING...
LIKE THIS IS THE THIS IS THE BEST IDEA I EVER HAD-- SOMETHING TELLS ME... THIS VOICE INSIDE ME--IT'S SCREAMING AT ME--THIS IS GOOD, THIS IS GOOD.
YES.

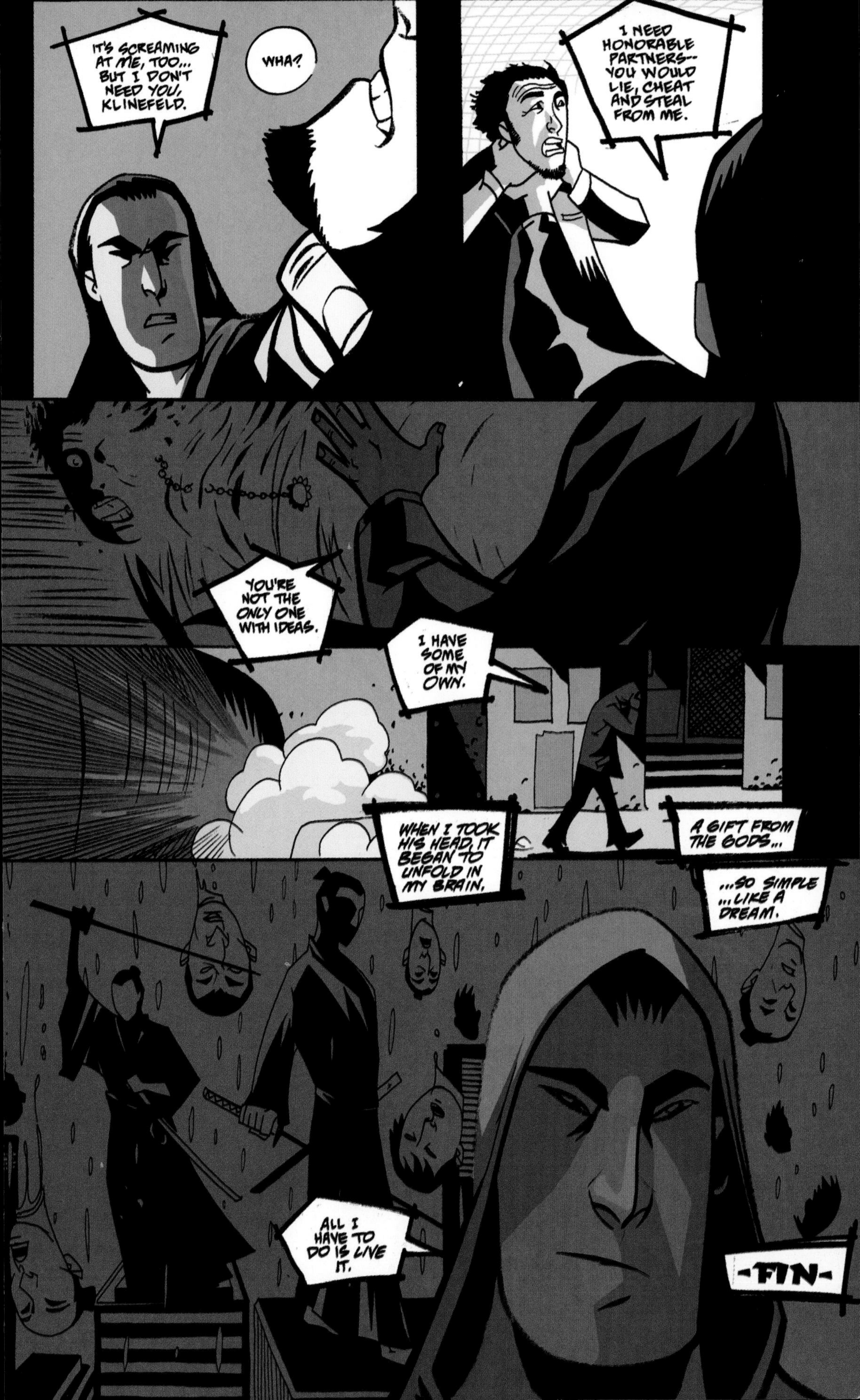
IT'S SCREAMING AT ME, TOO... BUT I DON'T NEED YOU, KLINEFELD.
WHA?
I NEED HONORABLE PARTNERS-- YOU WOULD LIE, CHEAT AND STEAL FROM ME.
YOU'RE NOT THE ONLY ONE WITH IDEAS.
I HAVE SOME OF MY OWN.
WHEN I TOOK HIS HEAD, IT BEGAN TO UNFOLD IN MY BRAIN.
A GIFT FROM THE GODS...
...SO SIMPLE ...LIKE A DREAM.
ALL I HAVE TO DO IS LIVE IT.
-FIN-

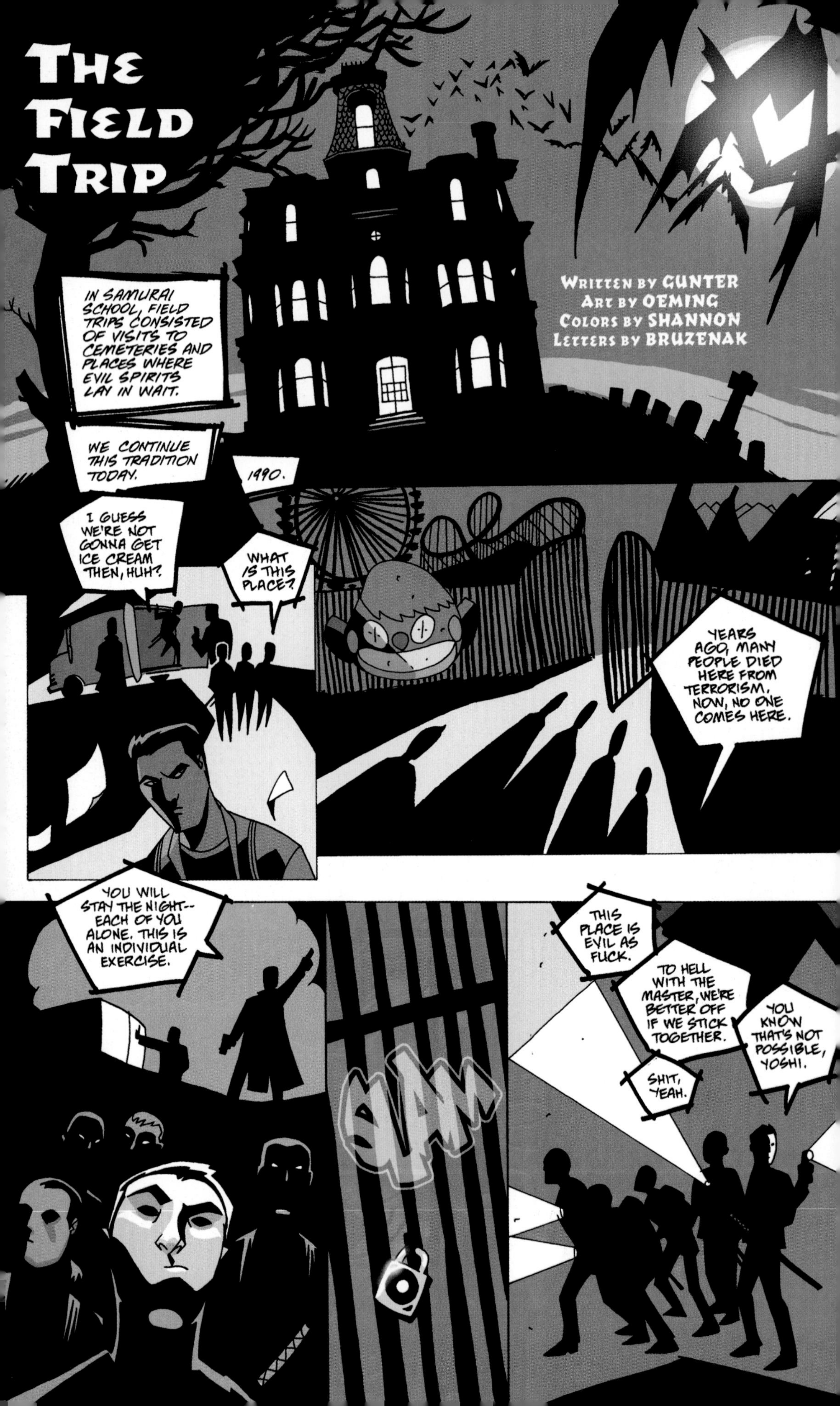
THE FIELD TRIP
IN SAMURAI SCHOOL, FIELD TRIPS CONSISTED OF VISITS TO CEMETERIES AND PLACES WHERE EVIL SPIRITS LAY IN WAIT.
WE CONTINUE THIS TRADITION TODAY.
1990.
WRITTEN BY GUNTER
ART BY OEMING
COLORS BY SHANNON
LETTERS BY BRUZENAK
I GUESS WE'RE NOT GONNA GET ICE CREAM THEN, HUH?
WHAT IS THIS PLACE?
YEARS AGO, MANY PEOPLE DIED HERE FROM TERRORISM. NOW, NO ONE COMES HERE.
YOU WILL STAY THE NIGHT-- EACH OF YOU ALONE. THIS IS AN INDIVIDUAL EXERCISE.
BLAM
THIS PLACE IS EVIL AS FUCK.
TO HELL WITH THE MASTER, WE'RE BETTER OFF IF WE STICK TOGETHER.
SHIT, YEAH.
YOU KNOW THAT'S NOT POSSIBLE, YOSHI.

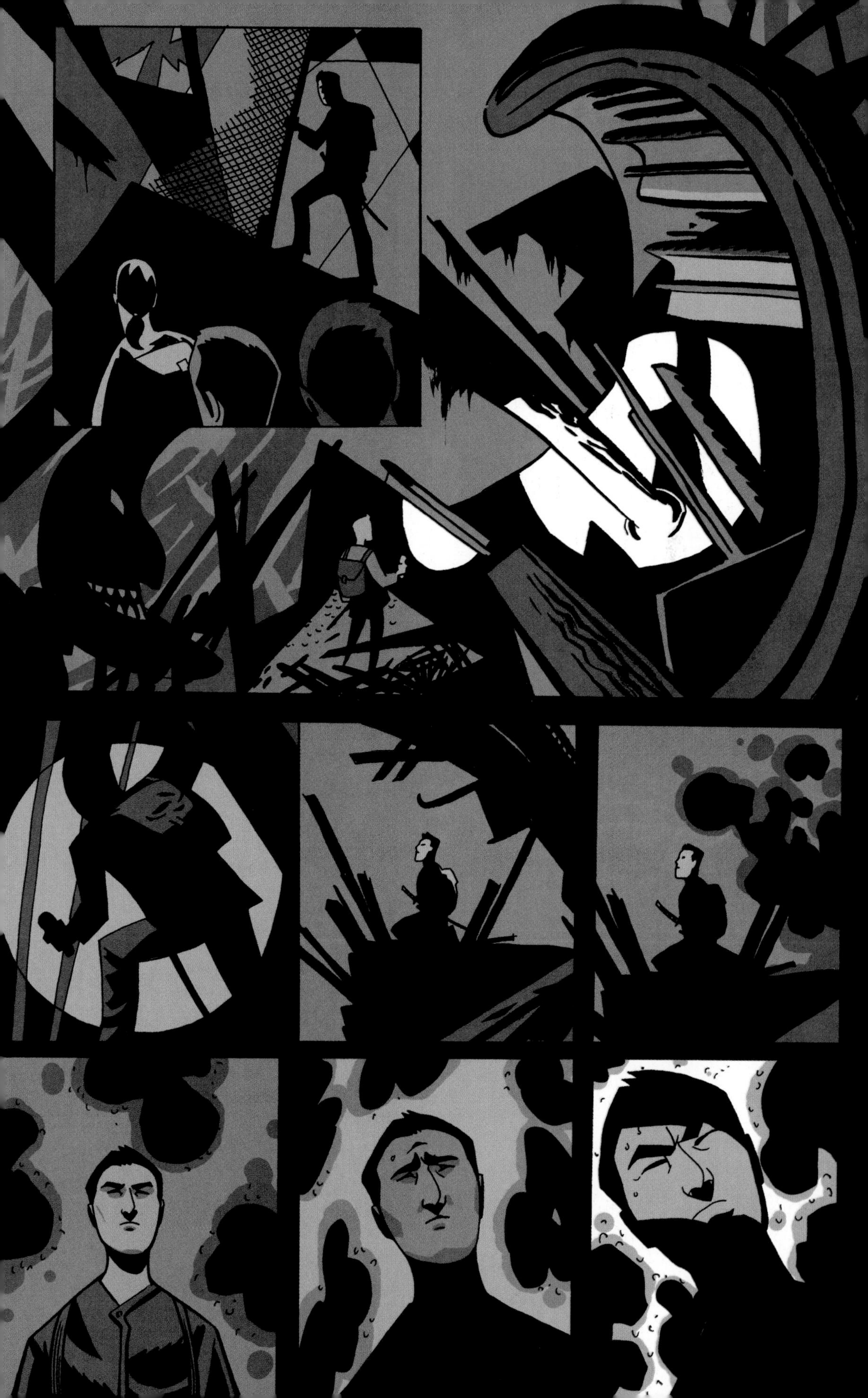

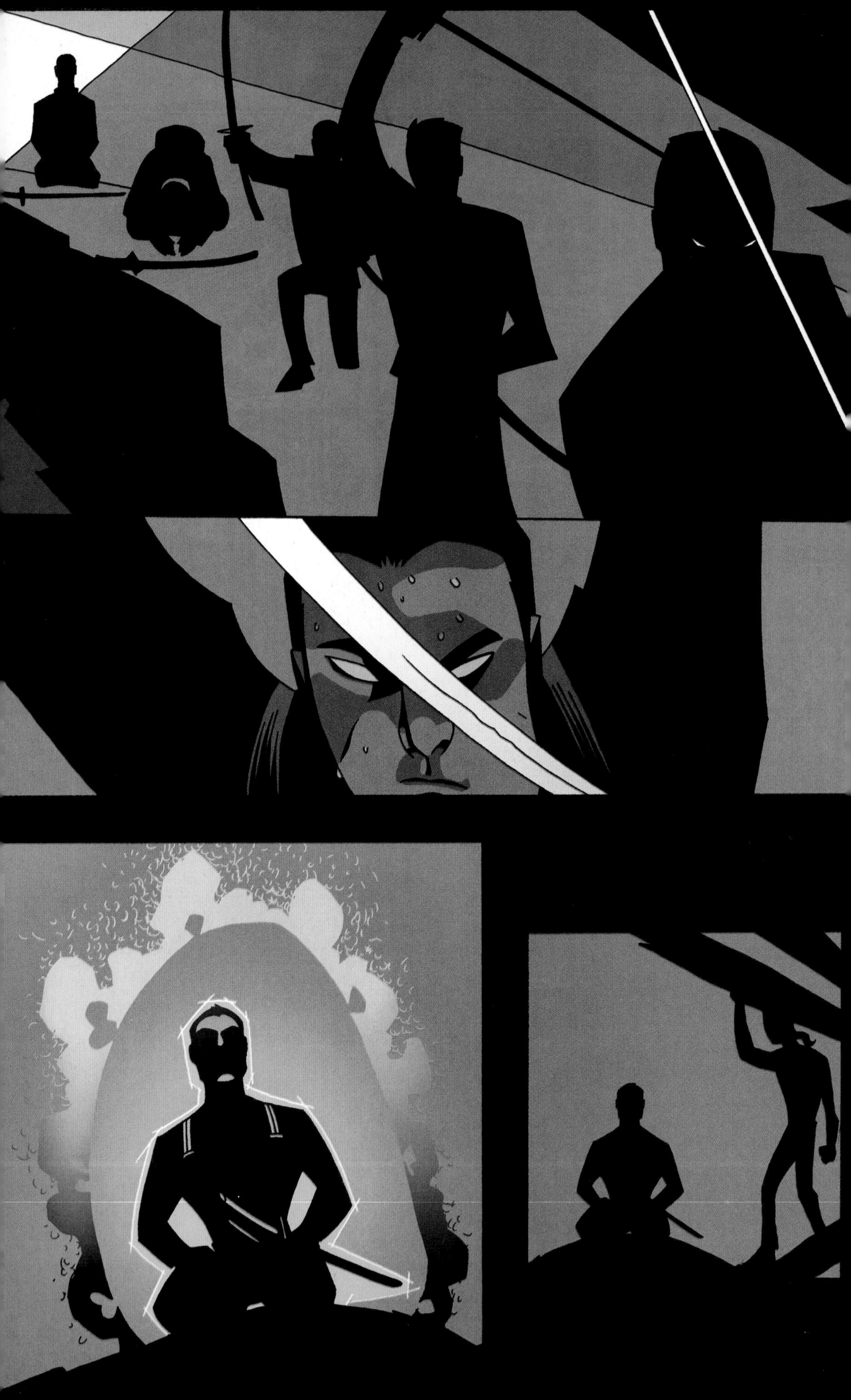

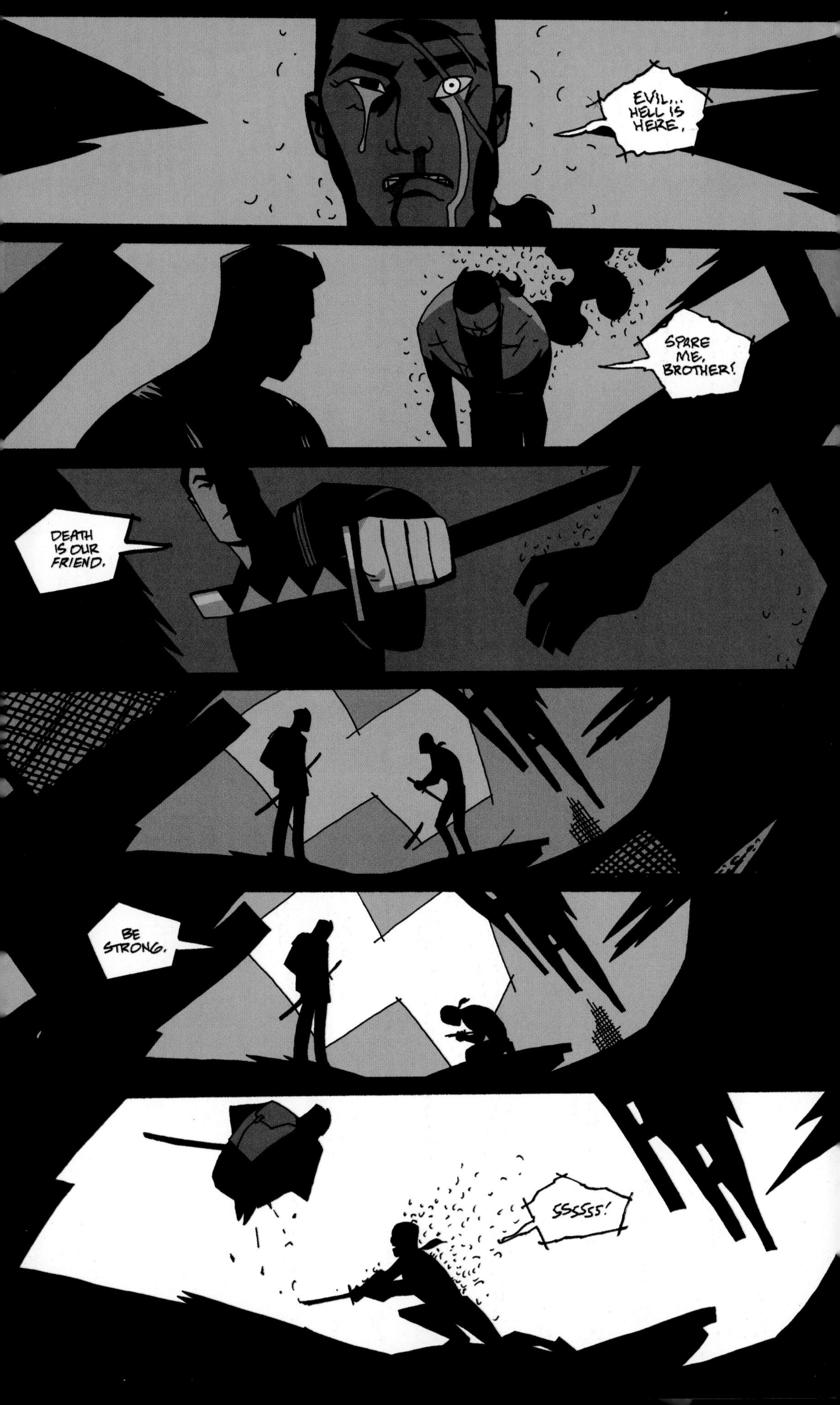

EVIL... HELL IS HERE.
SPARE ME, BROTHER!
DEATH IS OUR FRIEND.
BE STRONG.
SSSSSS!

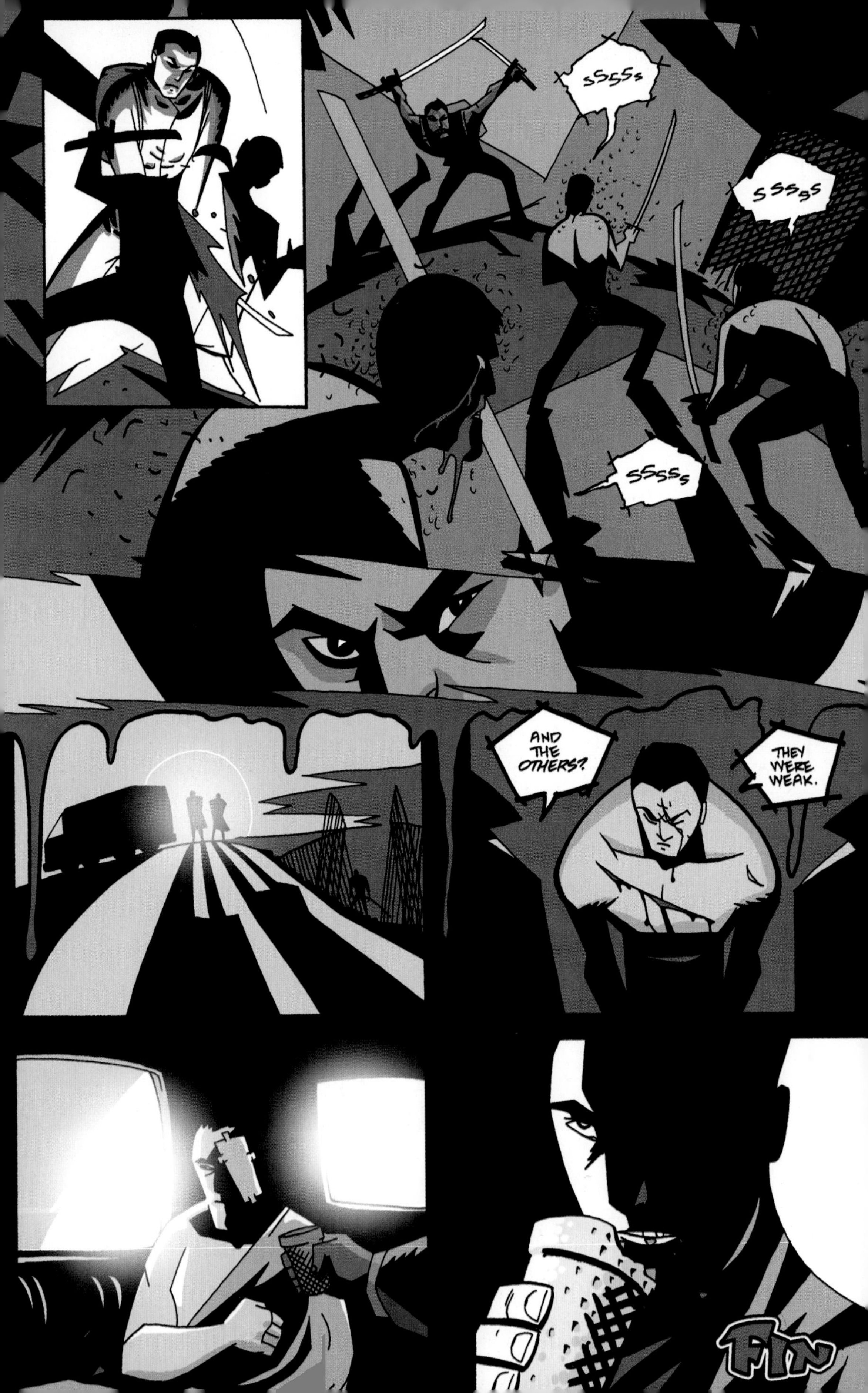
SSSSs
SSSSS
SSSSs
AND THE OTHERS?
THEY WERE WEAK.
FIN

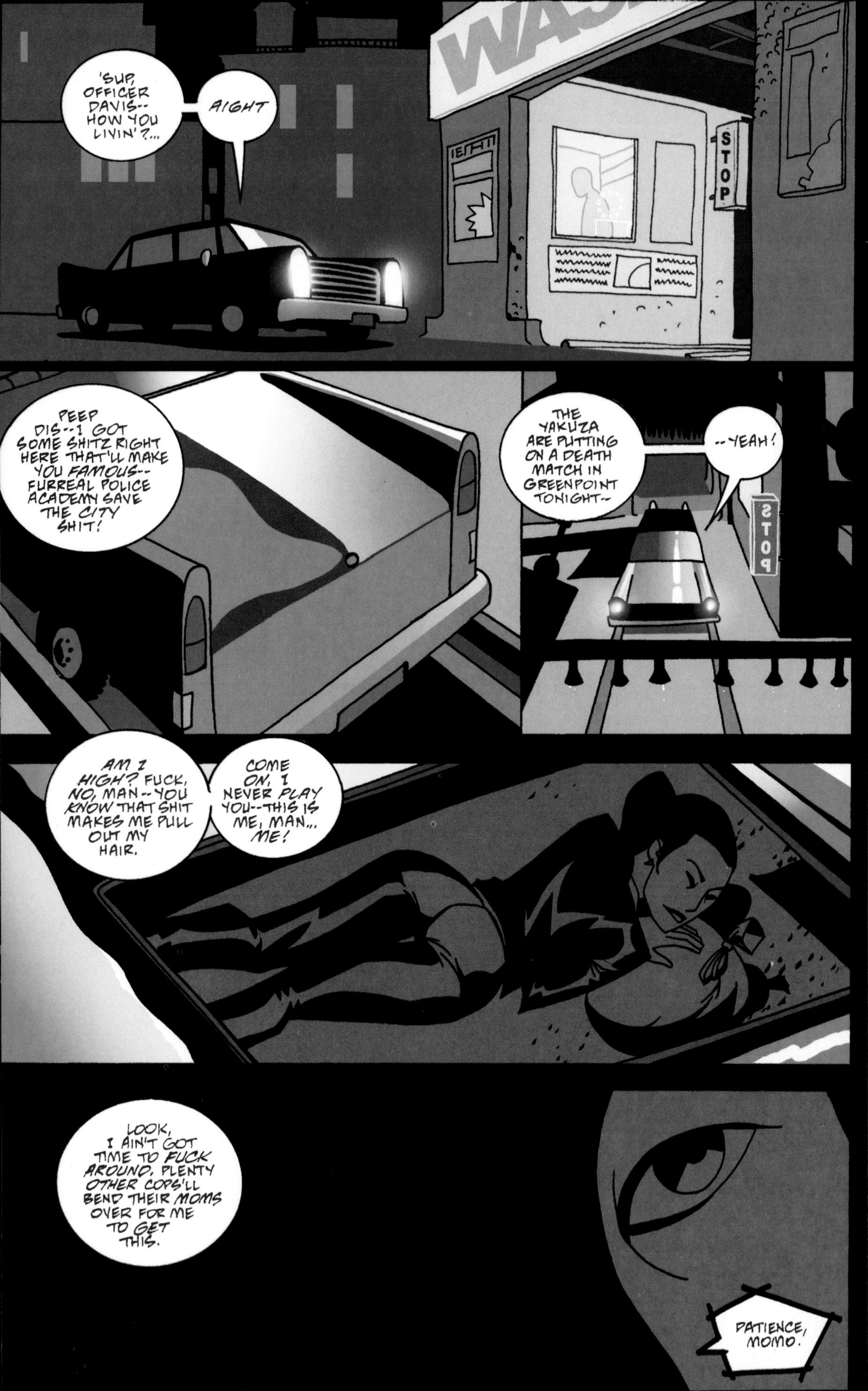
'SUP, OFFICER DAVIS-- HOW YOU LIVIN'?...
AIGHT
STOP
PEEP DIS--I GOT SOME SHITZ RIGHT HERE THAT'LL MAKE YOU FAMOUS-- FURREAL POLICE ACADEMY SAVE THE CITY SHIT!
THE YAKUZA ARE PUTTING ON A DEATH MATCH IN GREENPOINT TONIGHT--
--YEAH!
STOP
AM I HIGH? FUCK, NO, MAN--YOU KNOW THAT SHIT MAKES ME PULL OUT MY HAIR.
COME ON, I NEVER PLAY YOU--THIS IS ME, MAN... ME!
LOOK, I AIN'T GOT TIME TO FUCK AROUND. PLENTY OTHER COPS'LL BEND THEIR MOMS OVER FOR ME TO GET THIS.
PATIENCE, MOMO.

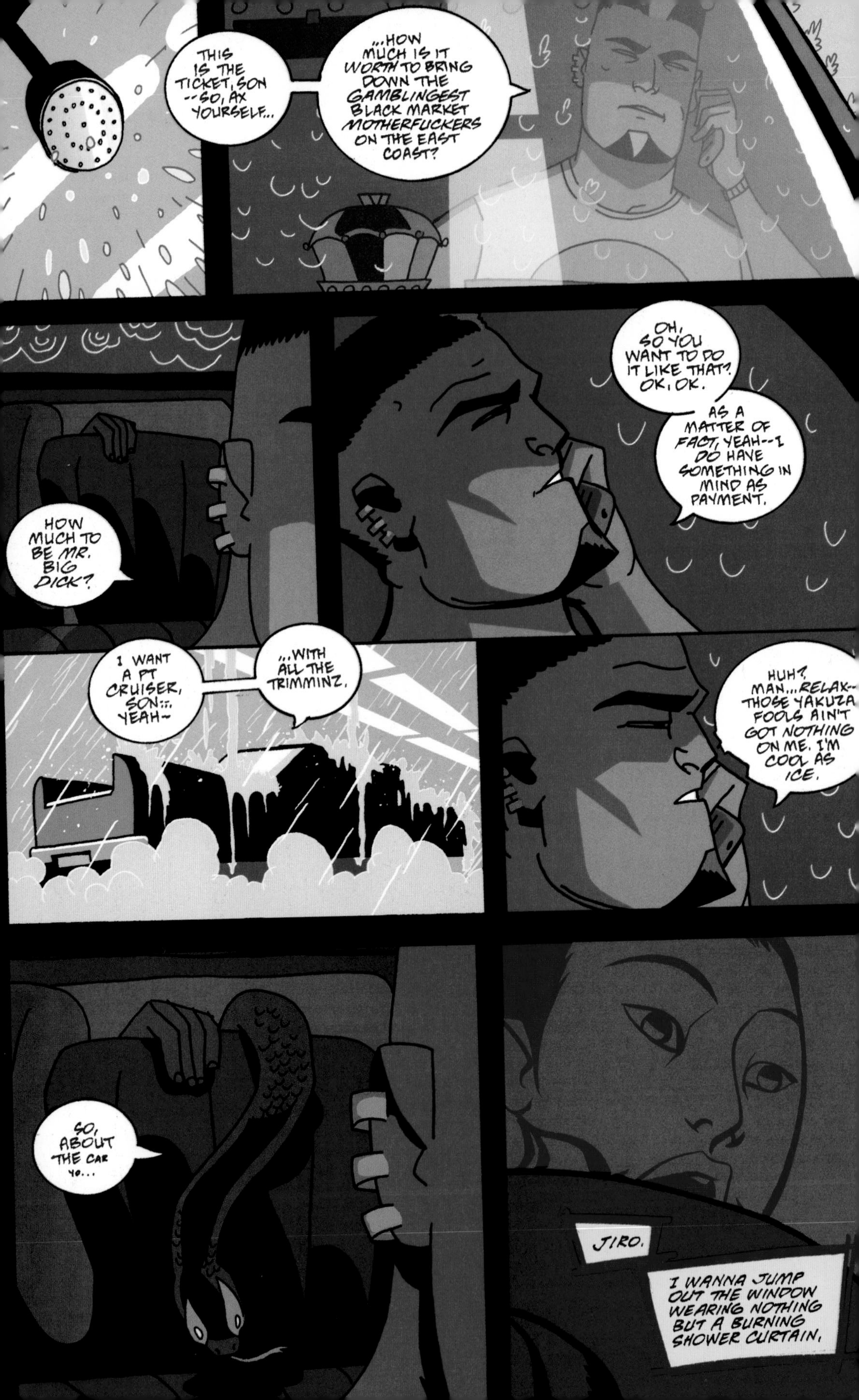
THIS IS THE TICKET, SON --SO, AX YOURSELF...
...HOW MUCH IS IT WORTH TO BRING DOWN THE GAMBLINGEST BLACK MARKET MOTHERFUCKERS ON THE EAST COAST?
HOW MUCH TO BE MR. BIG DICK?
OH, SO YOU WANT TO DO IT LIKE THAT? OK, OK.
AS A MATTER OF FACT, YEAH--I DO HAVE SOMETHING IN MIND AS PAYMENT.
I WANT A PT CRUISER, SON... YEAH--
...WITH ALL THE TRIMMINZ.
HUH? MAN...RELAX-- THOSE YAKUZA FOOLS AIN'T GOT NOTHING ON ME. I'M COOL AS ICE.
SO, ABOUT THE CAR YO...
JIRO.
I WANNA JUMP OUT THE WINDOW WEARING NOTHING BUT A BURNING SHOWER CURTAIN.

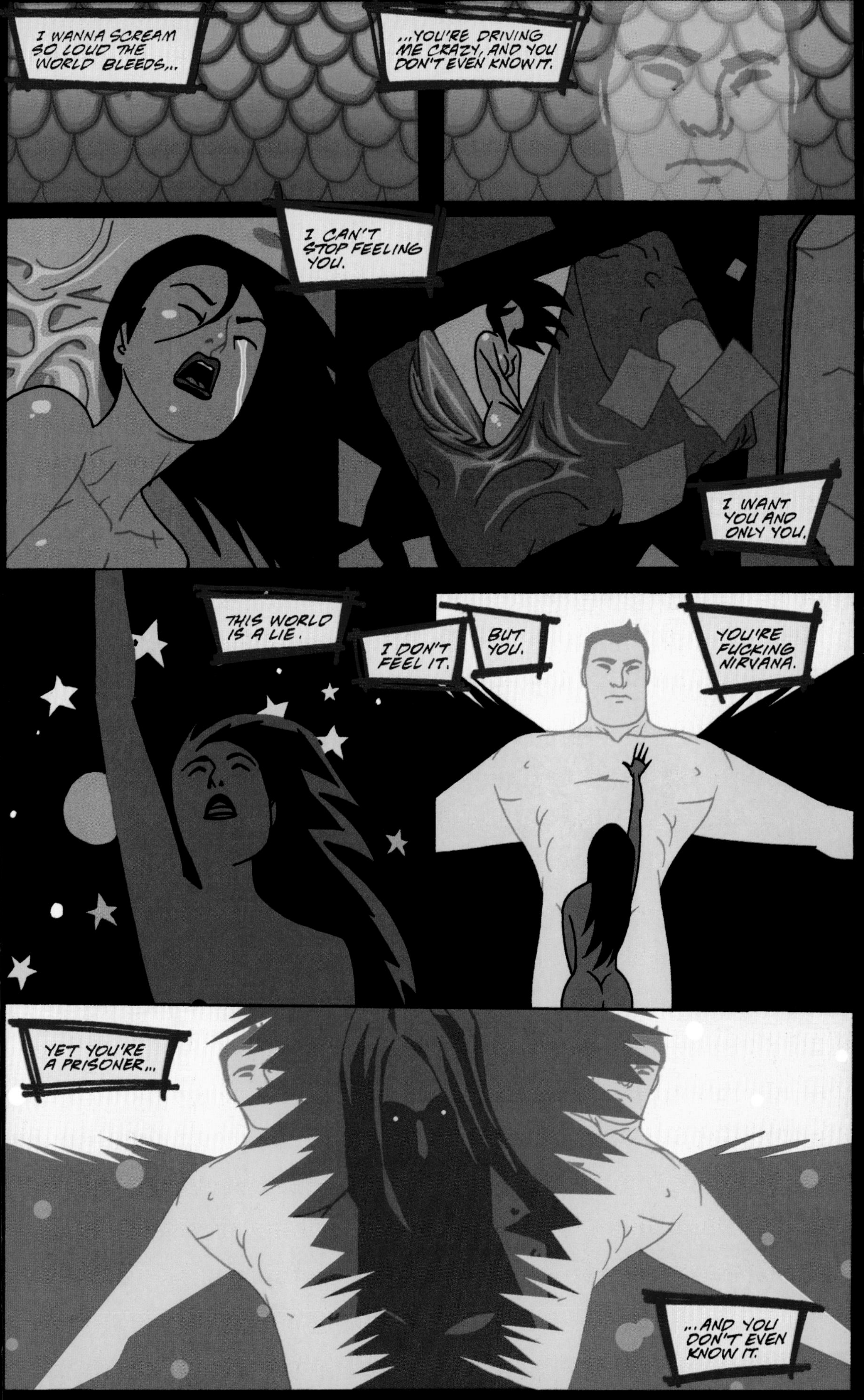
I WANNA SCREAM SO LOUD THE WORLD BLEEDS...
...YOU'RE DRIVING ME CRAZY, AND YOU DON'T EVEN KNOW IT.
I CAN'T STOP FEELING YOU.
I WANT YOU AND ONLY YOU.
THIS WORLD IS A LIE.
I DON'T FEEL IT.
BUT YOU.
YOU'RE FUCKING NIRVANA.
YET YOU'RE A PRISONER...
...AND YOU DON'T EVEN KNOW IT.

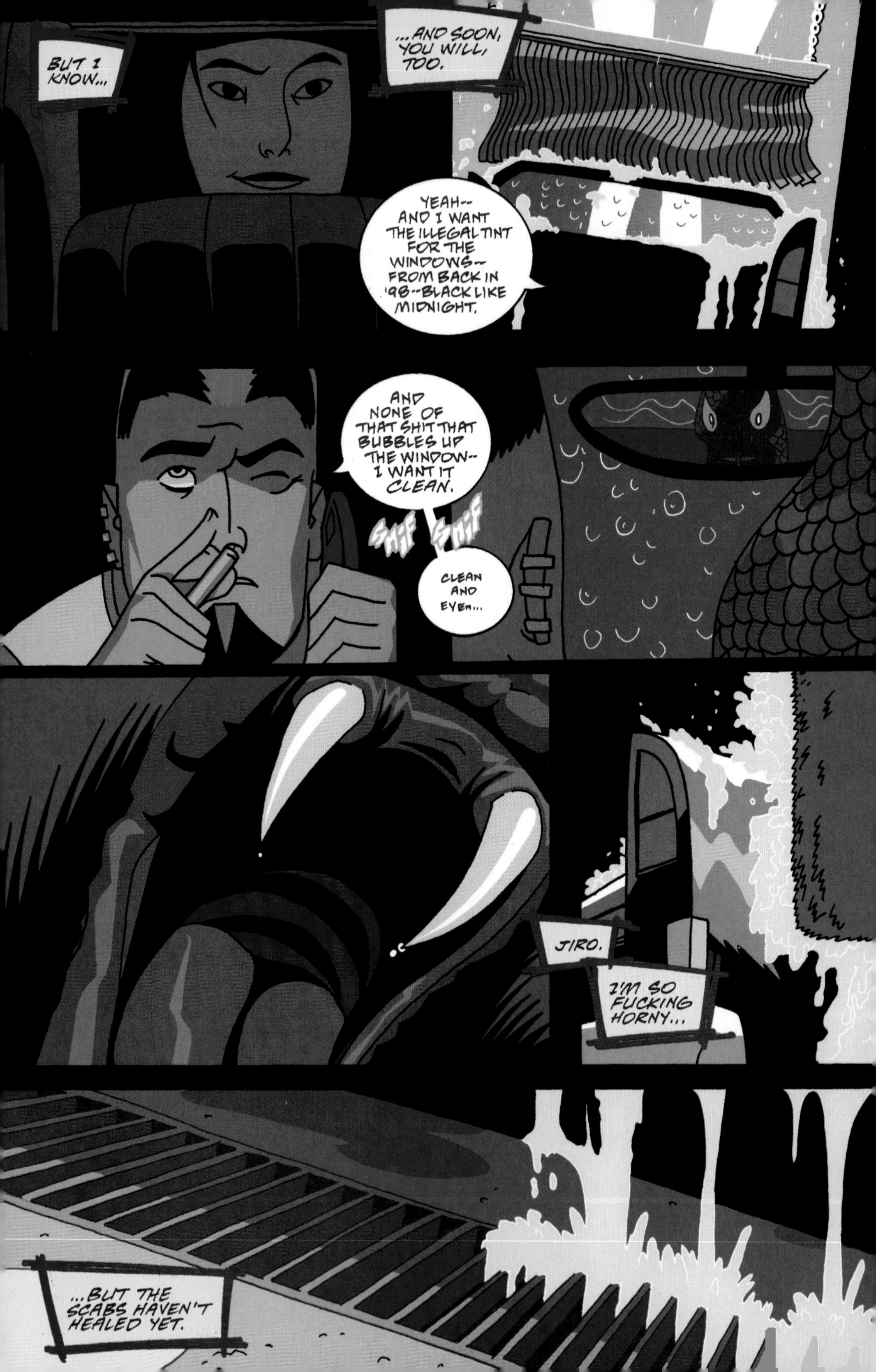
BUT I KNOW...
...AND SOON, YOU WILL, TOO.
YEAH-- AND I WANT THE ILLEGAL TINT FOR THE WINDOWS-- FROM BACK IN '98--BLACK LIKE MIDNIGHT.
AND NONE OF THAT SHIT THAT BUBBLES UP THE WINDOW-- I WANT IT CLEAN.
SNIFF SNIFF
CLEAN AND EVEN...
JIRO.
I'M SO FUCKING HORNY...
...BUT THE SCABS HAVEN'T HEALED YET.

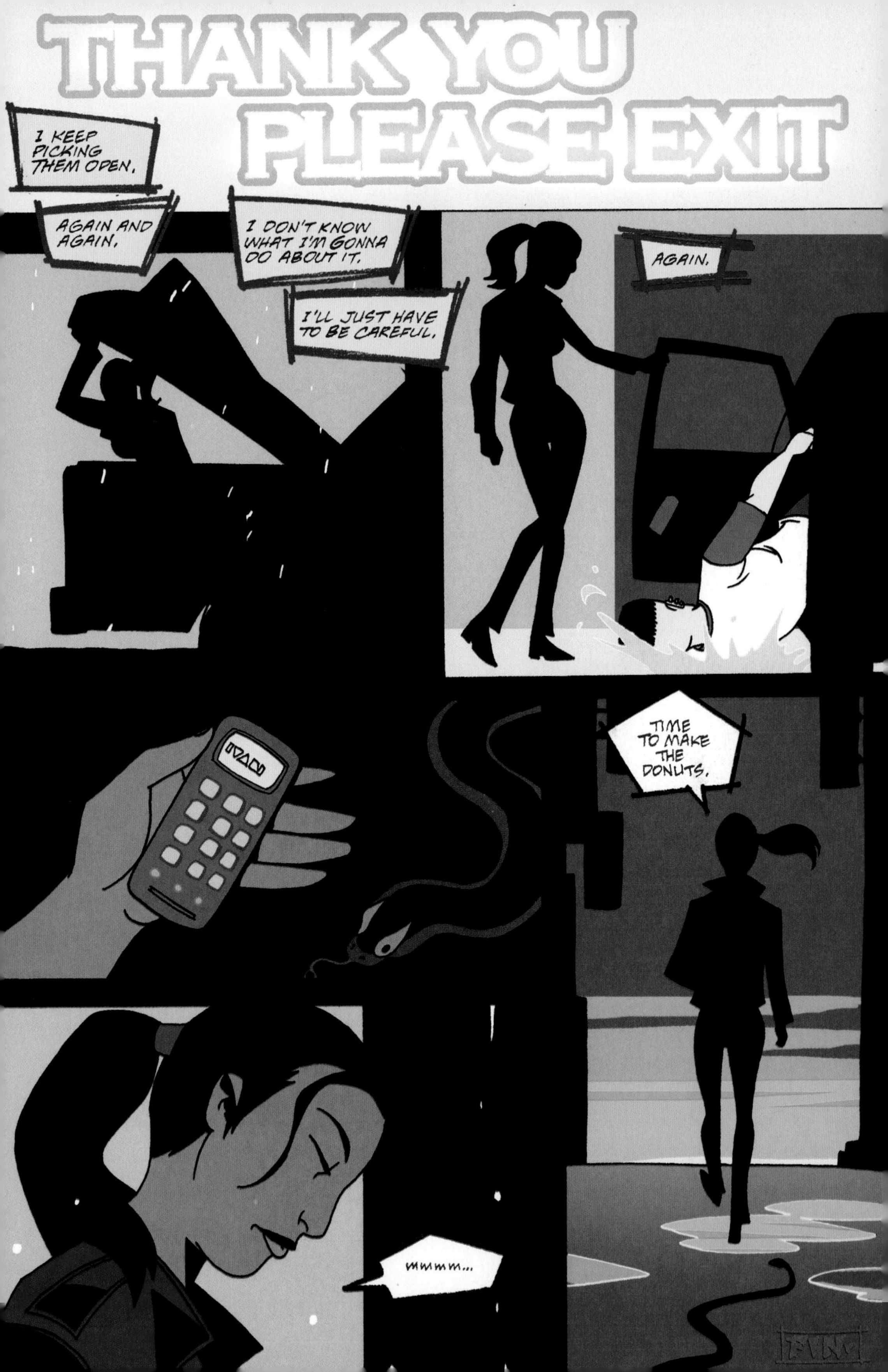
THANK YOU PLEASE EXIT
I KEEP PICKING THEM OPEN.
AGAIN AND AGAIN.
I DON'T KNOW WHAT I'M GONNA DO ABOUT IT.
I'LL JUST HAVE TO BE CAREFUL.
AGAIN.
TIME TO MAKE THE DONUTS.
MMMM...

BASTARD GALLERY

Dave Johnson
Jacen Burrows
David Mack
Brian Stelfreeze
Andy Lee

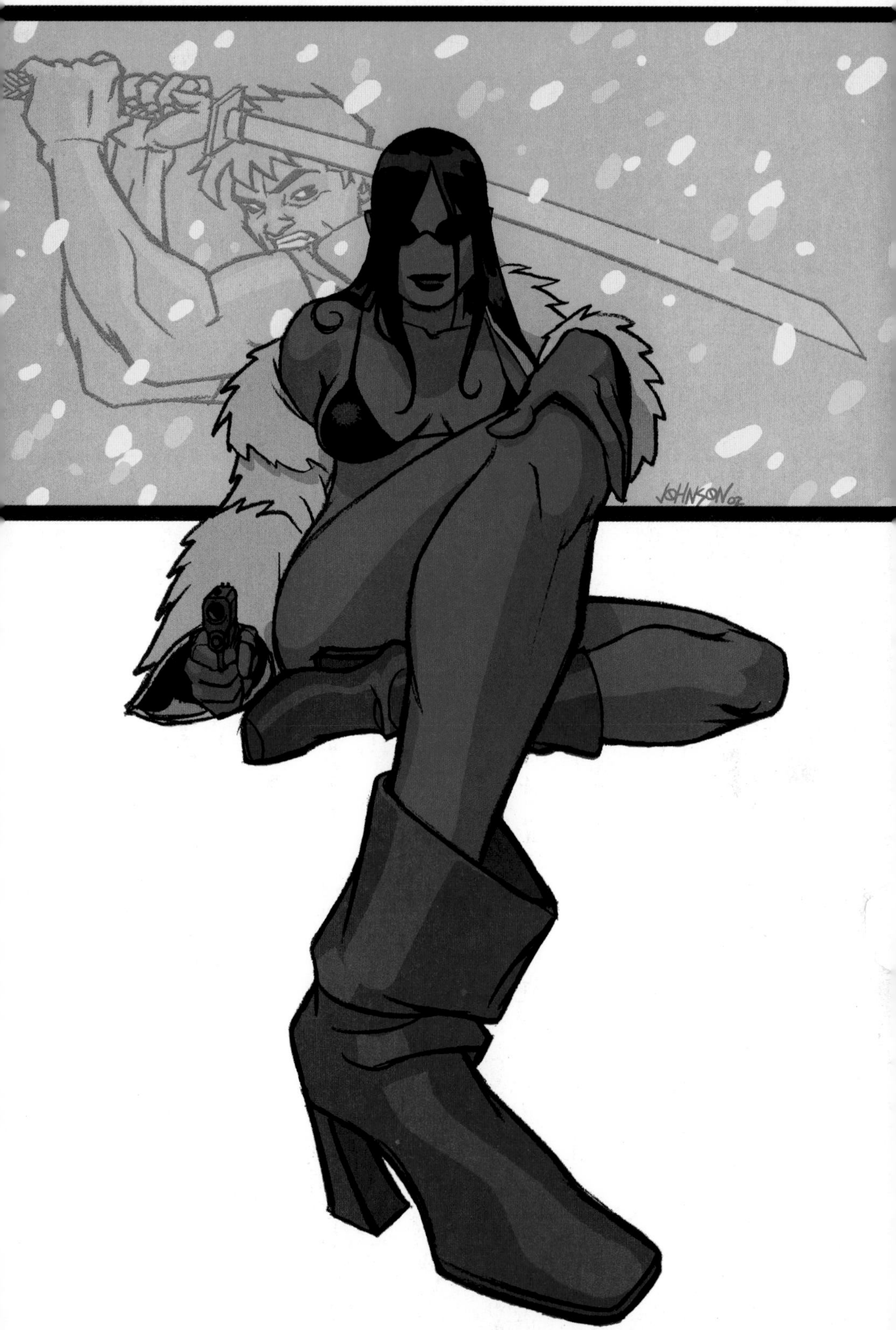
JOHNSON 02

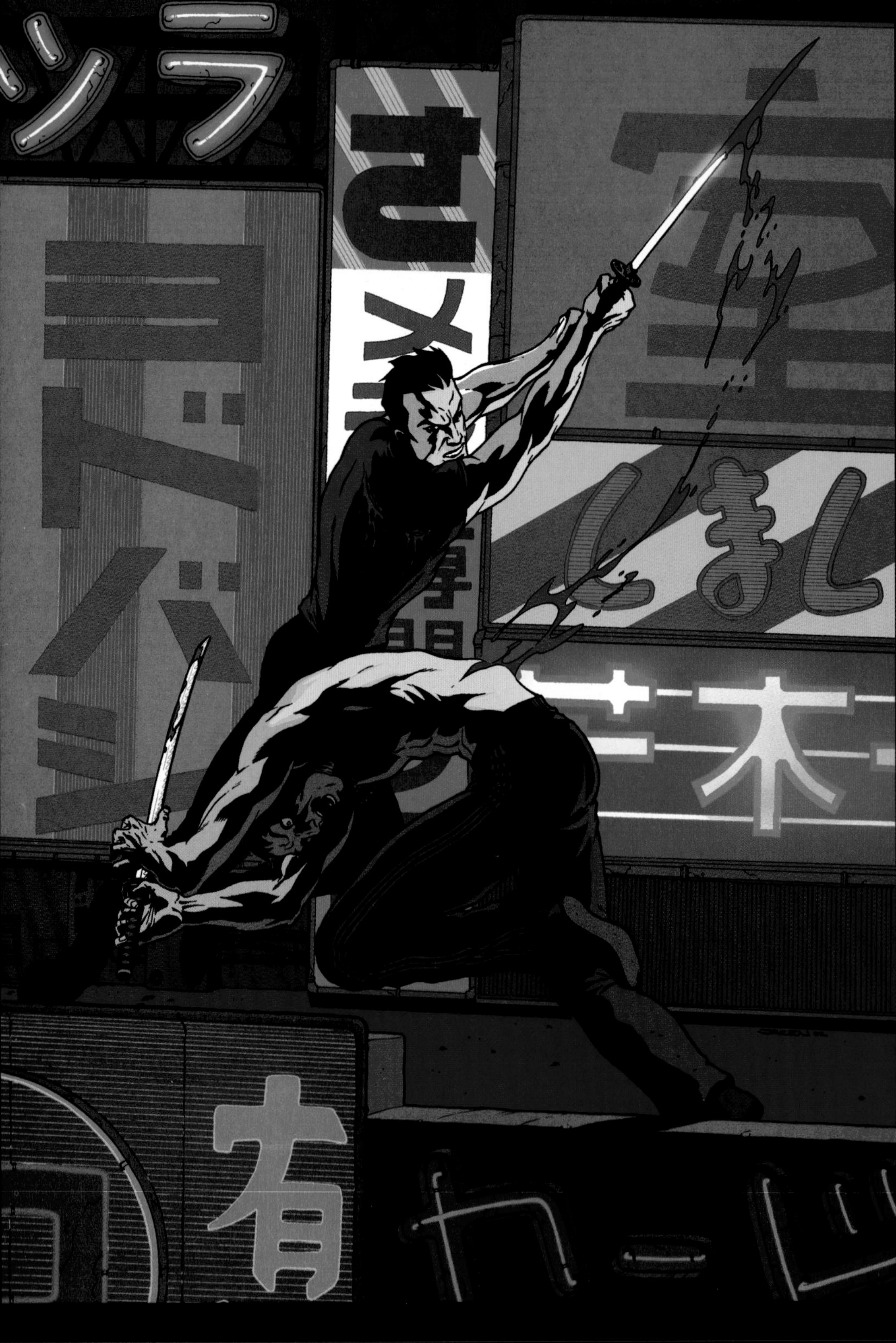
ツラ
しまし
本
有

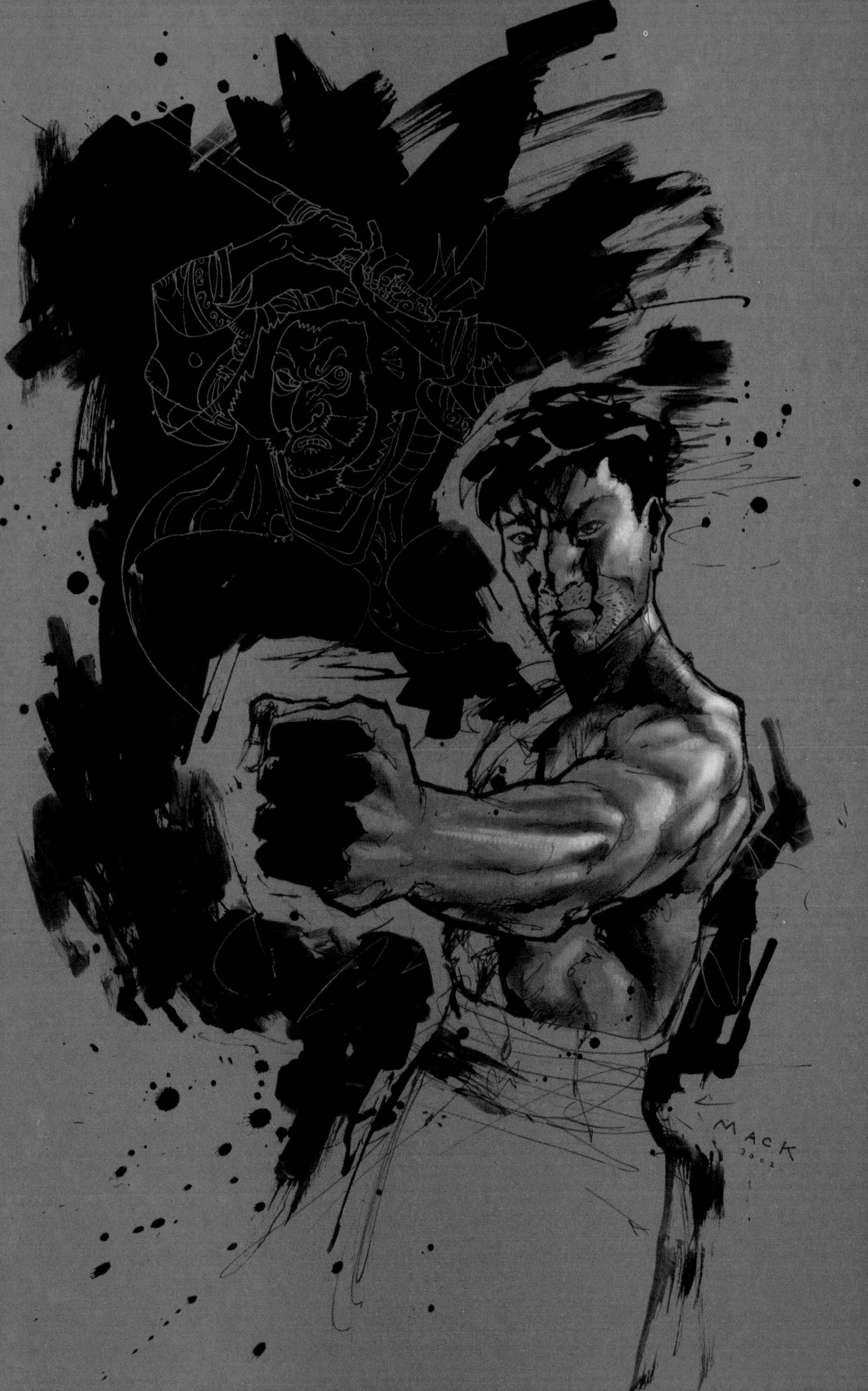
MACK
2002

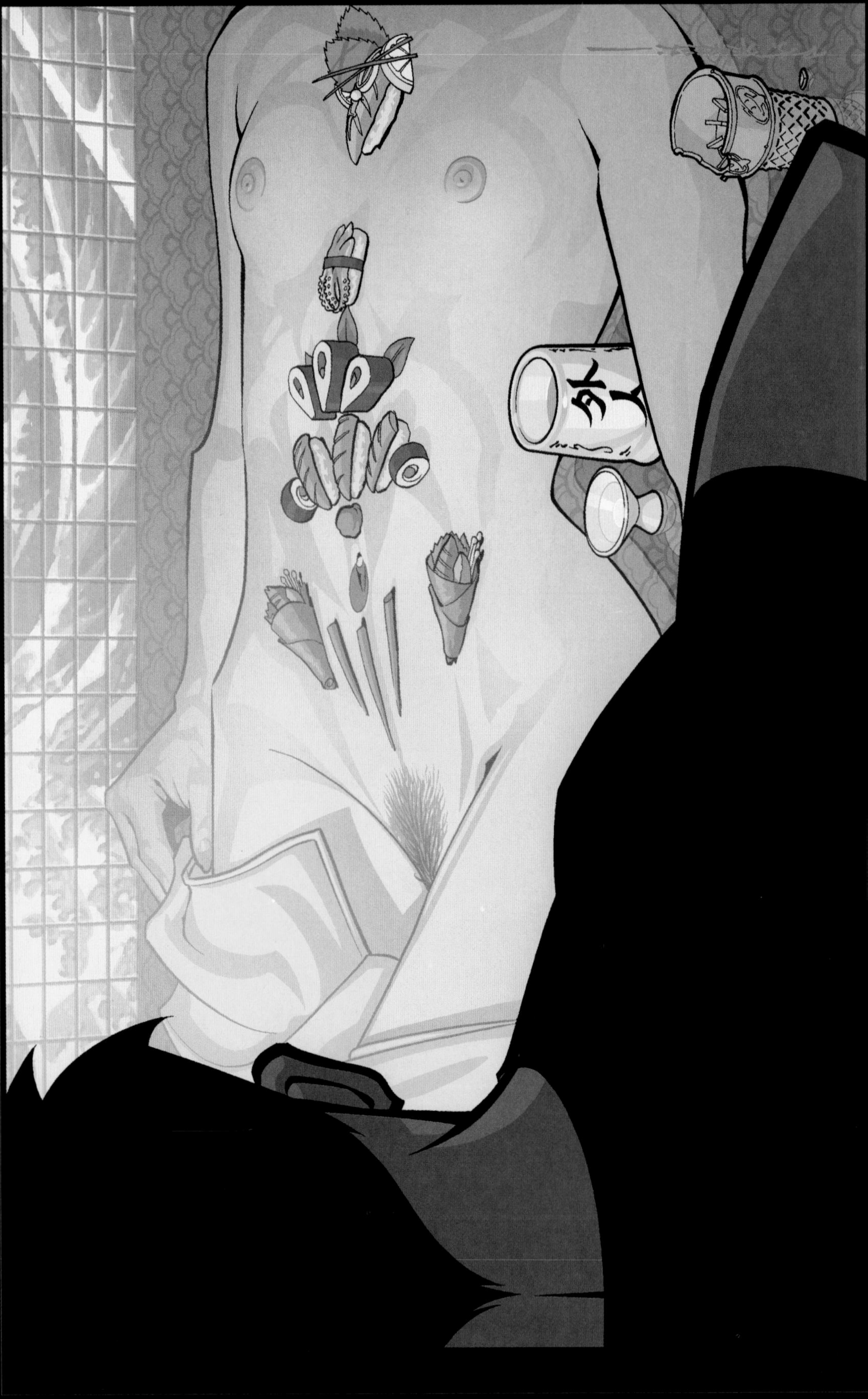

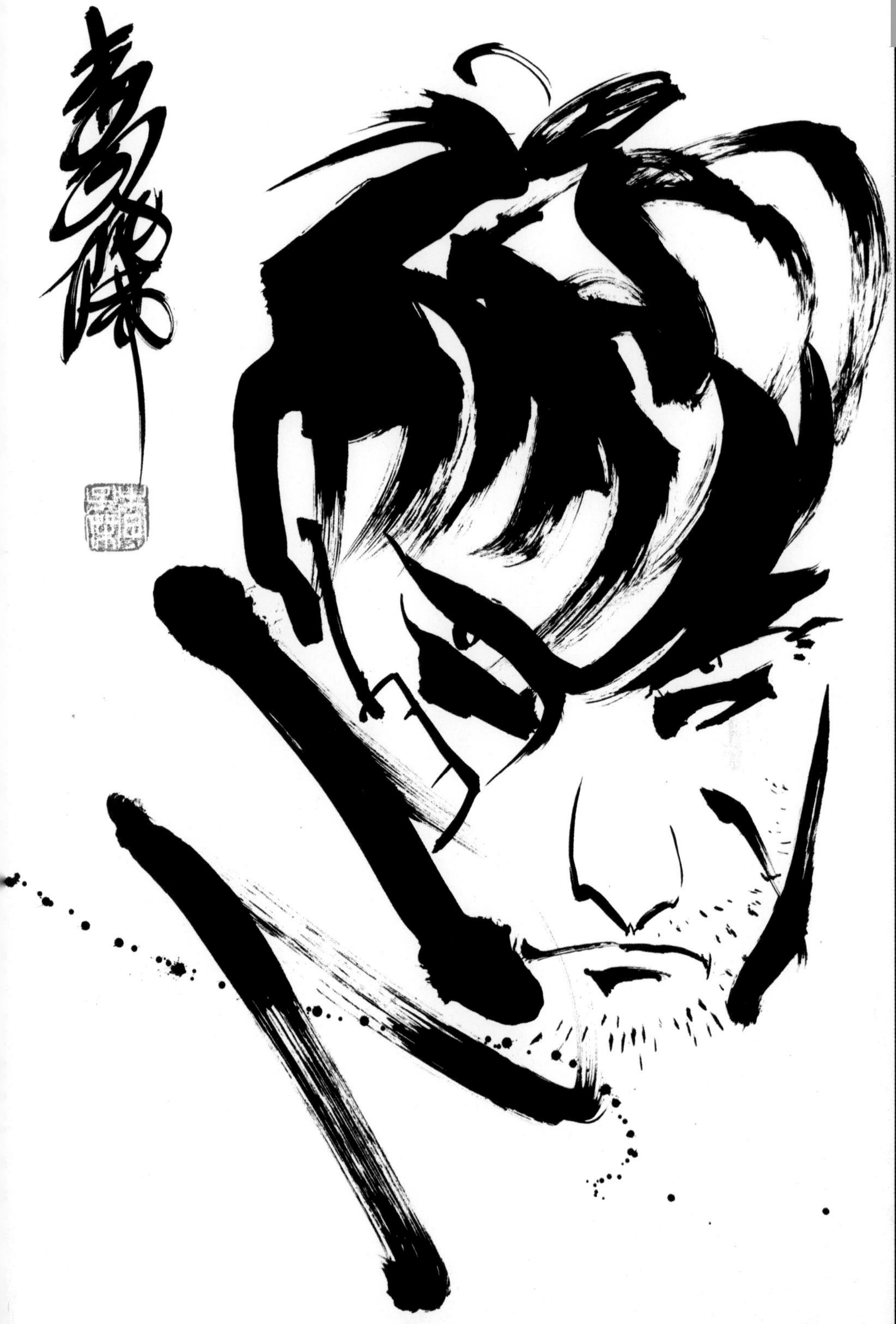

BASTARD SKETCHES

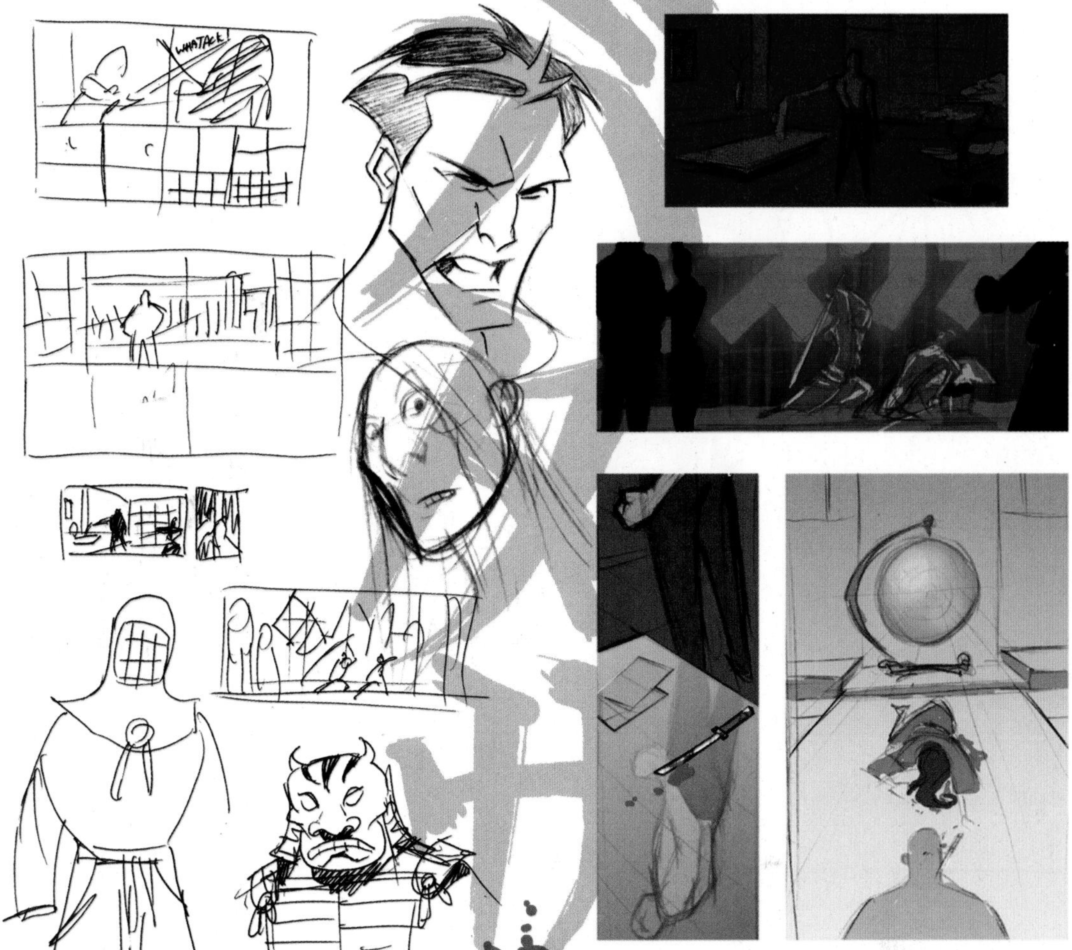

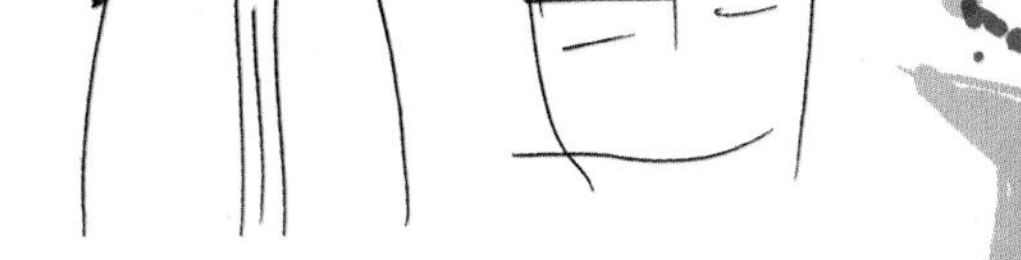

When we started this project it was important to create a distinct look for the story. Most of this was done before the script was even finished.

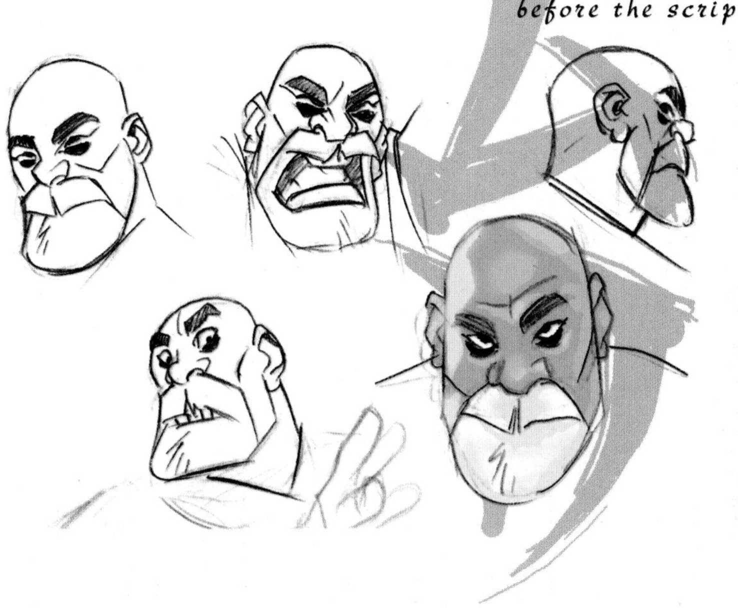

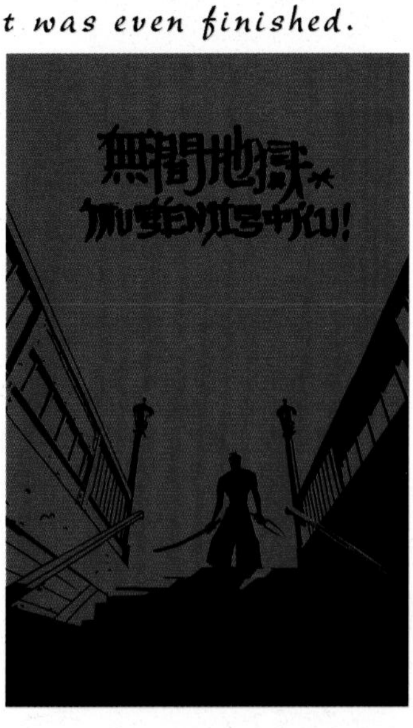
無間地獄
MUGENJIGOKU!

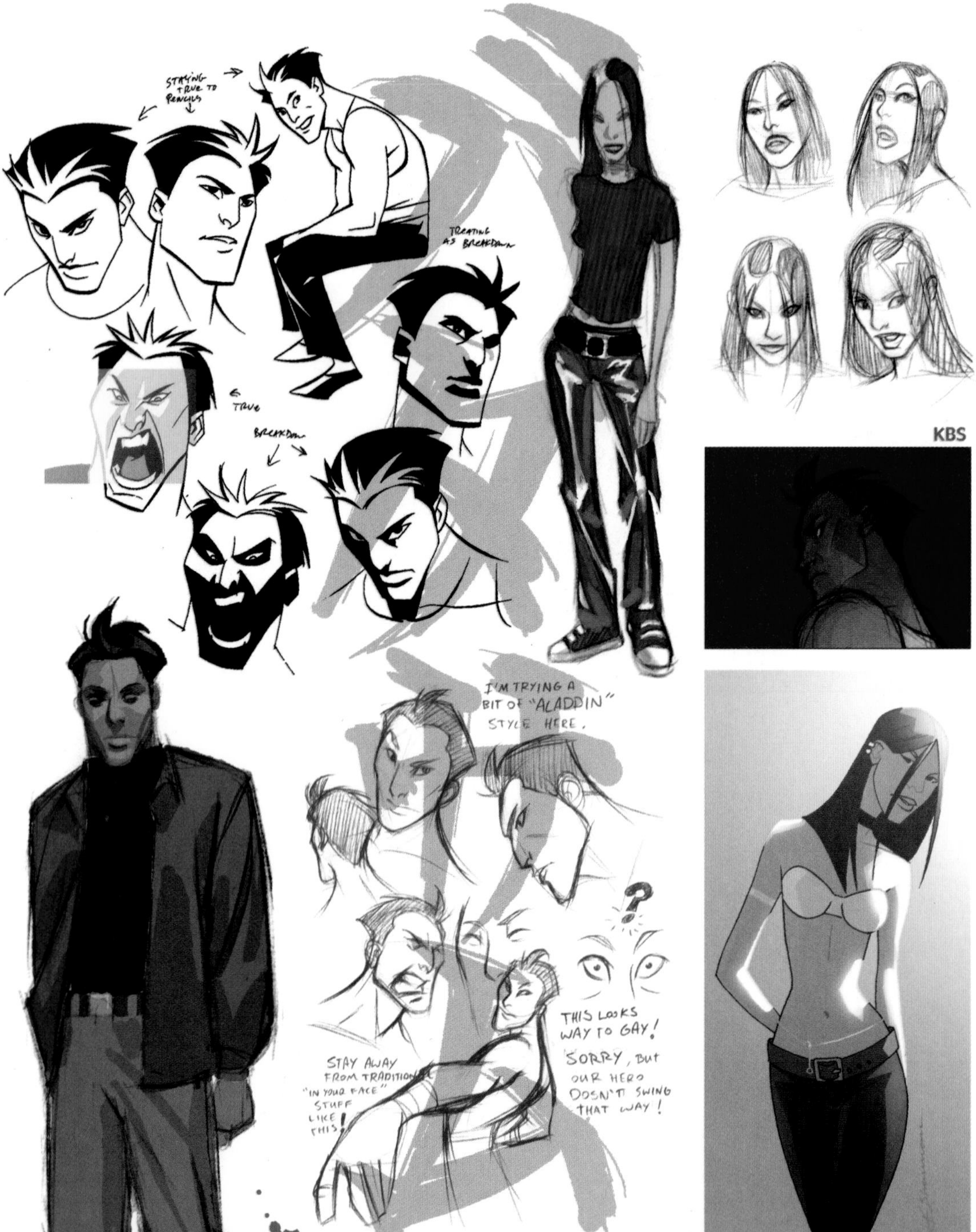
STAYING TRUE TO PENCILS
TREATING AS BREAKDOWN
TRUE
BREAKDOWN
KBS
I'M TRYING A BIT OF "ALADDIN" STYLE HERE.
?
THIS LOOKS WAY TO GAY!
SORRY, BUT OUR HERO DOSN'T SWING THAT WAY!
STAY AWAY FROM TRADITION "IN YOUR FACE" STUFF LIKE THIS!

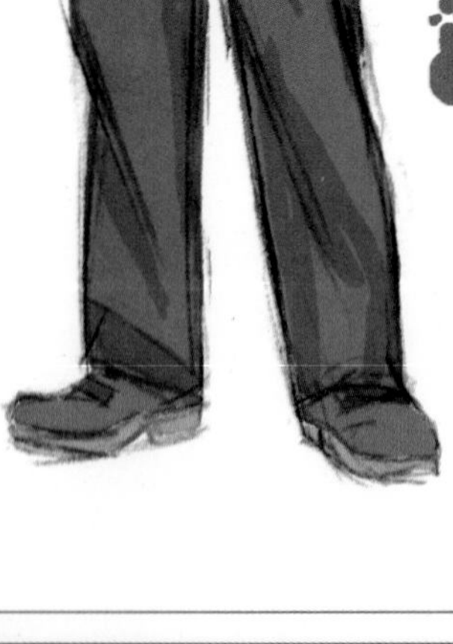

Part of the fun of working on your own book is getting the chance to design everything. A characters clothing, lighting, invironments, even hair style can all be used to help your story live.

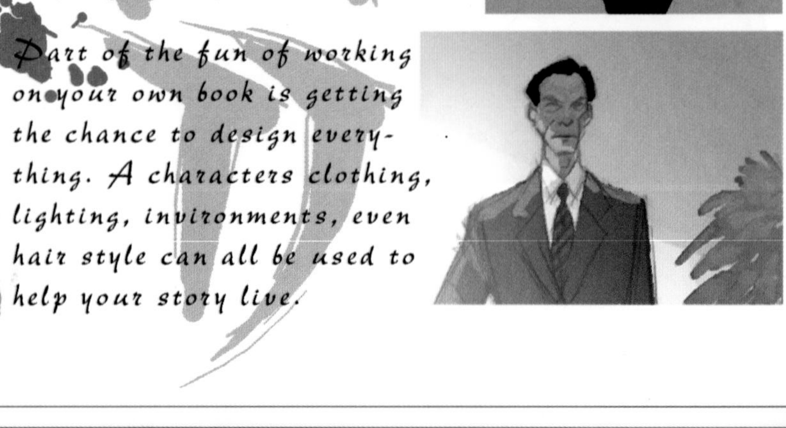

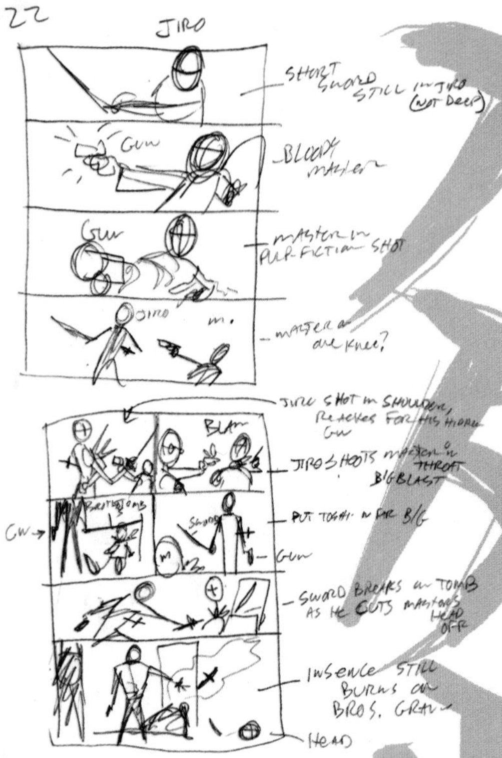
22
JIRO
SHORT SWORD STILL IN JIRO (NOT DEEP)
GUN
BLOODY MASTER
GUN
MASTER IN PULP FICTION SHOT
MASTER ON ONE KNEE?
JIRO SHOT IN SHOULDER, REACHES FOR HIS HIDDEN GUN
BLAM
JIRO SHOOTS MASTER IN THROAT
BIG BLAST
PUT TOSHI IN FAR B/G
GUN
SWORD BREAKS IN TOMB AS HE CUTS MASTER'S HEAD OFF
INSENCE STILL BURNS ON BROS. GRAVE
HEAD

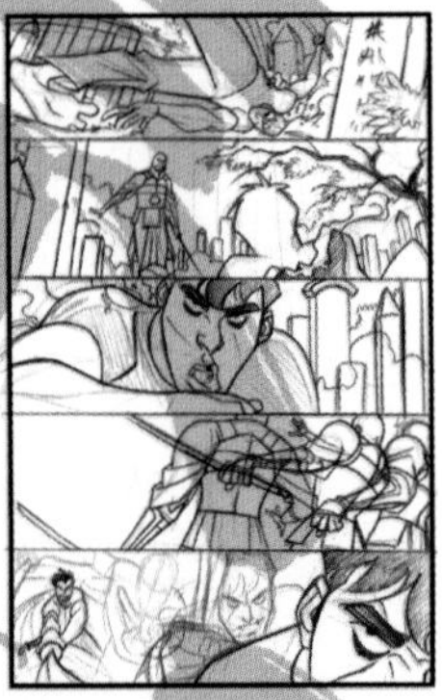

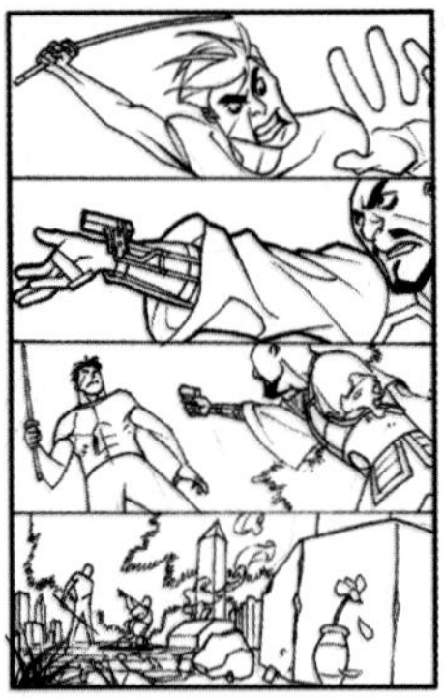

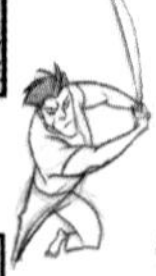

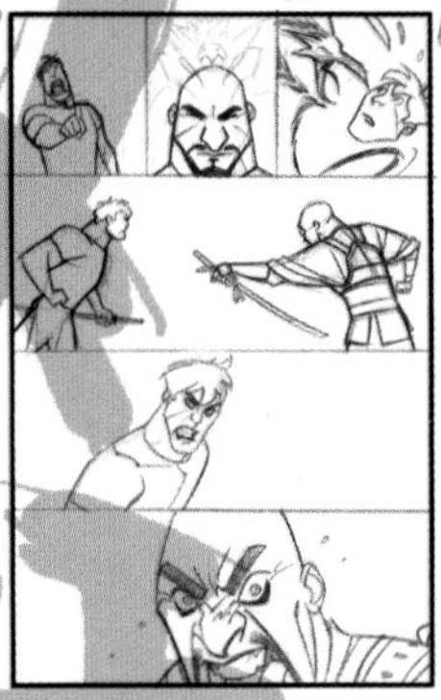

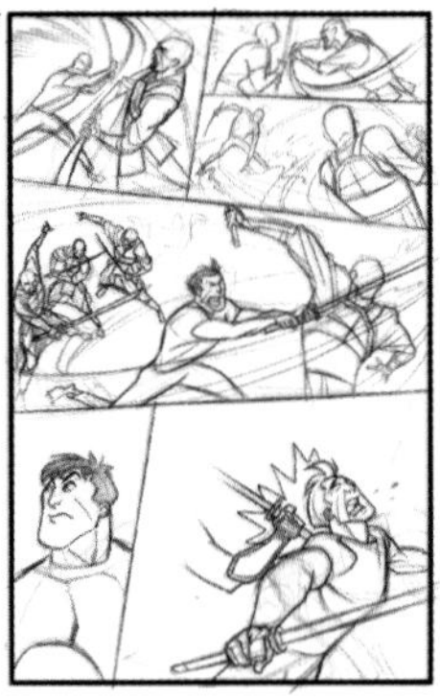

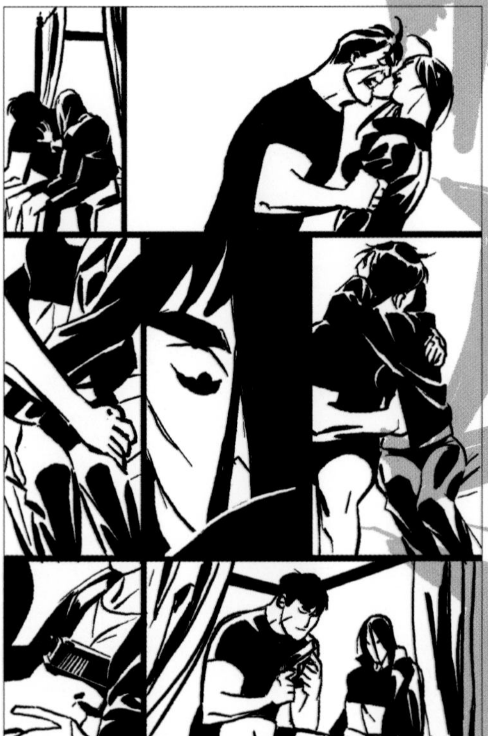

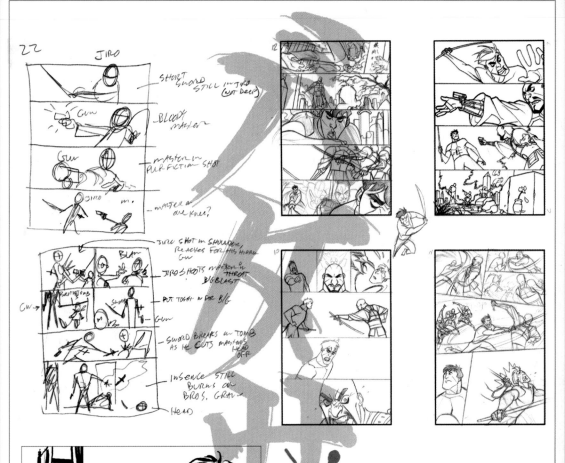

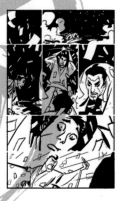

The layout stage is probably the most important step in drawing the book. If you don't get it right here then it's not going to work. Sometimes Mike would provide quick layouts (top left) to help speed up the process.

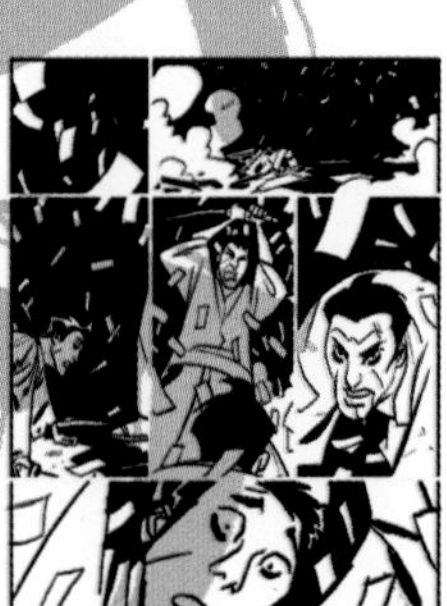

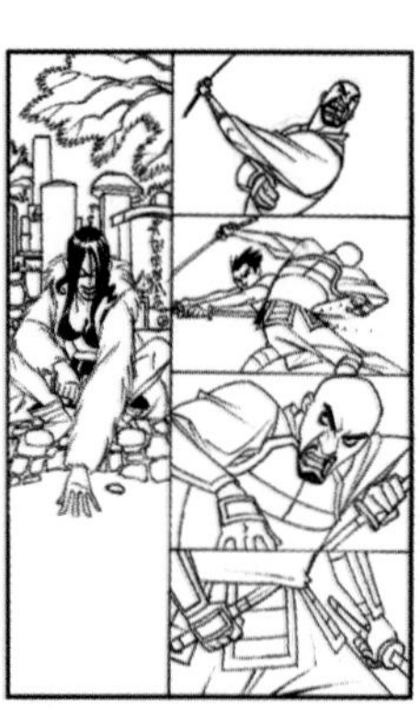

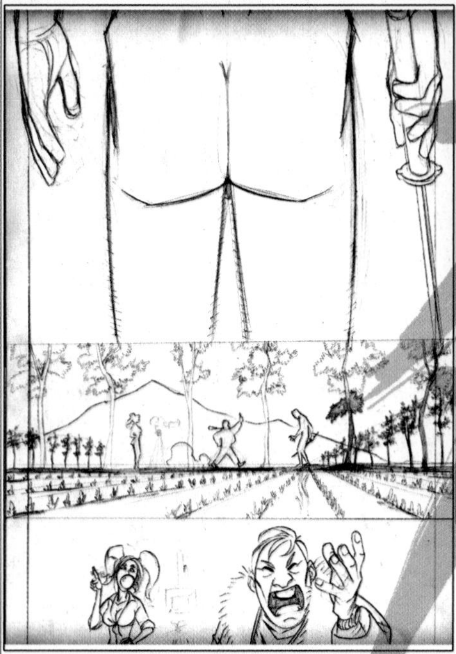

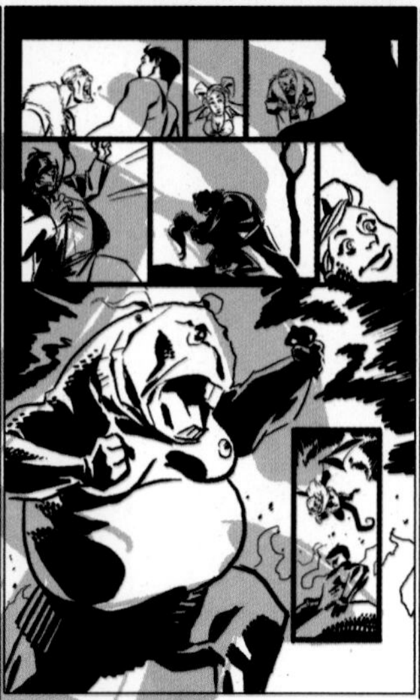

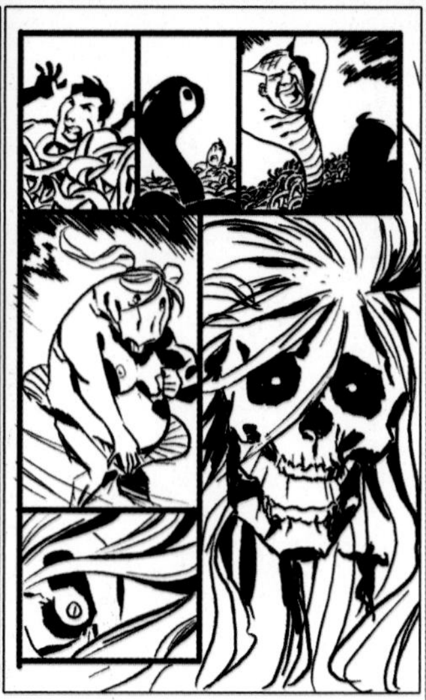

Originally the dream sequence that opens issue 2 started with a disoriented Jiro finding himself naked on the set of a Kurosawa film. Miles wanted to do the largest male ass shot in the history of comics for all the ass lovers out there. So Jiro is berated by Kurosawa and his teen pop star assistant whose name will not appear here for fear of legal action. The dream takes a Mignola turn for the worst as Jiro descends into hell. Kelsey decided to take a Venus of Willendorf approach to the demon and as you can see its pretty fucked up. In the end, the ass was too big, the demon too fucked and something didn't quite gel so we did a new sequence more akin to guitar feedback. Since Kelsey was so busy working on the end of the issue, Mike stepped in and drew the sequence; except the panel of Jiro hollering- that's all Kelsey.

M.G.

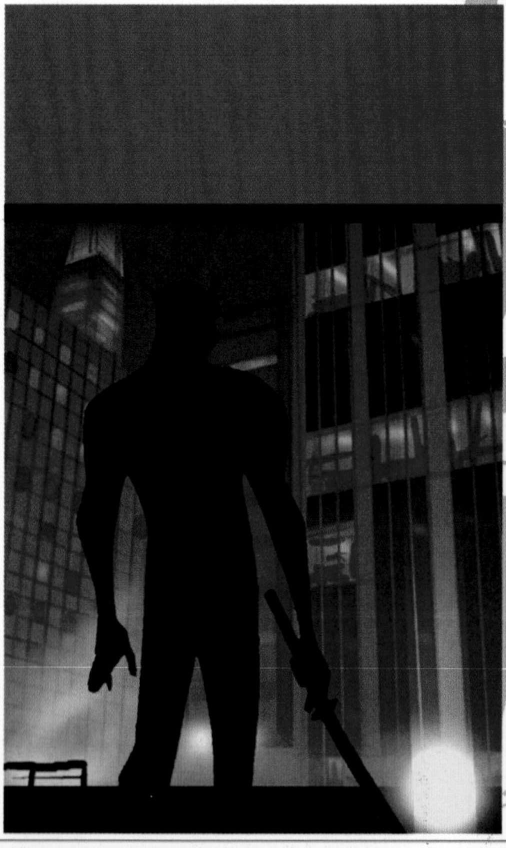

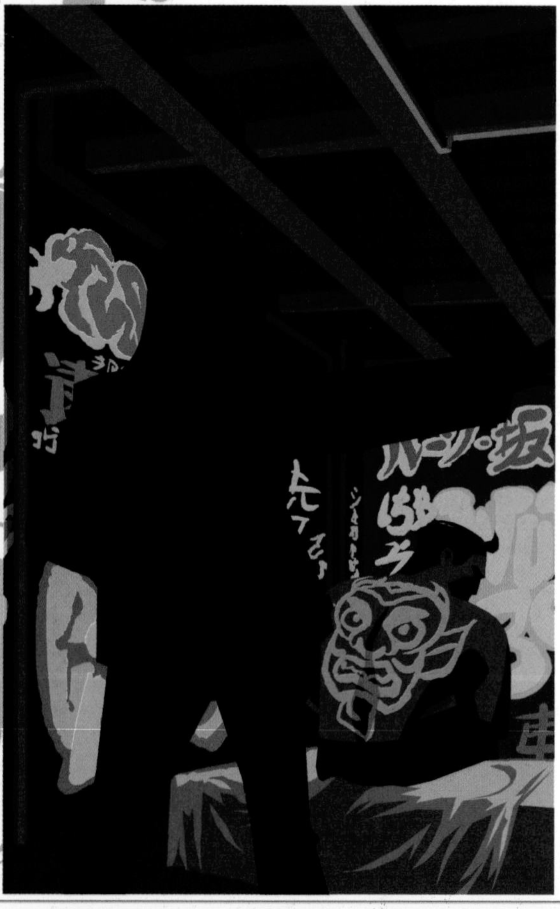

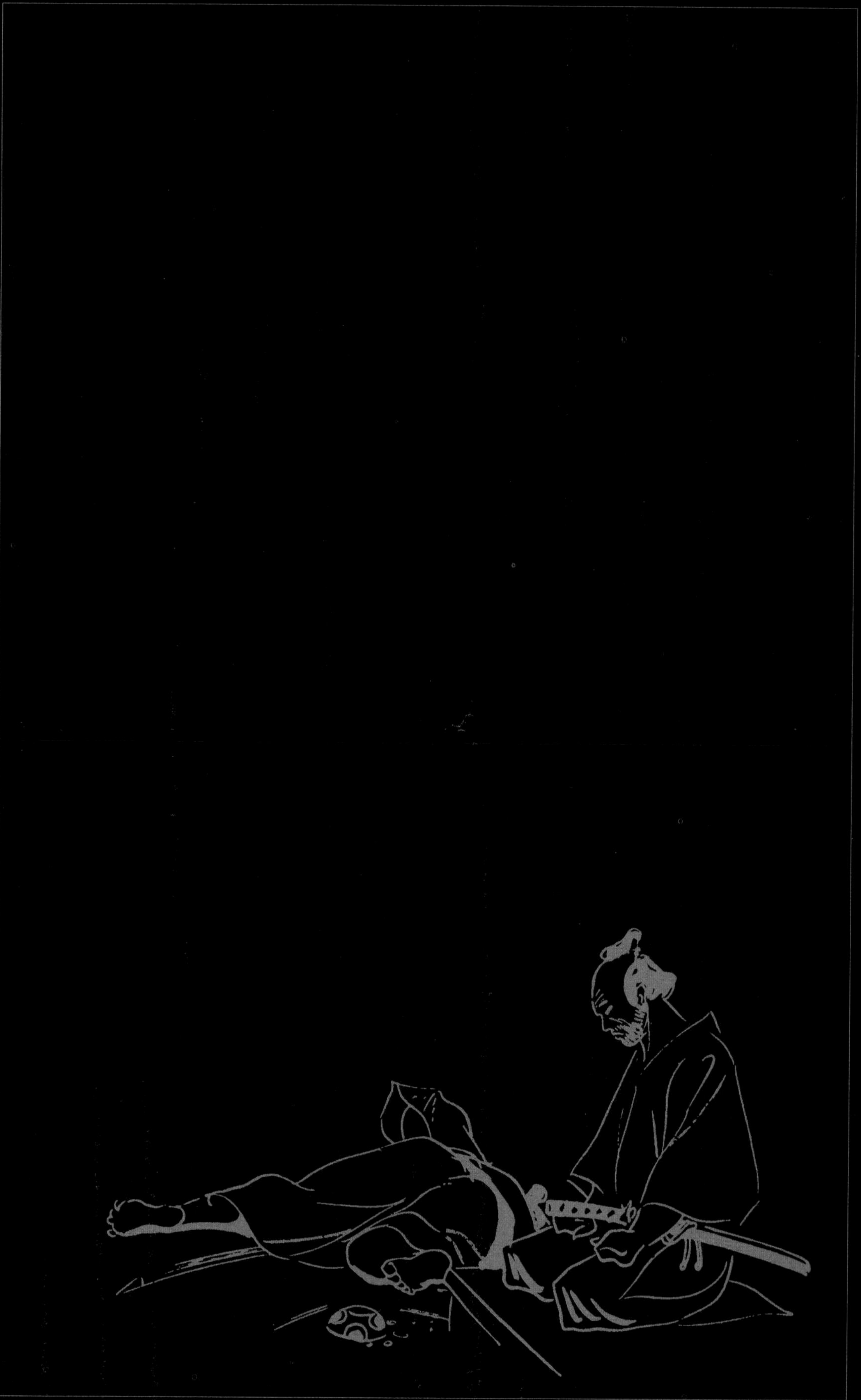

MORE GREAT COMICS FROM IMAGE COMICS

BEST MINI-SERIES OF THE YEAR
-PopImage
CROSS BRONX

THE CROSS BRONX, VOL. 1

Trade Paperback
ISBN: 978-1-58240-690-9
$14.99

HAMMER of the GODS
MICHAEL AVON OEMING & MARK OBIE WHEATLEY
MORTAL ENEMY

HAMMER OF THE GODS, VOL. 1: MORTAL ENEMY

Trade Paperback
ISBN: 978-1-58240-271-0
$18.95

POWERS
Who Killed Retro Girl?
BRIAN MICHAEL BENDIS
MICHAEL AVON OEMING

POWERS, VOL. 1: WHO KILLED RETRO GIRL?

Trade Paperback
ISBN: 978-1-58240-669-5
$21.99

POWERS
ROLEPLAY
BRIAN MICHAEL BENDIS
MICHAEL AVON OEMING

POWERS, VOL. 2: ROLEPLAY

Trade Paperback
ISBN: 978-1-58240-695-4
$13.99

COSTUMED CONSPIRACIES TAKE FLIGHT
POWERS
EXTRA!!
BRIAN MICHAEL BENDIS
MICHAEL AVON OEMING
SECRET ORIGINS NOT SO SECRET ANYMORE!

POWERS, VOL. 3: LITTLE DEATHS

Trade Paperback
ISBN: 978-1-58240-670-181
$19.99

POWERS
SUPERGROUP
BRIAN MICHAEL BENDIS
MICHAEL AVON OEMING

POWERS, VOL 4: SUPERGROUP

Trade Paperback
ISBN: 978-1-58240-671-5
$21.99

POWERS
ANARCHY
BENDIS
OEMING

POWERS, VOL. 5: ANARCHY

Trade Paperback
ISBN: 978-1-58240-331-7
$14.95

NOW A MAJOR MOTION PICTURE!
BULLETPROOF
MONK

BULLETPROOF MONK

Trade Paperback
ISBN: 978-1-58240-244-4
$9.95

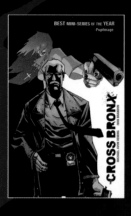

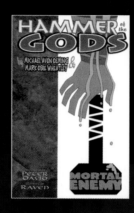

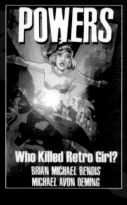

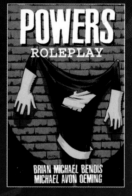

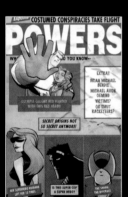

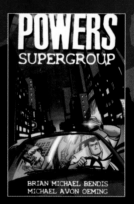

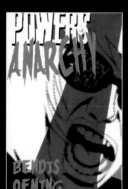

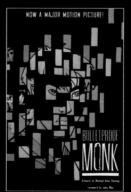

AND THE CREATORS OF BASTARD SAMURAI

NYC MECH, VOL. 1: LET'S ELECTRIFY TP

Trade Paperback
ISBN: 978-1-58240-558-2
$14.99

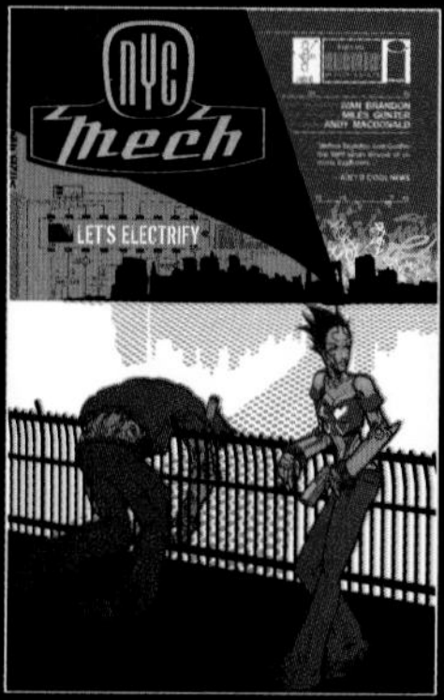
NYC
Mech
LET'S ELECTRIFY

24SEVEN

Anthology
ISBN: 978-1-58240-636-7
$24.99

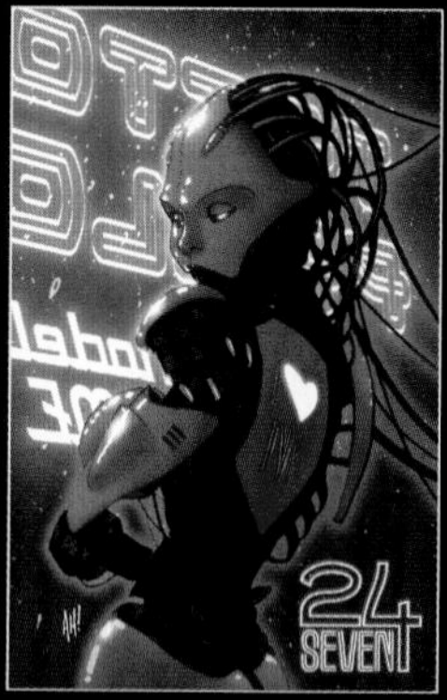
24
SEVEN

PARLIAMENT OF JUSTICE

Graphic Novel
$5.95

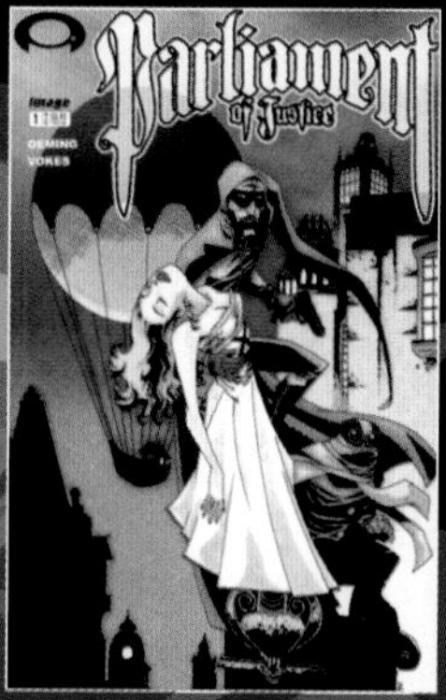
Parliament
of Justice
OEMING
VORES

SIX

Graphic Novel
ISBN: 978-1-58240-398-4
$5.95

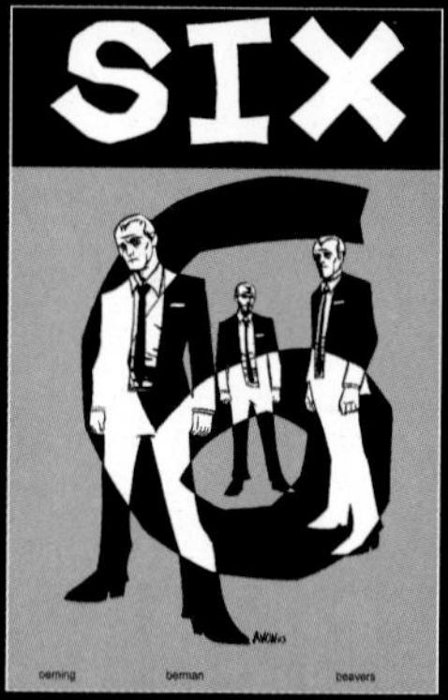
SIX
oeming
berman
beavers

THE WINGS OF ANASI

Graphic Novel
$6.99

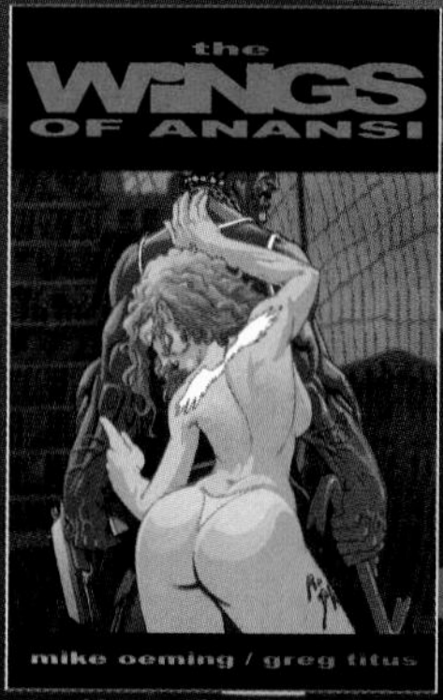
the
WINGS
OF ANANSI
mike oeming / greg titus

BLOOD RIVER

Graphic Novel
ISBN: 978-1-58240-509-4
$7.99

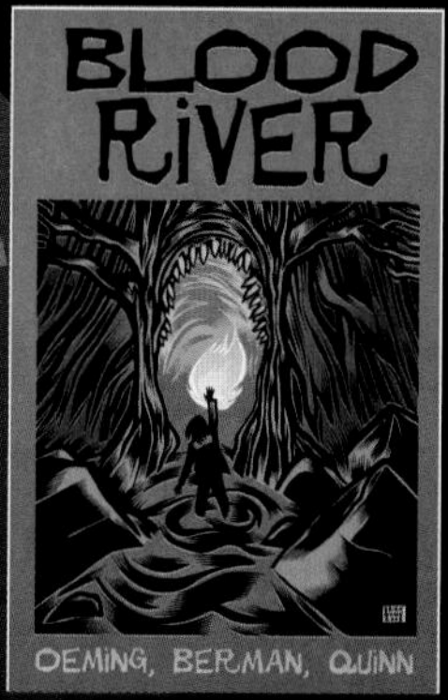
BLOOD
RiVER
OEMiNG, BERMAN, QUiNN

ZOMBEE

Graphic Novel
ISBN: 978-1-58240-662-6
$12.99

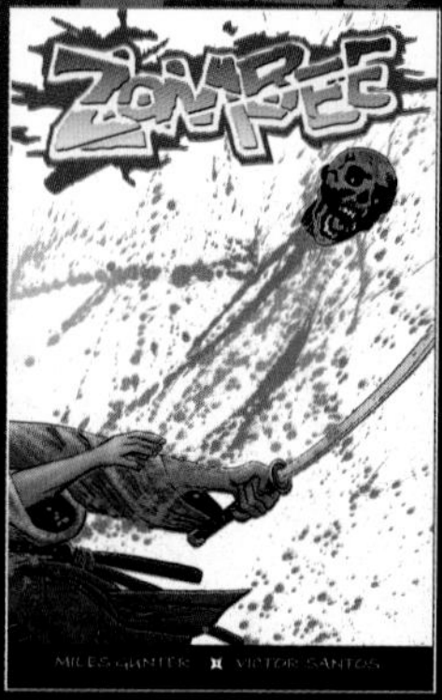
ZOMBEE

QUIXOTE, A NOVEL

Novel
ISBN: 978-1-58240-434-9
$9.95

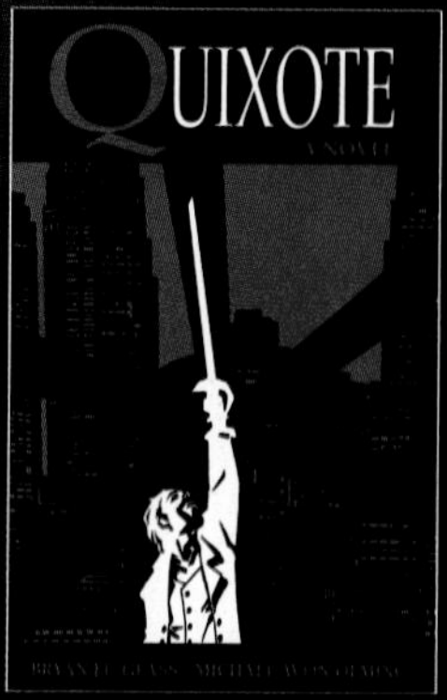
QUIXOTE
A NOVEL

40 OZ. COLLECTED TP
ISBN: 978-1-58240-329-8
$9.95

CASANOVA, VOL. 1: LUXURIA HC
ISBN: 978-1-58240-698-5
$24.99

CLASSIC 40 OZ.:
TALES FROM THE BROWN BAG TP
ISBN: 978-1-58240-438-7
$14.95

DEEP SLEEPER TP
ISBN: 978-1-58240-493-6
$12.95

DIORAMAS, A LOVE STORY GN
ISBN: 978-1-58240-359-5
$12.95

EARTHBOY JACOBUS GN
ISBN: 978-1-582409492-9
$17.95

FIRE: THE DEFINITIVE COLLECTION TP
ISBN: 978-1-58240-071-6
$9.95

THE FIVE FISTS OF SCIENCE GN
ISBN: 978-1-58240-605-3
$12.99

FOUR-LETTER WORLDS GN
ISBN: 978-1-58240-439-4
$12.95

GIRLS

VOL. 1: CONCEPTION TP
ISBN: 978-1-58240-529-2
$14.99
VOL. 2: ERMERGENCE TP
ISBN: 978-1-58240-608-4
$14.99
VOL. 3: SURVIVAL TP
ISBN: 978-1-58240-703-6
$14.99
VOL. 4: EXTINCTION
ISBN: 978-1-58240-753-1
$14.99

GOLDFISH:
THE DEFINITIVE COLLECTION TP
ISBN: 978-1-58240-195-9
$19.95

GRRL SCOUTS

VOL. 1 TP
ISBN: 978-1-58240-316-8
$12.95
VOL. 2: WORK SUCKS TP
ISBN: 978-1-58240-343-4
$12.95

HAWAIIAN DICK

VOL. 1: BYRD OF PARADISE TP
ISBN: 978-1-58240-317-5
$14.95
VOL. 2: THE LAST RESORT TP
ISBN: 978-1-58240-644-0
$14.99

HELLSHOCK:
THE DEFINITIVE COLLECTION TP
ISBN: 978-1-58240-504-9
19.99

JINX: THE DEFINITIVE COLLECTION TP
ISBN: 978-1-58240-179-9
$24.95

KABUKI

VOL. 1: CIRCLE OF BLOOD TP
ISBN: 978-1-88727-980-1
$19.95
VOL. 2: DREAMS TP
ISBN: 978-1-58240-277-2
$12.95
VOL. 3: MASKS OF NOH TP
ISBN: 978-1-58240-108-9
$12.95
VOL. 4: SKIN DEEP TP
ISBN: 978-1-58240-000-6
$12.95
VOL. 5: METAMORPHOSIS TP
ISBN: 978-1-58240-203-1
$24.99
VOL. 6: SCARAB TP
ISBN: 978-1-58240-258-1
$19.95

KANE

VOL. 1: GREETINGS FROM NEW EDEN TP
ISBN: 978-1-88727-340-3
$19.95
VOL. 2: RABBIT HUNT TP
ISBN: 978-1-58240-355-7
$12.95
VOL. 3: HISTORIES TP
ISBN: 978-1-58240-382-3
$12.95

VOL. 4: THIRTY NINTH TP
ISBN: 978-1-58240-422-6
$12.95
VOL. 5: THE UNTOUCHABLE RICO COSTAS AND OTHER SHORT STORIES TP
ISBN: 978-1-58240-551-3
$24.99
VOL. 6: PARTNERS TP
ISBN: 978-1-58240-704-3
$19.95

LAZARUS CHURCHYARD, THE FINAL CUT GN
ISBN: 978-1-58240-180-5
$14.95

MIDNIGHT NATION TP
ISBN: 978-1-58240-460-8
$24.99

NOWHERESVILLE TP
ISBN: 978-1-58240-241-3
$14.95

PHONOGRAM, VOL. 1: RUE BRITANNIA TP
ISBN: 978-1-58240-694-7
$14.99

PUT THE BOOK BACK ON THE SHELF: A BELLE AND SEBASTIAN ANTHOLOGY
ISBN: 978-1-58240-600-8
$14.99

PUTTIN' THE BACKBONE BACK TP
ISBN: 978-1-58240-402-8
$9.95

RISING STARS
VOL. 1: BORN IN FIRE TP
ISBN: 978-1-58240-172-0
$19.95
VOL. 2: POWER TP
ISBN: 978-1-58240-226-0
$19.95
VOL. 3: FIRE & ASH TP
ISBN: 978-1-58240-491-2
$19.99

RONINHOOD OF THE 47 SAMURAI
ISBN: 978-1-58240-555-1
$9.99

RUULE
VOL. 1: GANGLORDS OF CHINATOWN TP
ISBN: 978-1-58240-566-7
$19.99

VOL. 2: KISS & TELL
ISBN: 978-1-58240-540-7
$19.99

TORSO: THE DEFINITIVE COLLECTION
ISBN: 978-1-58240-174-4
$21.95

TOTAL SELL OUT TP
ISBN: 978-1-58240-287-1
$14.95

ULTRA: SEVEN DAYS TP
ISBN: 978-1-58240-483-7
$17.95

THE WALKING DEAD
VOL. 1: DAYS GONE BYE TP
ISBN: 978-1-58240-672-5
$9.99
VOL. 2: MILES BEHIND US TP
ISBN: 978-1-58240-413-4
$12.95
VOL. 3: SAFETY BEHIND BARS TP
ISBN: 978-1-58240-805-7
$12.99
VOL. 4: THE HEART'S DESIRE TP
ISBN: 978-1-58240-753-1
$12.99
VOL. 5: THE BEST DEFENSE TP
ISBN: 978-1-58240-612-1
$12.99
VOL. 6: THIS SORROWFUL LIFE TP
ISBN: 978-1-58240-684-8
$12.99
BOOK ONE HC
ISBN: 978-1-58240-619-0
$29.99
BOOK TWO HC
ISBN: 978-1-58240-759-3
$29.99

WANTED TP
ISBN: 978-1-58240-497-4
$19.99

THE WICKED WEST GN
VOL. 1 TP
ISBN: 978-1-58240-414-1
$9.95
VOL. 2: ABOMINATION & OTHER TALES
ISBN: 978-1-58240-661-9
$15.99